The Black Reproductive

The Black Reproductive

Unfree Labor and Insurgent Motherhood

Sara Clarke Kaplan

University of Minnesota Press
Minneapolis
London

Portions of chapter 2 are adapted from "Love and Violence / Maternity and Death: Black Feminism and the Politics of Reading (Un)representability," *Black Women, Gender, and Families* 1, no. 1 (Spring 2007): 94–124. Portions of chapter 4 are adapted from "Our Founding (M)Other: Erotic Love and Social Death in *Sally Hemings* and *The President's Daughter,*" *Callaloo: A Journal of African Diaspora Arts and Letters* 32, no. 3 (Summer 2009): 773–91; copyright 2009 Johns Hopkins University Press; reprinted with permission of Johns Hopkins University Press. The second epigraph in chapter 3 is from Mohammed Kacimi, "The Body of Memory / Le Corps de Mémoire," in *Le creux du corps* (Paris: Éditions Al Manar, 1996), reprinted with permission.

Every effort was made to obtain permission to reproduce material in this book. If any proper acknowledgment has not been included here, we encourage copyright holders to notify the publisher.

Published by the University of Minnesota Press
111 Third Avenue South, Suite 290
Minneapolis, MN 55401–2520
http://www.upress.umn.edu

ISBN 978-0-8166-9567-6 (hc)
ISBN 978-0-8166-9569-0 (pb)

Library of Congress record available at https://lccn.loc.gov/2020058454

Printed in the United States of America on acid-free paper

UMP BmB 2021

In gratitude to the workers and warriors who came before and showed us what was possible;

In memory of Tavi and Juli;

And, always, for Miles Martín, the rainbow after the storms.

Contents

Toward a Black Feminist Politics of Freedom

> In this play of paradox, only the female stands *in the flesh,* both mother and mother-dispossessed. This problematizing of gender places her, in my view, out of the traditional symbolics of female gender, and it is our task to make a place for this different social subject. In doing so, we are less interested in joining the ranks of gendered femaleness than gaining the insurgent ground as female social subject. Actually claiming the monstrosity (of a female with the potential to "name"), . . . "Sapphire" might rewrite after all a radically different text for a female empowerment.
>
> —Hortense J. Spillers, "Mama's Baby, Papa's Maybe"

> And here, the issue of reproduction . . . emerges right on time as it has to do not only with the question concerning slavery, blackness, performance, and the ensemble of their ontologies but also with a contradiction at the heart of the question of value in its relation to personhood that could be said to come into clearer focus against the backdrop of the ensemble of motherhood, blackness, and the bridge between slavery and freedom.
>
> —Fred Moten, *In the Break*

In the winter of 2017, a team of archaeologists and architects unearthed the long-hidden living quarters of Thomas Jefferson's enslaved concubine, Sally Hemings. The excavation of the buried chamber was part of the second phase of the Mountaintop Project, a multiyear initiative to restore dwellings and workplaces at Jefferson's famed plantation, Monticello, including those where Black captive and unwaged tradespeople, artisans, and domestic laborers lived and worked. One of the Mountaintop Project's stated goals was to demonstrate that slavery was neither peripheral nor marginal to Monticello—that, indeed, "there was no place on [the] mountaintop that slavery wasn't." The unearthing and planned restoration of Sally Hemings's quarters, however, applied this accepted fact of plantation history to an unprecedentedly intimate terrain.[1] Unlike the previously rebuilt cellar kitchens, slave quarters, and storehouses, this site was not located in one of the lower-level service halls (known, ironically, as "dependencies") or along the stretch of outbuildings known as Mulberry Row. It was buried in the South Wing of the main house, next to the suite of private rooms that made up the inner sanctum of the author of the Declaration of Independence and third president of the United States.

Lodged at the heart of Jefferson's never-quite-finished architectural paean to Enlightenment reason and aesthetics, the ghostly remains of Hemings's quarters serve as a spatial reminder of how closely entangled chattel slavery was with the emergence of U.S. liberal democracy. Adjacent to the bedroom where Jefferson slept, the cabinet from which he managed his holdings (including the 607 people he had inherited, bought, or bred), and the library where he honed his thinking on the inalienable rights of man, they demonstrate how chattel slavery was not only a ubiquitous and indispensable part of the political economy and racial ideology of the United States but also an intimate relation at the core of U.S. social formations. Slavery figured in all public facets of life on Jefferson's plantation—the crops harvested, the inventions built, the entertainments hosted—and also those most private aspects: morning ablutions, personal perseverations, nighttime sleep, and sex. The coerced and unwaged work of Black captives was not just essential to Monticello's productivity as a plantation; it was inextricable from the quotidian reproduction—the daily rising and repose—of Monticello and its master. Nor can the daily domestic tasks that required Hemings's proximity be divorced from her other reproductive labors. In her years of occupying that chamber or others like it, she bore her master at least six children, who increased his wealth in human capital at the same time that they embodied his deepest anxieties regarding the untenable fragility of racial categories—and, by extension, U.S. racial slavery itself.

The proclaimed archaeological discovery of Hemings's buried quarters (just where oral histories from Monticello's formerly enslaved residents had long asserted it had been) was in no small part motivated by the heralded genealogical discovery of Jefferson's DNA buried in the genetic code of Hemings's descendants (just as family oral traditions had long known it to be). Like the fragments of DNA that indelibly linked the Founding Father and descendants of enslaved offspring he never claimed, the fragmented remnants of the domestic space that Hemings occupied are a material reminder of the integral role that enslaved and unfree Black reproduction and reproductive labor have played in structuring the U.S. racial state. And yet, despite this—or, as I argue in the pages that follow, precisely *because of it*—for years, Hemings's living quarters had been disappeared as completely as her intimate labors as Jefferson's slave had been disavowed, her chamber paved over by a public men's bathroom.

This is not a book about Thomas Jefferson. There already exists an extensive body of work elucidating how Jefferson's iconic role as an Enlightenment thinker who espoused the self-evident equality of men was by no means inconsistent with his position as slave master who held deeds for more than six hundred Black people-cum-property. The best of this scholarship cogently illuminates a principle that grounds this book as well: that (white) liberal humanism has always been inextricable from and interdependent with the discourses of and practices of Black subjugation, commodification, and dehumanization. Nor is it solely about Sally Hemings, though she appears on many of its pages. This book is about the intimate relations of power and property, desire and difference, on which the United States has been built. Like the long-denied history of Hemings and the Founding Father who held her deed, it tells a story of slavery that perceives intimate labors to be as revealing as public sales and that understands slavery to be not just a relation of productivity but one of *re*productivity in all its senses: domestic, quotidian, and procreative. Like the unearthing of Hemings's buried chamber, which both resulted from and called for closer attention to how the reproductive politics of slavery continually surface to exert a claim on the present, this book digs down into the history of slavery and subsequent forms of Black unfreedom to explore the ongoing dynamics of race and gender, sexuality and political economy, history, memory, and national formation that undergird what I dub the *Black reproductive*: the constellation of national discourses, state policies, and individual practices through which Black reproductive acts, capacities, and labor have been imagined and administered in the United States for some 350 years.

This book tacks across historical periods, geographic scales, and academic fields to construct an alternative genealogy of blackness attentive to the workings of the Black reproductive. This revisionary genealogy is built on three foundational premises: First, that the expropriation, administration, and imagination of Black procreation, reproductive labor, and sexuality has been both necessary to and an endangerment of racial capitalism in the United States, alternately resolving and unsettling the sometimes contradictory demands of white supremacy, capitalism, and patriarchy. Second, that the conditions of Black subjection are fundamentally shaped in the antagonistic relation between the extraction and exploitation of reproductive labor, surveillance and management of biological reproduction, and instrumentalization of sexualized violence, and Black people's ongoing multifaceted opposition to these state and extralegal modes of control. And third, that the history of blackness—and especially the history of the Black reproductive—resides not just in archives or histories, political treatises or legal policies, but in the realm of contemporary cultural production. Through practices of mimetic reproduction, these cultural forms and texts do not simply remember or represent Black subjection but re-create and revise it, unraveling and undermining given categories of meaning such as woman, freedom, reproduction, and blackness itself.

If this project is built on these three fundaments, it is impelled by a critical preoccupation with the insights to be gained by theorizing the structures of Black subjugation and the conditions for Black freedom alongside and through the workings of the Black reproductive. It is this concern that shapes my interrogation of the intertwined discourses, structures, and practices of Black reproduction and Black (un)freedom, spurring, in turn, a set of attendant questions: How has the surveillance of, control of, and knowledge production around Black procreation, reproductive labor, and sexuality been a crucial site for the reproduction of racial-sexual common sense in the Americas? How can we reconcile this fixation on the production and reproduction of Black *life* with the material and discursive value of Black social, civil, and physical *death* to the racial capitalist state? And perhaps most significantly, how does attention to the unstable, illegitimate, and double-edged workings of the Black reproductive go beyond elucidating the historic and ongoing conditions of Black unfreedom to make room for the emergence of a Black feminist politics of freedom that eschews purity for proliferation, resolution for contradiction, and linear progress for aporetic undecidability?[2]

I explore these questions by reading a diverse set of late twentieth-century cultural representations of procreation, reproductive labor, and sexuality in African chattel slavery in order to locate a Black feminist political theory that posits unfree sexualized violence, procreation, and reproductive labor as integral to Black subjection. Reading these texts alongside and against a series of nineteenth-century literary, scientific, and political sources, I follow the effaced trace of Black reproductivity to chart a reconfigured theory and history of Black unfreedom and to imagine the possibilities of a radically reconfigured conception of the politics of Black freedom. All too often, discourses of Black subjectivity and subjugation—both dominant and counterhegemonic—either presuppose normative heteromasculinity as the default category for Black political oppression and resistance or instrumentalize discussions of gender and sexuality in service of a universalizing analytic of Black subjection that implicitly reinstantiates Black masculinity as the transparent category through and in which political meaning inheres. Approaching Black unfreedom as a social and racial formation that relies on Black reproductivity as a technology for the violent creation, negotiation, and evacuation of sexualized and gendered categories of meaning poses a crucial challenge to these heteromasculine frameworks. This alternative conceptualization of the relationship between violence, race, gender, and political subjectivity provides a critical framework through which to reconceptualize the racial calculus through which Black subjection is produced and maintained and to reimagine the conditions of possibility for Black freedom writ large.

This project is built on intellectual ground held in common by scholarship on the Black radical tradition and contemporary feminist studies of reproduction, including an analysis of capitalism as "'deeper' and 'broader' . . . than 'wage labour' and 'capital.'"[3] To this shared tenet I bring an understanding of race and reproduction as integrally connected aspects of the state and extralegal administration of life and death as well as a commitment to eschewing nationalist and heteronormative myths of singular, authentic, or pure origins. As an analytical framework and encompassing rubric, then, what I name the Black reproductive emerges at the intersection of these fields and their shared concerns to offer a heuristic for thinking through the dynamic relationship between heteropatriarchy and racial capitalism in the modern and postmodern eras.

Supplemental Declensions—Theorizing Blackness and Reproductivity

What follows situates the Black reproductive within broader conversations on blackness and on reproduction within feminist theory, queer theory, and African American and African diaspora studies, through an approach best described as *declension.* A grammatical term denoting a lexical variation in the form of a word or the act of enumerating such variations, *declension* also has an older, figurative denotation of falling away, deviation, or decay from an allegiance or standard. It thus seems an appropriate descriptor for a practice of *un*defining, in which seemingly stable and expected meanings are unraveled, allowing unexpected and unstable meanings to emerge.

In lieu of defining blackness or reproduction, I instead approach their meanings as contingent, contested, and changeable in relation to material contexts. By tracing that changeability, I map a set of dynamic relationships—between race and reproduction, reproductivity and normativity, slavery and blackness, blackness and the human—that constitute the material and discursive terrain on which this project is built.

First Declension: Blackness

Blackness is a material-discursive system of racial signification through which the "death-dealing displacement of difference" is produced, maintained, and contested.[4] Throughout this book, I use *blackness* to name that which operates *as* and *at* the limit of the human as well as the processes and practices by which that limit has been disrupted, leveraged against itself, transgressed, and even transformed. In this sense, it is at once a relation, a condition, and a form of consciousness.[5]

As the limit of the human, blackness names the fluid, interconnected relations of "dominance and abjection" that are imposed and rearticulated through political geographies ranging from the body to the home, the antebellum plantation to the postindustrial cityscape, the settler colonial nation-state to the African diaspora.[6] It describes the shifting and porous boundary that organizes both the opposition of and the "surreptitious traffic and exchange" between human and inhuman, person and thing, life and death, captive and free.[7] At the same time, blackness is a political geography itself: the horizon of the human through which differential value and vulnerability are produced and assigned to particular bodies. In this sense, blackness-*as*-limit is a terrain of violence—what Mary Pat Brady dubs, in another context, an "abjection machine."[8]

The history of blackness *as* and *at* humanity's limit is in itself a history of relations: namely, the power-laden interdependence of Black unfreedom, Western liberalism, and racial capitalism. I take these relationships in turn. First, as scholars of transatlantic slavery have argued for a century, the transmogrification of captive Africans to commodified Black slaves was integral to the emergence of modern racial capitalism as both mode of production and mode of life.[9] Not only did the hyperexploitation of Black labor, trade in Black bodies, and speculation on Black captivity and sale prove integral to the building of European and American capitalism, but in the United States, Black chatteldom determined the parameters of private property as a social and legal category. As Cheryl Harris argues, it was "the racial line between white and black" that came to determine those who could possess property in all its forms and those who could be possessed as property—that is, to demarcate the "line of protection from the potential threat of commodification."[10] The constitutive impossibility of Black self-possession in contradistinction to "whiteness as property" continues to constitute Black people as prior (and always potential) commodities—what Karl Marx describes as objects that can be possessed but that possess no inherent use value of their own, external to the social relations within which they are embedded.[11] In this sense, blackness names both a relation and a condition of being: the subject-as-commodity who is "by definition always already void of relationality."[12]

Second, the processes by which enslaved Africans were transported not beyond but *to the very limit of* humanity were crucial for the emergence of liberal conceptions of the universal human.[13] As blackness was instantiated as the marker of subjugated and less-than-fully-human status, it became a necessary social category against which (white) personhood and liberty—what C. B. Macpherson describes as "possessive individualism"—could be measured.[14] It is through this configuration of white possessive individualism and Black dispossession that whiteness became "the characteristic, the attribute, the property of free human beings."[15] In turn, devoid of the natural rights and attributes of the universal (white) human—including free will and reason—blackness remains simultaneously the "antiwill, the antithetical embodiment of pure will," and an unruly, unreasoning excess requiring unending domination, punishment, and containment.[16] Within this death-dealing "hierarchy of human and inhuman persons that in sum, form the category of 'human being,'" blackness is positioned at humanity's horizon.[17] Bound by liberal humanism's laws and norms but exempted from its protections, the Black subject-*at*-the-limit occupies the "vestibular" status of inhuman human, contingent life, and nominal freedom.[18]

It is this impossible condition of blackness as both void and excess, human and inhuman, person and object, life and deathliness, that Christina Sharpe has evocatively described as the "paradox" of "Black non/being" that she names "the wake." Sharpe's concept of the wake underscores the inseparability—indeed, the co-constitution—of the "conditions of Black life as it is lived near death, as deathliness in the wake of slavery," and a "form of Black *consciousness*" that seeks neither explanation nor resolution for Black abjection but confronts "the impossibility of such resolutions."[19] This book also meditates on the forms of consciousness that emerge in the context of blackness's impossibilities and irreconcilabilities. Instead of approaching this condition-cum-consciousness as paradoxical, however, this project draws upon a genealogy of Black dialectical thinking to read this impossibility within the framework of contradiction, thus emphasizing the generative potential of the contradictory, the irreconcilable, and the seemingly impossible.

As Saidiya Hartman most skillfully demonstrates, the postemancipation rearticulation of Black subjection within the lexicon of citizenship did not nullify the strategic contradiction underpinning the chattel slave's status as person-cum-property. Instead, that central contradiction was reconfigured to rationalize a Black legal subject exceptional in his civil obligations yet excepted from civil rights. At the same time, emancipation's signification of blackness as not only mute, objectified extralegality but also the threatened proliferation of alterity-in-excess both justified and obscured intensified state and extralegal campaigns of containment, intimidation, and punishment.[20] In this context, the captive African body's availability for metaphorical and physical constraint, expropriation, and enjoyment foreshadowed and enabled the ongoing production and exploitation of the nominally free Black subject as characterized by her "vulnerability to premature death."[21] The relationship between contemporary blackness and the slave, then, is perhaps best described not as one of supersession or instantiation but of *différance*.[22]

This differantial relation between blackness and the slave is materialized as both structural condition and political subjectivity. As a consciousness that coalesced in the context of slavery and European imperial expansion but was sedimented over centuries, blackness is neither entirely independent from nor reducible to the conditions of chatteldom. Formed amid the conditions of the Middle Passage, chattel slavery, and the ongoing modes of Black unfreedom that Hartman dubs "the afterlife of slavery," Black consciousness was nurtured by the epistemologies, subjectivities, practices, and political formations that predated those acts of mass kidnapping, captivity, and dispossession.[23] Thus, while blackness names a liminal category of (in)humanity that produces and is produced at the limit of the human, it also constitutes a negation of liberal humanism as a tool for and phenomenon of Black subjection.[24] An unassimilable stance shaped by "the meanings that Africans brought to the New World as their cultural possession" and transmogrified by "similar and interrelated systems of servitude and oppression," it is integral to European and American liberal and neoliberal racial capitalism, even as it exceeds and endangers those very systems of power and meaning.[25] At once immanent and unassimilable, it is a political subjectivity constituted in the crucible of racial subjugation but not *of* it.

Second Declension: Reproductivity

If theorizing the Black reproductive demands grappling with blackness's contradictions and impossibilities, so too does it require an expansion, supplementation, and resignification of reproduction. In this work, I signal that resignification through my use of the term *reproductivity.* Commonly defined as both one's reproductive ability and the state or condition of being reproductive, *reproductivity* is at once a quality and a capacity, a "dense transfer point for relations of power" and value, and a means of articulating ideological schema.[26] A variation of the older term *reproductiveness* (which is, in itself, one degree abstracted from the seemingly more concrete and self-evident *reproduction*), it simultaneously evokes both productivity and reproduction. At the same time, its variance marks it as a *supplement* to existing lexicons of meaning: an index of the unspoken yet ever-present networks of signification in which modern understandings of race, gender, sexuality, and capital are intertwined, and from which they emerge.

In one register, *reproductivity* is a way of naming the ensemble of discourses, state and individual practices, and collective fantasies through which modern notions of race, gender, and sexuality have been given form and meaning through the logics and language of reproduction. In this sense, this study's emphasis on reproductivity extends the work of feminist scholars on what Alys Weinbaum has dubbed "the race/reproduction bind"—that is, the inextricable interconnection of race and reproduction in the creation and maintenance of the modern nation.[27] In the context of U.S. racial capitalism, reproduction is always already a "racial project," structured by and interpreted through systems of racial meaning-making.[28] Conversely, modern racial categories and logics rely on notions of reproducibility—biological or otherwise—for their coherence. As perhaps it goes without saying, within the racial capitalist state, the co-constitutive entanglement of race and reproduction is never simply a dualistic bind; it is a complex articulation, structured in dominance with relations of gender, sexuality, and capital.[29] As it delves into distinct moments of Black reproductivity in the United States—from U.S. antebellum slavery, to post-Reconstruction, to the social and political mire of midcentury Black America, to the crisis in neoliberal capitalism at the end of the second millennium—one of the goals of this book is to trace how these complex relations of race and reproduction shift and change in different places and at different times.

In another register, reproductivity also refers to the material *work* of reproduction, including the production of the material and immaterial vital resources of human life and the production and reproduction of labor power. Procreation, waged and unwaged domestic work, and sexual labor and leisure are thus all part of the labor of reproduction.[30] Seemingly outside the networks of commodity exchange, the work of reproduction appears as "mere service" and thus as labor that produces no value. However, as Neferti Tadiar notes, it is precisely this apparent valuelessness that makes it possible for the reproduction of life and labor to "striv[e] against the conditions of commodification, objectification, and exploitation"—that is, to create ephemeral modes (or moments) of life unquantifiable by racial capitalism.[31] My point, here and elsewhere in this book, is not to imply an absolute recuperation or uncritical celebration of the reproductive; rather, it is to suggest that it is precisely these double-valanced characteristics of reproductivity that make it a critical terrain for subversion and transgression as well as exploitation and coercion.

In making this argument, I am, in part, responding to deployments of the reproductive within queer theory. The past decade and a half has heralded the emergence of a new body of critical queer scholarship on the politics of temporality that has drawn much-needed attention to how discourses of heteronormative procreation and the heteropatriarchal family have served to regulate temporality according to liberal notions of future progress and the interests and norms of bourgeois capitalism. Within the vast majority of this work, however, reproduction occupies a pivotal yet circumscribed role as an unquestioned delineator of the purview of (hetero)normativity. Lee Edelman's much-critiqued screed against "reproductive futurism," *No Future,* is not alone in casting reproductivity within the temporality of "generational succession . . . and narrative sequence, not toward the end of enabling change, but instead, of perpetuating sameness." Jack Halberstam contrasts queer time's opposition to "family, heterosexuality, reproduction" with "reproductive temporality," which, he argues, upholds "respectability, and notions of the normal on which it depends."[32] For Halberstam, reproduction is, on the one hand, the heteronormative master narrative that conceals the complex workings of social collectivity, and, on the other hand, the regressive and normative mode of generation that can and should be supplemented, if not supplanted, by alternative forms of construction, new modes of reanimation, and nonsexual processes of biological replication.[33]

Since the emergence of "queer time" as a popular critical theory catchphrase, a rich body of work has emerged to complicate how queerness, futurity, and temporality itself are conceived of. The most compelling and generative of these approaches effectively disarticulate futurity and childhood from the imperatives of white (hetero)normativity by resituating Edelman's and others' abstract conceptions of the future within material relations of race, class, or gender. Yet even these otherwise insightful works have largely failed to challenge the presumed role of the reproductive in the production and enforcement of normative temporality.[34] For example, José Esteban Muñoz's otherwise brilliant meditation on the profound political possibilities of a queer-of-color futurity in the here and now, *Cruising Utopia,* leaves unquestioned reproduction's "incredible mandate as a world-historical virtue"—a mandate about which women-of-color victims of state-sanctioned sterilization programs from North Carolina to Puerto Rico to Pine Ridge Reservation might, understandably, express skepticism.[35] Within each of these texts, "the reproductive" is repeatedly counterposed with "the queer"—or, in the case of Edelman, the "sinthomosexual."[36] As temporality's modifier, it is the lexical helpmate that keeps time straight.

In contradistinction to these readings of the reproductive as a mode of spatiotemporal regulation in the service of (hetero)normative idealizations of sameness and biopolitical narratives of linear progress, this book engages reproduction's other denotation as a copy, representation, or rendition—that is, as those objects and processes that displace authenticity in favor of plurality, undermine authority, and "shatter . . . tradition."[37] This sense of reproduction, I suggest, remains the indissoluble shadow to its more prominent, procreative usage. Given this, I draw upon feminist redeployments of mimesis unleashed—or *mimétisme*—to theorize how the feminized performance of replication is not bound to provide a faithful reproduction of an original referent but instead is "impossibly double, simultaneously the stake and the shifting sands: order and potential disorder, reason and madness."[38] To read reproduction as mimesis without guarantees is to perceive reproduction simultaneously as a system of stable origins and linear descent and as a practice that throws into crisis the very notion of true origins through the threat of repetition without referent or limit.

• • •

To speak of Black reproductivity is not simply a matter of particularization or specificity. *Black* is no mere modifier of reproduction, any more than *reproductivity* serves to narrow a broader study of blackness. Rather, blackness and reproduction are co-constitutive terms that, even in each other's absence, shape the parameters by which each is understood and deployed. Indeed, to argue for the centrality of Black reproductivity to the study of blackness, gender, and power in the United States is to first recall that blackness itself is "unavoidably reproducible and reproductive."[39] It is a dynamic terrain for the reproduction of hierarchies of power and difference within social formations. By lending meaning to existing structures and structuring relations of power, value, and difference, it reproduces the conditions for its own existence and transformation. At the same time, as a signifier, it is continuously reproducible, given new meanings and renewed force in different places and historical moments. It appears in unlikely venues, from Sigmund Freud's musings on hysteria to Founding Fathers' family trees, and in altered forms, such as the dis(re)membered body of an angry ghost or the vomited remains of a stolen lunch. This continuous rebirth of blackness as overdetermined signifier underscores its continuing efficacy for rationalizing and naming ongoing, uneven relations of power and difference in geographically and historically specific forms and contexts.

Even as Black procreation, domestic labor, and sexual labor and leisure have been materially vital to the growth of U.S. racial capitalism and white liberal democracy, Black reproductivity disrupts the linear progress narratives or stable ontologies on which such structures rely. It is a radical form of *mimétisme,* an "unremitting and interminable process of revision, reelaboration, mimcry, and repetition [that] prevents efforts to locate an originary or definitive point on the chain of associations."[40] A theory of Black reproductivity thus requires grappling with reproduction as a node of undecidability that encompasses both regulated procreation and unintended proliferation; names cumulative development and the accumulation of value in excess; and describes not only linear progress but also the political possibilities that emerge when, in the course of repetition and regeneration, systems go awry. In short, it is both the mechanism by which normativity is reproduced and the imminent glitch in that same machine, sometimes making possible the emergence of new formations, desires, and subjectivities.

Following the Trace of Black Reproductivity: Three Premises

A genealogy of the Black reproductive in the United States both enables and demands a revisionary theory of Black subjugation and of the conditions and practices of Black freedom. Such a theory, in turn, requires reexamining key concepts in Black studies with a Black feminist eye: looking closely at the interwoven histories of Black reproductivity and racial capitalism; attending to the gendered processes of Black subjugation and subject formation; and engaging cultural production as a vital site for creating historical knowledge about blackness. This section offers an initial foray into just such a Black feminist mode of inquiry, explicating the theoretical frameworks and methodological approaches that animate this text via three propositions, or premises, that provide the analytical scaffolding on which the following chapters are built.

The Black Reproductive as Enabling/Endangering Condition

I start from the premise that Black reproductivity is a condition of possibility for U.S. racial capitalism. For four centuries, the administration, expropriation of, and production of knowledge around Black sexuality, procreation, and reproductive labor have subtended the U.S. racial state and the colonial formations that preceded it. African chattel slavery in the Americas was not only the precondition for the emergence of European and U.S. industrial capitalism but also consubstantial with it.[41] In its mature form, chattel slavery in the United States was "capitalism with its clothes off": it both exposed and exponentially magnified modern capitalism's exploitation of labor (that is, the theft of labor power's value) and alienation of laborers (from their labor, humanity, and social relations).[42] In turn, enslaved women's procreation serves as late slavery's naked case exemplar, in which chatteldom's legal, economic, and social processes of expropriation and dispossession were themselves laid bare. Following the legal end of its participation in the transatlantic slave trade, the United States became the only slaveholding society in the Americas to successfully rely on so-called natural increase—that is, the multigenerational growth of an enslaved labor force and expansion of a plantation economy solely through the procreation of existing captives. It was only through natural increase that slaveholders could maintain and increase their cash crop production on the scale necessary for a quickly industrializing economy, that U.S. settler expansion into new slaveholding territories could continue throughout the first half of the nineteenth century, and that the domestic slave trade could emerge as a vital market economy of both exchange and speculation upon which white Americans, North and South, made their fortune.[43]

There was nothing natural about slavery's "natural" increase—rather, it was built on the legal foundation of *partus sequitur ventrem,* which consigned all children of enslaved women to lifelong slavery by tying the inalienable status of slave to one's maternal lineage. With its inversion of British common laws of patrilineal inheritance, *partus* produced a legal system in which white people's rights to property were passed down from free fathers, while Black people's status *as* property was inherited from enslaved mothers. In short, *partus* made social death—the status of social nonentity produced and maintained by the material and discursive structures of slavery—an inalienable matrilineal inheritance.[44] Under the rule of *partus,* the material and ideological conditions of the plantation economy—the multigenerational social death of the slave—were reproduced literally on, in, and through the enslaved woman's reproductive body, and through the management of Black intimate life.

The stakes of enslaved Black reproductivity were not just economic; the management of Black reproductivity was also central to the ideologies and semiotics of antebellum slavery. As Walter Johnson has argued, within the timocratic, or honor-based, society of the slaveholding South, white masculinity was measured by a man's mastery over slaves—both the possession of property in the form of other people and the correctly calculated deployment of threats and punishments, physical violence and sale, and even, occasionally, reward.[45] With the nineteenth-century expansion of a cash-crop plantation economy and the attendant demands to "rationalize plantation operations" for greater efficiency, the art form of white masculine mastery became a science in which existing tools of terror and brutality and strategies of negotiation were joined by the extensive biopolitical management of the physical and social lives of the enslaved. The idealized role of the slaveholder came to include not only the management of enslaved labor and discipline but also their domestic relationships and familial structures, their bodies and behaviors, and even their desires. This shift to the rationalized scientific management of slave populations coincided and converged with the professionalization of medical care and the emergence of women's health as an area of scientific inquiry and debate, inextricably entangling the surveillance and management of Black women's reproduction, the production of scientific knowledge about the female body, and the maintenance and expansion of U.S. racial capitalism in a material-discursive bind that to the present has yet to be undone.[46]

In emancipation's wake, the "natal alienation" of *partus sequitur ventrem,* the scientific and social rationalization of Black biological and social life, and the dispossession of body, home, and kin that characterized social death and gave meaning to chattel slavery in the United States ceased legally to structure Black existence.[47] And yet the expropriation, administration, and imagination of Black reproductivity have remained integral to the reproduction of the U.S. racial capitalist state, from policies of reproductive control to systems of social welfare, and from treatises on racialized pathology to liberal strategies for Black progress through inclusion and incorporation. As the last half century of popular panics over dysfunctional matriarchs, "crack babies," "welfare queens," and, more recently, "baby mamas" demonstrate, the Black reproductive—and, by extension, the Black female reproductive body—have remained a crucial terrain for political and ideological struggle.

At the same time, the structural viability and ideological coherence of both U.S. racial capitalism and the principles of American liberalism that undergird it have been built upon the disavowal and denegation of Black reproductivity. From Thomas Jefferson's excision of slavery from both the Declaration of Independence and his treatises on republican self-sufficiency to today, the maintenance of white possessive individualism, with its attendant idealization of self-sufficiency and self-improvement through the accumulation of property, has required obscuring white property owners' dependence on the low- and unwaged labor of Black people and other people of color for the reproduction of the necessary conditions for white life. Likewise, the antebellum slave codes, with their overweening commitment to the inalienable rights of white men to enjoy their private property in the form of other people, rendered the sexualized brutality and terror through which the Black female subject was made a slave a form of unrecognizable "negligible injury" and Black women's sexual consent a legal impossibility—a legacy that lives on in contemporary constructions of Black femininity as imminently vulnerable to sexualized violence.[48] And 350 years after *partus* and attendant legal codes delegitimized structures of Black kinship in order to maintain Black people as property, Black kin systems remain illegible to the surveilling eye of the welfare state outside the dominant narratives of criminality and pathology.

Rather than perceiving this foreclosure as merely a series of omissions to be rectified, I am interested in the generative possibilities that emerge if we see Black reproductivity as a historical *trace* immanent to the U.S. racial formation—that is, "the mark of the absence of a presence, an always already absent present . . . that is the condition of thought and experience."[49] Even as it serves as the "internal and positive condition of possibility" for the racial calculus through which Black subjugation is organized, rearticulated, and leveraged, Black reproductivity's undecidability and proliferation of alterity-in-excess threaten the ideals of racial purity and biopolitical control that undergird contemporary structures of racial capitalism and systems of racial and gendered meaning.[50] Alternately resolving and unsettling the sometimes contradictory demands of white supremacy, capitalism, and patriarchy, the Black reproductive is less the solution to a political conundrum than the posing of a conceptual problem; its potential lies not in the resolution (or solution) that it offers but in the contradictions that it exposes and the oppositions it destabilizes.

Black Reproductivity and Black Subjection

To posit Black reproductivity as an enabling condition for U.S. racial capitalism demands revising existing conceptions of the relationship between blackness, gender, reproduction, and subjection. This revision is the topic of my second premise: that Black subjection takes shape amid the antagonistic relation between the extraction and exploitation of Black reproductivity, on the one hand, and Black people's ongoing opposition to these state and extralegal modes of power, on the other. If the Black reproductive is integral to the U.S. racial capitalist state, it is equally inextricable from Black subjection—that is, both the multiscalar discourses and structures of Black subjugation and the myriad modalities of Black subject formation. Indeed, the surveillance and management of Black procreation, the extraction and exploitation of Black reproductive labor, and the deployment of sexualized violence on and against Black bodies have been crucial technologies for both the domination, containment, and punishment of Black people and the construction and negotiation of blackness as a racial and sexual category. Moreover, the historic dependence on and disavowal of Black reproductivity, the delegitimation of Black kinship, and the denegation of Black gendered subjectivity have produced an ongoing grammar of Black subjection structured by the necessary and impossible figure of the ungendered Black reproductive female.

As Hortense Spillers has argued, for Black Americans in the context and historic wake of chattel slavery, the management of Black reproduction, the leveraging of racialized brutality and terror, and the delegitimation of enslaved kinship through the laws of *partus* became inextricably linked in a racial system of meaning within which the slave is transformed from body—the precondition for personhood—to flesh, "that zero degree of social conceptualization" constituted by the severing of species life from human relationality and corporeality from embodiment.[51] Under the conditions of the flesh, sex and gender are denatured: in the absence of the social body, "the respective subject-positions of 'female' and 'male' adhere to no symbolic integrity," and the severing of reproduction from the claims of kin and the "mutilation, dismemberment, and exile" of the captive render "female *flesh* ungendered."[52] Rather than understanding Spillers's oft-cited concept of "ungendering" as a stripping away of difference that rendered all chattel genderless, a reading attendant to the trace of Black reproductivity identifies ungendering as the process of putting gendered subjectivity under erasure—that is, not its absence but the radical impossibility of its presence. Rather than suggesting the extraneousness or irrelevance of gender under the formative conditions of Black unfreedom, then, the ungendering of the enslaved Black female names how slavery's dispossession rendered Black gender itself as that necessary impossibility through which an altered lexicon of race, gender, and humanity was enacted, a divergent "theory and praxis" under which "'reproduction,' 'motherhood,' 'pleasure,' and 'desire' are all thrown into crisis."[53] Out of this crisis of meaning, the enslaved Black reproductive female emerges as a dissonance engendered by the articulation of an unimaginable political subjectivity, a rupture that "breaks in upon the imagination with a forcefulness that marks both a denial and an 'illegitimacy.'"[54] In short, she is "less an identity than what we might call a predicament": a subject who should not be a subject, whose very existence calls into question the categorical boundaries between production and reproduction, commodity and kin, social death and biological life.

To explicate Black subjection through the framework of Black reproductivity and the impossible subjectivity of the enslaved Black female thus revises how we narrate the conditions of Black subjugation and tracks a different trajectory of Black people's struggles against their own dispossession and for their freedom. Rather than attempting to counter the rupturing impact of enslaved Black reproductivity on Black subjectivity, this book follows in the tradition of contemporary Black feminist, queer, and trans scholarship by eschewing celebrations of Black men as the exemplary subjects of slavery and radical oppositional agents of freedom while also rejecting ongoing efforts to reclaim Black feminine subjecthood via the liberal norms of (white) women's empowerment. Instead, shaped by the simultaneous discursive impossibility and material necessity of Black reproductivity, it explores modes of resistance that do not seek liberation in the pure, the stable, or the knowable but instead seek to deploy the power of the impossible, the undecidable, the contingent, and the contradictory to produce instances of generative crisis and productive undecidability.

The Neoslave Narrative as Mimetic Reproduction

If the Black reproductive is the absented presence that subtends the U.S. racial formation, then how do we offer an accounting of that trace? This book starts from the premise that the history of blackness—and the historical trace of the Black reproductive—can be read for in contemporary Black cultural production. I thus ground my analysis in the realm of cultural production by Black women that grapples with the meaning, mechanisms, and afterlife of chattel slavery from the vantage point of the contemporary moment. I refer collectively to these cultural objects drawn from multiple contexts and genres as "contemporary narratives of slavery," intentionally invoking that defining genre of late twentieth-century African American literary production, the neoslave narrative.[55] While neoslave narratives were originally described by Bernard Bell in 1987 as "residually oral, modern narratives of escape from bondage to freedom" that use the structure and form of the antebellum fugitive slave narrative in order to recall and reflect upon the historical meaning of African chattel slavery, I follow more recent scholarship—most notably, that of Arlene Keizer—in expanding the genre to encompass not only historical narratives of slavery but also works set in the present and recent past that understand contemporary Black existence to encompass and reflect the residues of chattel slavery, as well as "hybrid works" that collocate past Black enslavement and present modes of racialized life and death.[56] Indeed, while my own interpretation is deeply influenced by Ashraf Rushdy's formative study of how late twentieth-century global and social economic crises produced the structural conditions for the burgeoning body of literature revisiting chattel slavery, this book expands the category of contemporary/neoslave narrative beyond what Rushdy narrowly describes as "contemporary novels that assume the form, adopt the conventions, and take on the first-person voice of the antebellum slave narrative." Its objects of analysis include film, visual art, and performance, in recognition that while literacy and literary production have fulfilled a vital function in African American cultural politics since the era of the talking book, Black narrativity has never been solely literary; thus, the intertextual and signifying relationships between orality, performance, and textuality that exceed the text also make up a critical part of Black cultural production.[57] Despite these divergences, I retain the term *neoslave narrative* as a means of indexing this longer legacy of cultural politics and literary criticism and of entering into conversation with recent generative rearticulations of the term, such as Joy James's description of abolitionist writings by incarcerated people as "(neo)slave narratives" and Dennis Childs's use of "narratives of neoslavery" to name those "prison and chain-gang centered soundings, writings, testimonies, and social practices" that bring into relief the "unsettling continuities of slavery" in its postemancipation afterlife.[58] Like James and Childs, I seek to track the uneven continuities between African chattel slavery and the contemporary systems of surveillance, dispossession, and containment that reproduce and maintain Black unfreedom—including the modern prison-industrial complex and contemporary politics and policies around raced reproduction.

As I argue in the early chapters of this book, contemporary neoslave narratives are both formal revisions of the antebellum fugitive slave narrative and revisionary historiographies of chattel slavery in the Americas that interrogate the processes through which both historical knowledge and racial subjects are produced, mediated, and articulated. Eschewing the practices of documentation in favor of citation, reiteration, and imagination, they enact a critical and textual practice of mimetic reproduction that does not simply remember or represent Black subjection and subjectivity but re-creates and revises them. By writing with, rather than against, the impossibility of fully testifying to slavery's raced and gendered processes of dispossession, the neoslave narrative as a genre has been a venue for the reconfiguration of the relationship between cultural production and social formation, a mode of unmaking and remaking history from the perspective of the present, and a method for the radical proliferation of revisionary theories and aesthetics of blackness.[59]

Accordingly, rather than using a body of critical and political theory to explore, expose, or analyze the form and content of cultural texts, I instead read the narratives of slavery in this book as constituting what Keizer dubs "fictional theories," deploying them as a refractory lens through which to reread and revise some of the central tenets of historical scholarship on Black freedom and unfreedom, and as meditations on the contemporary "complex set of relations of domination for which we do not yet have a literary or visual language."[60] In their practice of "re-memory," these contemporary narratives of slavery illuminate the entangled gendered and sexualized discourses and structures that constitute reproductivity as a critical technology of power through which Black subjectivity and subjugation are imagined and materialized.[61] My reading of these contemporary neoslave narratives as offering both a theory of history (not a history in itself but a political consideration of the production of history) and a theory of change (a material conception of how we might make alternative modes of living and dying possible) emerges from a belief in and commitment to the capacities of the "fictive" to signal the trace of the unspeakable, the foreclosed, and the must-be-forgotten that haunts histories of chattel slavery and social scientific studies of Black reproduction.[62]

Reading between the lines and against the grain of Black women's literature, art, and performance, I trace the ephemeral outline of a reconfigured feminist theory of Black reproductivity that expands existing parameters of both Black radicalism and Black feminism by interrogating the seeming stability of critical categories of meaning such as man/woman, white/Black, human/inhuman, living/dead as they operated in the context of African chattel slavery and subsequent systems of Black unfreedom. To do so, I follow a path that strays from both the conventions of literary close reading and the structures of political theory. Given that so many of Black feminist theory's earliest tenets emerged first in literature—novels, poems, plays, and creative nonfiction—the Black feminist reading practice at work in this project sits intentionally, albeit somewhat uneasily, at the interstices of the literary and the political. I approach each text discussed in this book as both a literary and cultural object and as a site for the articulation of a reconfigured theory of history and of change; I understand the theorizations of blackness, reproductivity, politics, and freedom that emerge to be neither overlooked elements inherent to these relatively well-known texts nor extrinsic theories constructed and applied by a creative reader. Rather, I understand the Black feminist theory articulated throughout this book to be *created* just as much as it is *located,* through dogged attention to the points of undecidability, contradiction, and impossibility that constellate around each text's engagement with Black reproductive politics, logics, and practices.

• • •

This book begins with an examination of the infamous Black reproductive icon Aunt Jemima. Consumer brand, cultural icon, and racist trope, Aunt Jemima illuminates three claims integral to this book's overarching argument: that the extraction and exploitation of Black women's reproductive labor and the commoditization and consumption of Black female bodies have been integral to the reproduction of U.S. heteropatriarchy, white supremacy, and racial capitalism; that the material history and cultural imagination of enslaved and subservient Black female reproductivity constitute a vital enabling imaginary of U.S. racial capitalism; and finally, that the Black female reproductive body—that is, the reproductive body-made-*flesh*—remains a dynamic and contested terrain for the negotiation of racial, gendered, and sexual meaning. This first chapter lays out the intertwined and mutually constitutive relationship between Black procreation, reproductive and domestic labor, and sexuality that I expand on throughout the book.

Chapter 2 reads enslaved maternity and domesticity through the lens of the Black reproductive. In it, I revisit and extend a question posed by Hartman in *Scenes of Subjection* that remains unanswered: "What happens if we assume that the female subject serves as a general case for explicating social death, property relations, and the pained and putative construction of blackness? . . . What possibilities of resignification would then be possible?"[63] To answer it, I juxtapose Toni Morrison's *Beloved* with the legal histories of enslaved women and girls charged with infanticide in the mid-nineteenth century. I argue that *Beloved* offers up a theory of the history of enslaved maternity and domesticity that posits the enslaved maternal body as the exemplar of and structuring condition of Black social death.[64] Through its attention to the intimate forms of sexualized and gendered racial violence that constitute enslaved maternity, domesticity, and kinship, Morrison's novel enables us to rethink the relationship between love, violence, and reproduction on the ostensibly private scales of the antebellum plantation and to envision the political possibilities of claiming the monstrous figure of the insurgent, infanticidal, enslaved mother.

Chapter 3 shifts focus to rethink the politics of unfree sexual labor and sexualized violence as integral aspects of Black reproductivity. I start with a reading of the nineteenth-century fugitive slave narrative *The History of Mary Prince* to explore how Prince's narrative relies on the effacement of her history of sexualized violence and elides the complexity of enslaved female sexuality in order to render her legible as a subject of injury. Juxtaposing Prince's memoir with Gayl Jones's 1975 narrative of slavery and its aftereffects, *Corregidora,* I argue that in her depiction of an embodied genealogy of unfree and coerced sexual labor and violence and her enactment of a literary practice of hysteria, Jones restructures the vexed relationship of hypervisibility and invisibility that structures the nineteenth-century bondwoman's narrative and overdetermines the enslaved female body, reproducing an oblique narrative of the sexualized relations of racial violence and coerced reproduction as deeply imbricated with what Michel Foucault enumerates as a key moment in the transition to biopower: the psychosexual medicalization, or "hystericization," of women's bodies. Using Jones's text to argue that Freud and Ida Bauer's notion of the female hysteric is implicitly haunted by the figure of the racially impure and sexually endangering mulatta, I contend that Jones's use of the blues and hysteria as both narrative tropes and aesthetic forms offers a glimpse of the potential for a Black feminist political practice in the wake of chattel slavery that prioritizes mimetic reproduction over reproductive linearity, feminine jouissance over heteronormative desire, and a Derridean politics of justice over those of restitution.

Chapter 4 brings the previous three chapters' analyses of procreation, domestic labor, and sexual labor and violence to bear on a single historical figure: the iconic-yet-erased figure of Sally Hemings as she appears from the nineteenth century to today in historical texts, written scholarly debates, mainstream news media, and popular novels. Leaving behind the debates over the facticity of Hemings's sexual relationship with Thomas Jefferson, I seek to understand why such a relationship, as signified through the iconic and ephemeral figure of Hemings herself, remains such a heated and visceral concern in the American popular imagination. I argue that Hemings's status as disavowed founding mother lays bare the racial-sexual logics of the U.S. nation-state, indexing the sexual coercion, natal alienation, and total domination through which the United States as a slaveholding nation reproduced itself as well as the disavowed cross-racial desire and consumption that constitute a crucial American structure of feeling. At the same time, the possibility of Hemings loving and desiring within such constraints signifies an articulation of will that irrevocably destabilizes the socio-legal construction of the female slave as socially dead sexual subject—an object without will.

The final chapter extends the previous four chapters' study of enslaved Black reproductivity to consider its continuing crucial function in the twentieth century. I use the history of mainstream reproductive politics in the United States as a framework through which to explore the role that Black reproductivity has played in linking liberal projects of social reproduction to the racial state's management of biological reproduction on and through the Black female body. In it, I read three visual texts: the 1940s public education materials for the Birth Control Federation of America's Division of Negro Service; Lee Daniels's Oscar-winning 2009 film, *Precious*; and the billboard images of recent national public campaigns linking abortion service provision to Black genocide and antiabortion campaigns to activism against anti-Black racism. I argue that these temporally disparate visual texts share a common logic in which the regulation, exploitation, and curtailment of Black women's reproduction remain the acceptable collateral damage for other people's freedom. In contradistinction, I propose the late twentieth-century activism and writings by feminist reproductive justice workers on the politics of freedom as a model for imagining the political potential of a Black liberatory project that centers an analysis of reproductivity within its enunciation of a politics of Black freedom.

The Work of Imagining Freedom

The chapters that follow offer an alternative genealogy of blackness through the lens of Black reproductivity. In so doing, they outline a supplemental theory of history that encompasses not only the historical processes of raced and gendered subjection and subjugation but also the conditions of and for Black freedom. One reading of this book, then, is as a response to legal scholar Dorothy Roberts's exhortation to reimagine liberty through the logics and lexicons of Black reproduction.[65] I argue that attending to how the surveillance, exploitation, and criminalization of Black procreation, reproductive labor, and sexuality have been necessary to maintaining Black unfreedom offers crucial insights into the nature and practice of

Black freedom. Indeed, taking reproductivity seriously, in all its unstable and proliferating forms, might offer up alternative ways of conceptualizing freedom altogether.

Certainly, within the historical context of U.S. liberal democracy in general, and African chattel slavery in particular, the notion of freedom is, at best, vexed, and certainly without guarantees. Indeed, as Orlando Patterson argues in his epic study of slavery, the modern liberal conception of freedom as individual sovereignty rendered slavery a "self-correcting institution" in which the enslaved subject's desire for freedom was used to motivate and discipline her. By leveraging the slave's desire for freedom—especially, but not only, through labor—"manipulating it as the principle means of motivating the slave, who desires nothing more passionately than dignity, belonging, and release . . . the master provides himself with a motivating force more powerful than any whip," Patterson concludes.[66] If notions of freedom as personal authority over one's life and labor served to reproduce the conditions of domination within systems of slavery, then the discourse of racial equality as distorted under the postemancipation regimes of plantocratic white supremacy produced new structures of Black unfreedom. As Hartman has convincingly illustrated, the Reconstruction period marked a moment in which the "very language of persons, rights, and liberties" was quickly seized upon to facilitate continuing "relations of domination" and to enable "new forms of bondage." In this way, the hegemonic discourse of humanity central to how the United States imagined itself, and its attendant vocabulary of natural rights and personal liberty, served to engender for its formerly enslaved subjects "travestied liberty, castigated agency, and the blameworthiness of the individual"; in short, the formal domination of slavery was transmogrified, rather than replaced, by minimally restructured Black unfreedom.[67]

Nor is the concept of freedom within the liberal nation-state unproblematic for those (white) sovereign subjects whose interests liberal racial democracy ostensibly serves, and to whose status rights-based racial justice struggles have typically aspired. Rather, the ideal of freedom as rooted in the presumed primacy of the sovereign individual and defined through an attendant body of ostensibly natural rights and licenses remains rife with dangers. As Chandan Reddy has argued, the construction of freedom as synonymous with the liberal state's protection from the arbitrary, irrational, and illegitimate serves to legitimate its monopoly on violence, transforming what Wendy Brown has dubbed "liberty with license" into an uneven form of domination.[68] Given this, I follow Brown—and the work of women of color feminists over the past fifty years—in defining freedom not as protection from the exertions of power but as a collective political practice able to account for the myriad deployments of power within a regime or set of regimes and to transform how power is produced, deployed, and shared. In this sense, I understand the politics of Black freedom not as a quest for a set of individual rights and authorities but as a conjuncture of "the desire for some degree of collective self-legislation, the desire to participate in shaping the conditions and terms of life," and the collective practice of "struggling for futures" with the understanding that "our survival is mutual."[69]

This book locates the practice of freedom not in legalized emancipation, the achievement of equal rights, or romanticized notions of everlasting liberation but in the "transient and fleeting expression of possibility" engendered in moments of heightened contradiction.[70] Such an approach keeps in mind Hartman's admonition that the "travestied liberty" of post-emancipation Black life renders any unambiguous claim to the status of Black freedom impossible. But it also insists that it is in precisely these aporetic instances of the contingent and ephemeral, the unsustainable and the ruptural, the still-not-achieved yet not-quite-impossible, that the generative potential for Black freedom lies. It is a politics of freedom without guarantee or political end point, a practice of Black "liberation in the future anterior tense."[71] As Gayatri Chakravorty Spivak reminds us, to deploy the future anterior requires us to reject the certainty of a future based on present identities, policies, or strategems and instead, in the moment of crisis, to surrender to radical undecidability as the ethical condition of future possibility.[72] It is a politics of Black liberation that calls forth "manifestations of the future in the degraded present," while concomitantly turning to the past not as the origin for the present but as the prior manifestation of the present's possibilities and failures.[73] Such a politics appears in instances that are only fleetingly intelligible, at least from a stance squarely in the present: the arrival and the banishment of an angry ghost child; a voice that simultaneously hurts and holds; the private bedchamber under the public bathroom.

Thus, while Brown carefully distinguishes her approach from one that renders freedom simply "aesthetic," I would suggest that as critical as it is to resist the aestheticizing of freedom, it is equally important that we seek to imagine the *aesthetics* of freedom—that is, the principles by which a practice of freedom makes itself perceptible in the arena of cultural production.[74] I locate the aesthetics of freedom in that cultural/political labor of Black women that Grace Kyungwon Hong has named "the work of imagination"—the leap of vision and expression that "defies the real . . . in order to be impossibly airborne, even if for a moment"—and that Christina Sharpe describes as "wake work": that is, a way of "re/seeing, re/inhabiting, and re/imagining the world" such that

> we might continue to imagine new ways to live in the wake of slavery, in slavery's afterlives, to survive (and more) the afterlife of property. In short, I mean wake work to be a mode of inhabiting *and* rupturing this episteme with our known lived and un/imaginable lives. With that analytic we might imagine otherwise from what we know *now* in the wake of slavery.[75]

As postcolonial feminists have argued, imagination is neither a form of escapism nor a promise of escape. Rather, it is an act of political confrontation and ethical engagement with that which is radically other and seemingly impossible. Nor is imagination separate from or in opposition to historicization. For even as the work of imagination refuses to "concede the future to the present, but imagines it as something still in the balance, something that can be fought over," it concomitantly underscores the past not as linear origin for the present but as the prior material manifestation of both the possibilities and the failures of the present and the future.[76]

This book explores how Black women's cultural narratives of unfreedom do the political work of imagination. I embark on this inquiry from a Black feminist political and critical position, although my objects of analysis and critical points of entry are not limited to those writers who work or those articulations that are made under the proper name of Black feminism. Indeed, my usage of *Black feminist* as a modifier for the theory of Black reproductivity that emerges in these pages may, at first glance, seem catachrestic: many of the authors, thinkers, and artists within have understood and announced themselves to be working parallel to, if not antagonistically with, that which operates under the sign of feminism. What I ascribe to Black feminism, however, is less a uniform ideology or institutionalized political structure marked by membership or fealty than an ethical and analytical stance, and a political praxis.

In this, I am defining feminism as both the "political commitment to women and to the changes that women desire for themselves and the world" and "a theoretical revolution in the ways in which terms such as art, culture, woman, subjectivity, [and] politics" are understood.[77] This kind of revolutionary theoretical practice is, as Linda McDowell has noted, no small task: "It demands nothing less than the dismantling of the basis of everyday social relations, most institutions and structures of power and the theoretical foundations on which current gender divisions stand."[78] More specifically, it requires a trenchant critique of the deeply embedded and closely held attachments within intellectual and popular circles to a naturalized notion of dichotomous categorical difference; a continuing acknowledgment that such categories are not only binary but also hierarchical; and a close consideration of how they are produced through interrelated axes of sociopolitical power, including race as well as gender. By this I mean not only masculine and feminine, or Black and white, but also the attendant terms through which humanity is measured and social value is calculated: radical and reform, active and passive, oppositional and complicit, life and death. The Black feminist reading I seek to practice in these pages demands attention to how these raced and gendered dichotomies are constructed and maintained in the most intimate of places and the most public—an endeavor that, in itself, necessitates a destabilization of gendered distinctions between the public and private spheres, the local and the global.[79] Moreover, such a strategy operates from an understanding that challenging the hierarchized categorical dichotomies through which the political geographies of race and gender are constituted both enables and demands a trenchant reevaluation of the category of womanhood itself.

The blackness of this feminist reading practice is more than an identity-based amendment; rather, it names a mode of analysis that acknowledges the inextricability of blackness from modern processes of gender construction—that is, a reading strategy that, as Evelynn Hammonds describes it, "make[s] visible the distorting and productive effects" of Black female genders and sexualities on seemingly transparent and stable notions of womanhood, maternity, and sexuality.[80] The following pages thus trace the outlines of what Spillers suggests in the epigraph to this introduction might be possible through "claiming the monstrosity" of the enslaved Black reproductive female: "a radically different text for female empowerment" that relies not on established categories of subjectivity, emplacement, or political recognition but on the very possibilities inherent in the thorough dismantling of such categories and the hierarchies on which they are built.[81]

From its inception, this project has emerged from and evidenced the insufficiency of discrete modes of classification, including those of personal, political, and intellectual; it remains founded as much in affect and activism as in academic theory. I write about Black cultural production because it was in fiction and in verse, on screens and on stages that I first saw the political possibilities of Black feminism literalized. In the writings of Black women, queer and straight, the raced and gendered violence that I could not yet put word to was made language; in their narratives of the "unthinkable," I saw a radical imagination of freedom given form. I consider these literary texts in dialogue with more explicit treatises on the social and political causes and consequences of material structures because it was from women of color writers, artists, and activists in social and political movements that I learned how such ideas could and must be actualized. Ultimately, then, I consider this book to be evidence of the late Barbara Christian's astute observation that in the end, we write to save our own lives.[82]

1

Ain't Your Mama on the Pancake Box?

Aunt Jemima and the Reproduction of the Racial State

> "Peaches" and "Brown Sugar," "Sapphire" and "Earth Mother," "Aunty," "Granny," God's "Holy Fool," a "Miss Ebony First," or "Black Woman at the Podium": I describe a locus of confounded identities, a meeting ground of investments and privations in the national treasury of rhetorical wealth. My country needs me, and if I were not here, I would have to be invented.
>
> —Hortense J. Spillers, "Mama's Baby, Papa's Maybe"

> This is for Hattie McDaniels, Butterfly McQueen, Ethel Waters
> Sapphire
> Saphronia
> Ruby Begonia
> Aunt Jemima
> Aunt Jemima on the Pancake Box
> Aunt Jemima on the Pancake Box?
> AuntJemimaonthepancakebox?
> auntjemimaonthepancakebox?
> Ainchamamaonthepancakebox?
> Ain't chure mama on the pancake box?
>
> Mama, Mama
> Get off of that damn box
> And come home to me
>
> —Kate Rushin, "The Black Back-Ups"

In August 2014, D. W. Hunter and Larnell Evans filed a $3 billion class-action lawsuit against Quaker Oats and its parent company, PepsiCo, on behalf of all descendants of their great-grandmother, Anna Short Harrington. The daughter of sharecroppers from Wallace, South Carolina, Harrington was hired by Quaker Oats in 1935 to portray Aunt Jemima, the kerchief-wearing, griddle-toting brand icon for the company's boxed pancake mix. For the next fifteen years, Harrington was the face, voice, and body of Aunt Jemima for all print advertisements, radio spots, and public appearances. When Quaker Oats trademarked the Aunt Jemima logo in 1937, it was a commercial artist's rendering of Harrington's visage that they submitted. Yet when presented with an existing copy of the 1937 trademark application filed at the U.S. Office of Patents and Trademarks, a death certificate declaring that Harrington was employed by Quaker Oats before her death from diabetes, and innumerable advertisements emblazoned with Harrington's likeness that declared, "I'se in town, honey!" or inveighed readers to "let ol' Auntie sing in yo' kitchen," Quaker Oats and PepsiCo claimed no knowledge or record of Harrington, or of her relationship to the Aunt Jemima brand.[1] In the face of this, Hunter and Evans argued that they were owed not only back royalties for the use of Harrington's image but also revenues for sixty-four original recipes that Quaker Oats had ostensibly stolen from Harrington and used to create foods marketed under the Aunt Jemima brand. The pancakes sold under the Aunt Jemima name, they alleged, were in fact based on Harrington's family recipe, stolen and marketed without permission or remuneration.[2] The case of Harrington's descendants versus Quaker Oats was short-lived: by February 2015, a U.S. District Court had dismissed the case on the grounds that Hunter and Evans had failed to prove themselves as legitimate claimants; indeed, even if they had had legitimate standing as executors of Harrington's nonexistent estate, the court ruled, the statute of limitations for such a claim was long expired.

The case of Harrington's descendants against Quaker Oats offers generative insights regarding Black women's productive and reproductive labor, Black gendered dispossession and commodification, and the relationship between reproduction, kinship, personhood, and property in the afterlife of chattel slavery. Her story certainly is not unique: while her descendants were the first to seek remedy in court, Harrington was one of many named and unacknowledged Black women who helped build Quaker Oats by embodying Aunt Jemima at fairs and exhibitions, promotions, and media appearances for more than seventy years.[3] Just as significant, Hunter and Evans's recounting of their great-grandmother's low-wage exploitation, blatant co-optation, and historical erasure indexes a long history of similar stories. For more than three centuries, the bodies and labor of Black women in what is now the United States have been expropriated and exchanged for the use, enjoyment, and profit of others. Yet even as the commodification of their bodies and the exploitation of their labor have created surplus value, biological and social life, and racial meaning for institutions, individuals, and the state, their ongoing dispossession has been naturalized by legal, political, and cultural logics in which their blackness and femaleness make their only recognizable value that which can be extracted by others. Within these logics, Black women are valuable, but they have no claim on this value: neither the value of their labor power, coerced by masters or sold to corporations for scant wages, nor that of their bodies, displayed, studied, bred, and denigrated; no value to pass on to the children of their children, or for which to claim recompense after years of forced seizure. It is this dispossession that enables the commodification of the Black female body and the appropriation of her toil in the service of racial capitalism, just as it is this devaluation that enables the legal, economic, political, and cultural practices of strategic forgetting and disavowal that serve to undermine historic claims such as Hunter and Evans's.

The state's vested interest in protecting racialized relations of capital is matched by equally strong national cultural investments in maintaining the proprietary fantasy of an idealized, subservient Black maternalism that is expressed solely through the nurturance of non-Black America. By suing Quaker Oats, Evans and Hunter demanded the courts weigh the claims of Harrington's actual, living, Black kin against PepsiCo's (and U.S. consumers') right of unfettered (and uncompensated) access to and income from the abstract Black maternal figure of Aunt Jemima. Thus, when the U.S. District Court dismissed Harrington's descendants as illegitimate claimants, it demonstrated how processes of Black female dispossession and commodification historically have relied on and rationalized the delegitimation of Black kinship claims in order to protect national investments in Black reproductive servitude. From enslaved Black females' coerced production of future generations of property to be exploited, sold, financially leveraged, or bequeathed by their masters even before their birth; to the expectation that Black domestic wage workers reside away from their own children and/or partners to better serve "their" white families; to Black women's exclusion from early social welfare benefits for widowed mothers through state exemptions for "necessary workers," the support and expansion of U.S. racial capitalism has relied on the exclusion of Black people from the dubious forms of protection and recognition granted to the white heteropatriarchal family. As Black feminist scholars have long noted, within the structures of chattel slavery and its enduring afterlife, Black lineage neither bears the imprimatur of patrimony nor enables the claims of kin;

rather, it marks racialized availability to possession by the master, the state, or the corporation.[4] The resulting contradiction of Black maternity in the face of Black dispossession—a subject that I return to in subsequent chapters—is at the heart of the Black reproductive.

The case of Anna Short Harrington and her delegitimized heirs found its rationale and hit its limit of possibility in this elision of Black lineage and Black availability for possession. As Alexander Weheliye argues, the limit of the law as a tool for recognition or redress for racialized subjects lies in its indissoluble linking of subjectivity and property. That is, juridical recognition as persons under the law operates through the codification of personhood as property—a form of self-possession that is guaranteed to white people and conditionally granted to racialized others.[5] If the legal construction of personhood as property is rooted in the hierarchical differentiation between and among groups, then in the United States, it is inextricable from U.S. racial capitalism's emergence out of African chattel slavery and the seizure and settlement of Indigenous lands.[6] In this sense, while Hunter and Evans's suit contested Quaker Oats' ongoing, unremunerated extraction of value from Harrington's labor and image long after her years of employment, their demand for remedy in the form of back royalties ceded to the racialized conflation of legal recognition and property rights. Within the framework of trademarks and contracts, the objectification, commodification, and natal alienation of Black women like Harrington remained unspeakable, outside the parameters of the law.[7]

The Harrington descendants' failure to achieve such juridical recognition, however, is also instructive in what it reveals about the quotidian operation of the law in regard to Black personhood/property.[8] Here, it is helpful to return to Weheliye's case exemplar of the law's foundation in personhood-as-ownership and its undergirding in white supremacy and (settler) colonialism: the writ of habeas corpus. Habeas corpus—literally translated as "you shall have the body"—names the recourse in law that requires imprisoning officials to present a prisoner before a judge to legally justify their ongoing imprisonment.[9] However, in a state in which Black captivity, containment, and punishment are the norm and nonwhite bodies presented before the court all too frequently have been returned to unjust and unlawful imprisonment, the notion of habeas corpus functions unevenly and inadequately as a prerogative writ, while the broader injunction to "produce the body" operates as the unspoken, ubiquitous mandate for all Black people seeking remedy before the courts. From the legal prohibitions against enslaved Black people offering testimony, which required instead for them to exhibit their brutalized bodies as evidence of injury done, to the demand for increasingly high-tech visual evidence—videotapes, iPhone recordings, body cameras—to "prove" over and over again to skeptical prosecutors and juries the unrelenting epidemic of police violence against Black bodies, this expansive sense of habeas corpus undergirds a system of law in which Black people have always been required to present their bodies for a "comparative tabulation of suffering" as the precondition for a juridical recognition of subjectivity that is all too often denied.[10]

This unspoken injunction to produce a (Black) body for juridical recognition created a conundrum for the descendants of Anna Harrington. For if, as Weheliye argues, "the writ of habeas corpus—and the law more generally—anoints those individualized subjects who are deemed deserving with bodies" that form the precondition for their legal personhood, what form of juridical recognition could the courts possibly offer the descendants of Aunt Jemima, the iconic idealization of Black maternal servitude available for purchase and consumption in almost any grocery store in the nation? As the romanticized portrayal of the enslaved Black female as commodity, Harrington qua Aunt Jemima exemplifies what Spillers describes as the Black female "stand[ing] *in the flesh,* both mother and mother-dispossessed."[11] Her costumed figure and trademarked visage instantiate Spillers's observation that in slavery's afterlife, the slave's status as *flesh*—that is, not body but that which both precedes the body and is produced through its mortification—continues to authorize the treatment of Black people as "a kind of raw material," to be commoditized at will.[12] In the face of this, Hunter and Evans's efforts to produce the legal body of their great-grandmother—her Black face smiling from advertisements and trademark applications; the certification of her Black body in death; the literal bodies of her Black descendants, standing in court with their sworn affidavits—inevitably were measured and found wanting in the face of Quaker Oats' eighty-year claim on her *flesh.*

The court may have declared the historical claims of Anna Harrington's descendants to be a case long closed, but the vexed history of Aunt Jemima as a brand icon remains a subject of enduring popular debate and academic interest. For the past several decades, demands for the brand to be discontinued—accompanied by rehearsals of its fraught history—have occurred nearly annually, culminating in Quaker Oats' June 2020 announcement that the Aunt Jemima name and image would be removed from all products within the next six months.[13] Meanwhile, museum exhibits, websites, and popular media stories have been devoted to exploring the history and significance of Aunt Jemima, with approaches ranging from nostalgia to outrage. Scholarship on Aunt Jemima has become what one such researcher has dubbed an academic "cottage industry," with a multitude of critical monographs, book chapters, and journal articles written about the origins of the Aunt Jemima image, its rise to the status of ubiquitous consumer brand, and its evolution in the face of shifting U.S. racial politics.[14] What explains this ongoing proliferation of discourse about a 130-year-old ready-mix brand? No mere relic of the past or simple outdated stereotype, Aunt Jemima remains a sociocultural convergence point of discourses and structures, ideologies and imaginaries, systems of labor and schema of desires. For more than a century, the Aunt Jemima brand and the women who have embodied it have been dynamic repositories for white racial fantasies of Black reproductive servitude and domestic sustenance. More than a consumer brand, Aunt Jemima is an icon of the quotidian forms of Black gendered commodification, expropriated labor, and coerced intimacy that produce gendered racial meaning. A commercialized chronotope invented to suture the break between chattel slavery and its postemancipation afterlife, she exceeds the historical moment of her creation even as she reflects its particular tropes and technologies of Black subordination.

This ongoing fascination with Aunt Jemima in all her incarnations indicates the unexpected importance of the consumer brand in reproducing relations of race, gender, and capital in the United States. As the go-to ready-mix for white housewives in the rapidly industrializing North and Midwest of the early twentieth century, Aunt Jemima offered effortless sustenance for white bodies and the seamless reproduction of white supremacy for white people and aspiring nonwhites alike. Moreover, Aunt Jemima's role in reproducing the nation-state cannot be separated from the icon's construction as the face of Black female reproductive servitude. A distillation of dominant fantasies of the ideal Black woman as purely objectified reproductive labor power, the brand promised eager consumers a "slave in a box": an "ever-smiling producer of food . . . [and a] nurturer who [has] no appetite and make[s] no demands."[15] Not just reproductive, the Aunt Jemima icon itself has been endlessly reproduced: her frequently remade image has been replicated in one version or another on everything from mass-produced quick-cook foods to dolls, cookbooks, cookie jars, and other quotidian cultural artifacts of idealized white domesticity built on aestheticized Black servitude. Her fungibility is that of both blackness and the commodity; indeed, as innumerable advertisements assuring the unmatched pleasure of consuming "Aunt Jemimas" illustrate, the marketing of Aunt Jemima pancake mix has relied on a "symbolic slippage" in which she both "*prepares* and *is* food."[16] This slippage occurs along a chain of commoditization and consumption in which the mass-produced foodstuff to be consumed is signified by the highly consumable image of the commodified Black labor of the cheerful (former) slave, as embodied by a series of Black women whose historic dispossession rendered them interchangeable commodities to be made and remade in the enslaved mammy's image. In short, Aunt Jemima condenses in a single figure what Michael Rogin describes in a different context as "black labor in the realm of production, interracial nurture and sex . . . in the realm of reproduction, and blackface minstrelsy in the realm of culture."[17]

Indeed, Aunt Jemima—the brand, the icon, and the women who came to embody it—is a complex instantiation of Black reproductivity in all its forms, including reproductive and domestic labor, procreation and maternity, and sexual labor and leisure. The mythical cook and housekeeper's salience as a vehicle for producing meaning around Black domestic labor is perhaps self-evident: the trademark offered consumers a nostalgic and romanticized memory of enslaved reproductive and domestic labor that naturalized its expropriation and disavowed the violence of its coercion. Yet even as Aunt Jemima's imagined and ready-mixed slave labor was successfully marketed as preserving white domesticity by "saving dinner" for desperate housewives, its advertised origins in southern slave kitchens worked to conceal its actual reliance on the industrial labor of a largely white, female industrial workforce whose employment was currently transforming notions of white urban domesticity.

Less immediately evident, and far more vexed, are the complex and ambivalent negotiations of Black procreation, maternity, and sexuality that were negotiated in and through the image of Aunt Jemima. The grinning cook in apron and kerchief was a manufactured postbellum iteration of the archetypal mammy, whose surrogate maternal status relied on her nurturance of white families at the expense of her own. However, Aunt Jemima's central role in sustaining the postbellum heteronormative household concomitantly required her inscription within heteropatriarchal norms; thus, one of the brand's most successful marketing ploys was a giveaway of rag dolls portraying her nuclear family, including a husband and two children (Figure 1).[18] And while the long skirts and starched aprons worn by Harrington and a host of other Aunt Jemima spokeswomen held the promise to conceal and contain all traces of wayward Black sexuality, effectively confining the women within to the asexual role traditionally ascribed to the archetypal plantation mammy, Quaker Oats' advertising campaigns all too frequently revealed the sheer force with which anxieties and fantasies about Black female hypersexuality permeated the white cultural imaginary. "Buckwheats with the 'tang' men hanker for," one such ad declared (Figure 2); "Men just can't resist 'em!," another promised. By bringing Aunt Jemima into the kitchen, such ads suggested, virtuous white housewives were able to leverage the racialized sexual allure attributed to the so-called Black jezebel to ensure the security of their home life and continuity of their marriage.

It is this multivalanced instantiation of Black reproductivity in all its senses—procreation, reproductive labor, and sexuality—that makes Aunt Jemima a generative entry point for exploring Black reproductivity. What follows uses the case of Aunt Jemima—consumer brand, cultural icon, and racist trope—to illuminate three claims integral to this book's overarching argument. First, the 130-year history of the Aunt Jemima brand offers insight into how the extraction and exploitation of Black women's reproductive labor and the commoditization and consumption of Black female bodies, both physical and fictional, have been integral to the reproduction of U.S. heteropatriarchy, white supremacy, and racial capitalism—from sustaining white families, to unifying a divided nation, to fueling nationwide systems of mass production. Second, Aunt Jemima's ongoing cultural salience and commercial success illustrate the extent to which U.S. racial capitalism is enmeshed with and buttressed by the material history and cultural imagination of enslaved Black female reproductivity—indeed, fantasies of Black reproductive subservience such as Aunt Jemima constitute one dominant imaginary of the Black reproductive. And finally, exploring the proliferation of discourses, cultural texts, and representational forms that currently circulate under the name "Aunt Jemima" offers an opportunity to meditate on how the Black female reproductive body—that is, the reproductive body-made-*flesh*—remains a dynamic and contested terrain for the negotiation of racial, gendered, and sexual meaning.

Figure 1. An early twentieth-century advertisement for Aunt Jemima Pancake Flour includes an offer for ragdolls of her family: Uncle Mose and her two "little pickaninnies." *New-York Tribune,* November 7, 1909. *Chronicling America: Historic American Newspapers.* Image provided by Library of Congress, Washington, D.C.

Figure 2. A magazine advertisement suggestively promises housewives that Aunt Jemima's buckwheat pancake mix has the "kick" their husbands are "longing" for. *Ladies' Home Journal,* January 1927. Copyright 2015, ProQuest LLC.

The Most Famous Colored Woman in the World

As an icon of Black reproductive labor, Aunt Jemima has many origin stories but no single origin. Because Quaker Oats bars access to its company archives, virtually every account of the brand's creation—popular and academic alike—begins with Arthur Marquette's unsubstantiated 1967 corporate hagiography, *Brands, Trademarks, and Good Will: The Story of the Quaker Oats Company.*[19] According to Marquette, it was 1889 in St. Joseph, Missouri, when white vaudevillian Pete F. Baker appeared on the minstrel stage in the "apron and red-bandanna headband of the traditional southern cook" to perform a "jazzy, rhythmic New Orleans style cakewalk to a tune called 'Aunt Jemima.'" Upon witnessing this performance, journalist Chris Rutt had a brainstorm: he could appropriate the name and image of this model of "southern personality personified" to market the heretofore unnamed and underselling ready-made pancake mix with which he hoped to save the nearly defunct flour mill he had recently purchased.[20]

Four years later, after Rutt and his partner Charles Underwood had sold their flour mill and ready-mix recipe to the R. T. Davis Milling Company, Aunt Jemima the brand was first rendered corporeal. Marquette once again narrates the revelatory moment when R. T. Davis realized that his newly acquired brand required a living spokeswoman and hired former slave Nancy Green to portray Aunt Jemima at the 1893 World's Columbian Exposition. Marquette assures his readers that there was nothing Green enjoyed more than sharing stories and songs from her childhood in slavery while making pancakes for a rapt crowd of hungry fairgoers. Billed as an unmitigated success, Nancy Green's World's Fair appearance was only the first of many, just as she was only the first of a series of Black women—among them Anna Short Harrington—to function as a living trademark by appearing at World's Fairs and expositions, in advertisements, and on variety shows. As undifferentiated Aunt Jemimas, the women would cook pancakes, sing "old home" songs, and spout apocryphal stories of their happy years as an enslaved cook and housekeeper.[21]

In the years since its publication, Marquette's breathless tale of how the minstrelized spectacle of Black feminized subservience served as the unintended spark for masculine white innovation has become a well-worn legend. Yet it is not the only account. Even as Quaker Oats limited access to its private archives, it publicly marketed an alternative narrative. "The Life of Aunt Jemima, the Most Famous Colored Woman in the World" first appeared as a booklet written by Purd Wright and printed by the R. T. Davis Milling Company to commemorate the appearance of Aunt Jemima (that is, Nancy Green) at the World's Colombian Exposition. A mash-up of Green's own sanitized accounts of her life in slavery, glowing reports of the success of the Aunt Jemima World's Fair exhibition, and various outrageous tales of antebellum pancake hijinks on the mythical plantation of Colonel Higbee, "The Life of Aunt Jemima" provided Quaker Oats a foundation for multiple advertising campaigns when it purchased the brand from the Davis Milling Company.[22] Over time, Marquette's corporate history and Wright's plantation stories began to blur in the popular imagination, producing an artful amalgamation of corporate brand management, racist plantation nostalgia, and fables of white male genius and Black female abnegation "saving the day"—or at least, breakfast.

One could be forgiven if such origin stor(ies) of Aunt Jemima call up an image of her as a Black Athena, repeatedly springing forth, fully formed, from the Zeus-like heads of Baker, Rutt, Davis, and Wright. Unsurprisingly, critical attention to the political economic context of the brand's emergence complicate this apocryphal tale. With his midshow "brainstorm," Rutt joined in a nascent marketing trend of the 1870s to leverage the postbellum craze for cuisine, music, and popular literature associated with romanticized notions of the antebellum plantation in order to boost sales. Yet Aunt Jemima and other turn-of-the-century brand-name mammies were not just strategic tools in the mass marketing of the romanticized antebellum South in order to sell mass-produced domestic products to white urban dwellers in the North. If the 1893 World's Fair marked a national economic rapprochement between the South's agricultural cotton industry and the North's textile and consumer commodity production in the service of a new American empire, the messengers for this renewed national unity were Aunt Jemima and her ilk. Along with millions of units of boxed breakfast food, these various Aunt Jemimas were selling something far more important: a nostalgic vision of Black maternalism and domesticity that unified white America—industrialized North and modernizing South—in a shared antebellum fantasy of white supremacy and Black submission, revised for a postemancipation era still reliant on the thoroughgoing political, social, and economic disenfranchisement of Black people.[23] Read through this history, Aunt Jemima could be said to operate as a kind of second-order simulacrum, created at the convergence point of mass-commodity production and the mass reproduction of images, such that the "semiotic production and consumption" of Aunt-Jemima-as-icon was inseparable from the "material production and consumption" of Aunt-Jemima-as-commodity.[24] What started as a brand became a signifier of Black female subservience that supersedes the enslaved Black women whose historic work the product ostensibly replicates and precedes contemporary Black women who are indelibly marked by the brand's insistent naturalization of their cheerful desire to serve.

And yet there is still more to this story. Historians of Black popular culture have noted that the minstrel song "Old Aunt Jemima" was written in 1875 by celebrated Black musician, songwriter, and minstrel performer Billy Kersands, who made it famous through his numerous performances of it throughout the 1870s and 1880s. Baker was likely one of the many white vaudevillians who had adapted Kersands's song for their performances of the standard postbellum minstrel show character of the mammy.[25] The dance he supposedly performed, the cakewalk, was best known until the early 1870s as a plantation dance form popular within enslaved communities. Before its adoption by white minstrel performers, it served as a performance practice of pleasure and embodied artistry that simultaneously mocked the sense of entitlement and superiority expressed by white plantation residents. From this perspective, Black women's portrayals of Aunt Jemima as we know them were "a black female's adaptation of a white male businessman's appropriation of a [white] vaudevillian's imitation of a black male minstrel's parody of an imaginary black female slave cook," performing a dance appropriated by white minstrels and partygoers from former slaves' satirical send-ups of white supremacist elitism.[26]

I offer these multiple origin stories not to suggest that any single one—or even the strategic conglomeration of them all—can provide the "true story" of Aunt Jemima, or of the various men and women who portrayed her. Rather, I present them as what Rosalind Morris describes as "alternative histories"—that is, "not as the disclosures of a final truth, but as the assemblages of utterances and interpretations that might have emerged from a different location." As Morris reminds us, alternative histories neither escape the brush of ideology nor provide access to the real truth; instead, they make visible the instability of the truth claims on which dominant histories rest, offering other modes of making meaning from the past.[27] Read through these alternative histories, the story of Aunt Jemima appears less as one of mythic innovation than a dynamic and contested process of mimetic iteration: from Black to white to Black again; commodified body to embodied commodity; the flesh seized upon, displayed, and celebrated in the service of masculine sovereign embodiment, white domestic sustenance, and—lest we forget—Black financial survival.

Indeed, as this proliferation of creation narratives demonstrates, the image and idea of Aunt Jemima has served as a semiotic terrain for the creation, reflection, and renegotiation of raced and gendered discourses, ideologies, and desires, all mediated through the shifting structures and demands of postbellum to postindustrial racial capitalism. If the multiple narratives constructed and meanings made of Aunt Jemima have served to sustain and codify raced and gendered hierarchies of subject/object, consumer/consumed, body/flesh, this ongoing process of revision and reiteration has simultaneously created openings for the construction of alternative genealogies and political imaginaries. These counter(hi)stories, radical revisions, and insurrectionary reimaginings are made up of what Weheliye describes as those "practices, existences, thoughts, desires, dreams, and sounds" that "persis[t] in the law's spectral shadows."[28] Operating in a different register than that of legal trademarks or property laws, these other genealogies and mimetic remakings of Aunt Jemima offer what Hunter and Evans's lawsuit could not: a glimpse into the "politicopoetic imaginary of the flesh" that emerges in the wake of the violence that sundered the enslaved from her body.[29] It is to two of these iconoclastic transfigurations that the remainder of this chapter attends.

Re/membering Aunt Jemima

When the curtain comes up on Glenda Dickerson and Breena Clarke's *Re/membering Aunt Jemima: A Menstrual Show,* it reveals a nearly bare stage, "somehow reminiscent of a circus or carnival sideshow." The lighting is harsh, the floor littered with sawdust. The five Black women performers take their places in the loose semicircle that a nineteenth-century audience would immediately recognize as the traditional opening staging of a blackface minstrel show. At a command from the master of ceremonies, La Madama Interlock-It-Togethererer, the "stereotypes extraordinaire" are seated. The performer farthest stage left begins to play the tambourine; the one farthest stage right strikes up the bones. They welcome the audience with a song:

Welcome to the circus of our minds
The carnival of our intentions
The menstruation of our bodies
The minstrelsy of our souls
The Aunt Jemima Traveling Menstrual Show[30]

What the audience is watching appears at first to be a modern-day minstrel show. Yet these performers are not minstrels; they are *menstruals.*

With this sleight of tongue, *Re/membering Aunt Jemima* provocatively links the process of menstruation to the performance practices of blackface minstrelsy, signaling what is to follow: a spectacle of mimicry and mimesis centered on the sexed Black female body as a material-discursive linchpin between the politics of reproduction and the politics of representation. Equal parts broad parody and revisionist Black feminist history, Dickerson and Clarke's modern-day minstrel-cum-menstrual show sets itself a mission: to "rescue" the lucrative brand icon and denigrated stereotype from more than a century of consumer capitalist mammy-hood by deconstructing the raced and gendered politics of representation that underpin her transhistorical appeal and shamefulness.[31] To do so, the players in Aunt Jemima's Traveling Menstrual Show offer yet another origin tale for the infamous pancake queen, following Aunt Jemima from her apocryphal birth on a fictional antebellum plantation, to her emergence as commoditized icon of Black reproductive servitude, and through the countless iterations of Black feminized sexual deviance, dangerous excess, and availability to violence that she embodies in her remaining years. In the process, they produce a performative genealogy of representations of Black women in the United States that engages with race and gender, spectacle and sexuality, reproduction and commodification, and that interrogates the possibilities, limits, and dangers of representation as a strategy for Black women's social and political empowerment.

Unlike Dickerson and Clarke, I am not convinced of the feasibility—or, indeed, the desirability—of rescuing cultural figures such as Aunt Jemima. I am, however, deeply invested in what is revealed about the vexed politics of representation and reproduction by their performative re/membering of the "most famous colored woman in the world" via the genre of the blackface minstrel show. In particular, I am interested in how *Re/membering Aunt Jemima* invokes and reconfigures the forms of gender essentialism that all too often underpin racial and reproductive politics to create a mimetic reproduction of Aunt Jemima as mythic embodiment of enslaved Black reproductive labor, artifact of Black gendered commodification, and fungible index of white racial fantasies of Black servitude. The result—minstrel show as menstrual show—enables a critical reconsideration of how Black women can be seen, heard, and remembered within the constraints of a racial capitalist order within which Black reproductivity and racialized, gendered violence are inextricably entangled. Next, I explore each of these issues in turn.

Of Minstrels and Menstruals

From the appearance of standard minstrel players such as the interlocutor and paired end men, Tam and Bones, to its promise to reveal the "true copy" hidden behind the performers' masks, the Aunt Jemima Traveling Menstrual Show deploys the forms and archetypes of the nineteenth-century minstrel show where Aunt Jemima first emerged to explore raced and gendered "relations of mastery and servitude," mimicry and brutality, desire and subjection, as they are imagined, reenacted, challenged, and instantiated through the performance of blackness. Like the Black-cast minstrel shows of the nineteenth century, Aunt Jemima's Traveling Menstrual Show is a contested venue for the performance of blackness, a vexed "nexus of race, subjection, and spectacle" that at once includes the expression of "racial and race(d) pleasure, enactments of white dominance and power, and the reiteration and/or rearticulation of the conditions of enslavement."[32] The Aunt Jemima players' parodic minstrelsy is no exception to these fraught politics of performing blackness. They self-consciously use their status as "creature[s] of white imagination" to skewer the racialized and sexualized fantasies of white masculine mastery and Black feminized subjugation that undergird contemporary structures of white supremacy. Invoking the ritualized politics of *bo akutia*—the Ashanti practice of censuring those in power by publicly performing one's grievance to a less politically powerful proxy—the players flag their performances as an indirect form of speaking truth to power.[33] At the same time, the menstruals threaten to "defile and mutilate" each other's bodies, reminding contemporary audiences that it was the "mutilation, dismemberment, and exile" of captive African bodies that transmogrified them into enslaved flesh, and that minstrelsy's staging of the excesses and pleasures of blackness was predicated on the subsequent reenactment of such acts of seizure, containment, possession, and punishment.[34]

Even as they draw upon its conventions, however, Dickerson and Clarke depart from representations of nineteenth-century minstrelsy—and antebellum slavery—as an ongoing contestation over the conditions, excesses, and limits of Black and white masculinity, instead emphasizing the centrality of the Black female reproductive body to Black captivity as well as to ongoing forms of dispossession and bodily exploitation. By rearticulating the minstrel show as *menstrual* show, they frame their production as a womanist exploration of the conjoined thematics of blood and sex, replacing the usual masculine pantheon of sly Jim Crows, cocksure Daddy Blues, and laughable Zip Coons with a cast of tragic mulattas, Sapphires, welfare queens, and race women. As the name of their interlocutor, La Madama Interlock-It-Togethererer, suggests, *Re/membering Aunt Jemima* refuses to disaggregate considerations of race, gender, sexuality, and capital, instead following in the tradition of Black feminists such as the Combahee River Collective to understand "systems of oppression [as] interlocking" and the "synthesis" of those oppressive structures as "creating the conditions of [Black women's] lives."[35]

As minstrels-cum-*menstruals,* the players in the Aunt Jemima Traveling Menstrual Show both reiterate and refashion normative tropes and lexicons of womanliness, reproduction, and embodiment. Their initial promise to reveal to the audience "the menstruation of [their] bodies," not to mention the play's deployment of menstruation and menopause as structuring narrative elements, seems to locate both femininity and feminism in the biological essentialism of uterus and ovaries, procreation and menstruation. Yet their subsequent minstrelesque performances as what they describe as "true copies" of "the distaff side of the Sable Genus of Humanity" complicate any easy characterization of *Re/membering Aunt Jemima* as in thrall to biological essentialism. The menstruals instead present their race and gender as an unceasing series of mimetic performances and citational practices—that is, as iterations without a stable referent or origin.[36] These true copies enact what Elin Diamond has described as the impossible doubleness of mimesis, in which the promise of representation reflects social desires for universality and coherence while simultaneously "unraveling that unity through improvisations, embodied rhythm, . . . and . . . impersonation."[37] By donning the minstrel/menstrual mask, then, the Traveling Show's players invoke the seemingly universal and essential character of race, gender, and sex, only to then "denaturalize" and "undermine [their] givenness," presenting them instead as the variable and unpredictable results of a complex practice of signifying and matrix of signification, in which every copy—and thus, no copy—is the true one.[38] The menstruals' mimetic reproduction of Black femaleness is neither natural nor given; rather, it is a vexed and contradictory performance of both "order and . . . disorder"—a quality that characterizes Black reproduction itself.[39]

The Grand Mammy of American Myth

With its promise to "present a true copy of the . . . life of Aunt Jemima," the traveling m(i/e)nstrual show that bears her name constructs a mimetic history of "the Grand Mammy of American Myth" and of the nation she sustains. Even as it parrots and parodies the specific narrative introduced in Wright's "Life of Aunt Jemima," *Re/membering Aunt Jemima*'s frequent intertextual references to numerous other iconic iterations of Black mammyhood, from *Gone with the Wind*'s Mammy to *Imitation of Life*'s Aunt Delilah, posit "Aunt Jemima" as one proper name for the complex constellation of fantasies, functions, and figurations that make up antebellum and postbellum constructions of the enslaved Black mammy.[40] A near-ubiquitous presence in more than a century of literary, historical, and popular cultural representations of slavery in the U.S. South, the figure of the mammy is "a meeting ground of investments and privations in the national treasury of rhetorical wealth," whose meaning, purpose, and even physical embodiment are revised and remade in and through dynamic historical and geographic contexts.[41] A signifier of racial and gendered domestic order in the antebellum South, her reappearance as a minstrel show standard, novelistic trope, and consumer brand logo in the post-Reconstruction era offered an embodied reconciliation for a regionally fractured nation through the nostalgic embrace of a Black surrogate mother who was always happy to serve, even as she provided a vehicle through which contested ideations and heightened anxieties about emancipated Black women's sexuality, maternity, and relationship to heteropatriarchy were explored, albeit not resolved.[42]

As a neoslave iteration of the iconic mammy, Dickerson and Clarke's Aunt Jemima eschews the cheerful acquiescence of the idealized antebellum cook and housekeeper in favor of an anachronic embodiment of Black reproductive servitude that indexes the dynamic, and sometimes contradictory, processes of raced and gendered abjection, dispossession, and commodification that have been integral to the construction of blackness since the inauguration of the African slave trade. "Born in a box" that is both crib and coffin, she embodies what Orlando Patterson has dubbed "social death"—the status of social nonentity produced and maintained by the material and discursive structures of slavery.[43] A formulation neither identical to nor entirely divergent from Spillers's concept of the flesh, social death marks not just the stripping away of rights—rightlessness—but the total legal, philosophical, and material dispossession of self that relegates the enslaved to a liminal existence between life and death, insider and outsider, human and nonhuman. In the antebellum United States, it was the construction of people as property through the alchemy of social death that both produced and marked captive Black people as existing *as* and *at* the limit of the human—a liminal position that, as I argued earlier, continues to shape the meaning of blackness in slavery's afterlife. In the context of chattel slavery, the Black captive's existence as and at the limit of the human had both material and discursive significance. Materially, it meant that even as the enslaved were foreclosed from personhood-as-property, they were rendered a form of property *without* personhood—that is, subject to laws and norms but nonexistent in terms of their protections. Discursively, the liminal category of (Black) slave fulfilled the essential function of embodying the not-quite-human against which (white) humanness was created and reproduced.[44]

From the moment of her birth, Aunt Jemima's existence is shaped by the "constituent elements" of social death. The brand on her forehead serves as the mark of what Patterson describes as the total and absolute subjection of the enslaved. The letters burned into her skin, KKK, simultaneously index historical processes of punishing and commodifying Black slaves, invoke the modes of racial and sexual terror used to maintain the subordination of Black people in the wake of their ostensible freedom, and recall the sexualized violence enacted on the flesh of fifteen-year-old Tawana Brawley more than 120 years after emancipation.[45] Like Harriet Beecher Stowe's infamous Topsy, Jemima "springs up" without origin or maker on Colonel "Uncle Sam" Higbee's plantation. The product of unknown parents, she exemplifies how slavery relies on what Patterson dubs the "natal alienation" of past, present, and future kinship networks.[46] "Discovered covered with feces," her submersion in human waste indexes what Patterson describes as the social and personal degradation of slavery by marking her as what Julia Kristeva names the "abject"—that radically excluded and defiled object at the border of human life.[47]

If Aunt Jemima's racial-sexual dispossession, alienation, and abjection constitute her as socially dead, her attendant status as property-without-personhood situates her within the material-discursive structures of U.S. racial capitalism. Indeed, even as she comes into being as objectified and degraded body and mutilated Black flesh at the limits of (white) human sociality, Aunt Jemima's ongoing existence is inextricable from the structures of U.S. racial capitalism that she is created to sustain. Her years living in the pancake box that bears her image constitute another branding of her—this time as a mass-produced commodity to be desired and consumed by white America. As the cook on Higbee's plantation, she nurtures the U.S. racial state with her reproductive and affective labor and the "clean, sweet, pure pancake flour" that carries no trace of her embodied racial contamination.[48] Her coetaneous existence as the dispossessed, mortified, and alienated flesh of chattel slavery and as the raw material on which early commodity capitalism relied underscores the inseparability of modern capitalism's emergence and the subordination, expropriation, and exploitation of captive Black people.

Dickerson and Clarke's hyperbolic history of Aunt Jemima as the Grand Mammy of American Myth thus constructs an alternative genealogy of blackness in the United States that centers the integral role that Black female reproductive servitude—real and imagined—has played in reproducing relations of race, gender, and capital in the United States. Using oral history, African American idiomatic traditions, and feminist performance methods, Dickerson and Clarke restage the history of the United States through the lens of Black reproductivity, rearticulating its key moments, figures, and debates as indelibly marked by ever-present anxieties, fantasies, and ideologies regarding Black reproductivity, and structured by state, corporate, and individual efforts to exploit, administer, and contain it. Or to put it differently, the Aunt Jemima that Dickerson and Clarke seek to re/member offers a performative reminder that the United States was built on Black *flesh*.

I return to Spillers's notion of the flesh here for what it offers to enrich and expand Patterson's concept of social death—namely attention to the "messy corporeality" that constitutes Black procreation, domesticity, and sexuality in the context of chattel slavery.[49] Significantly, *Re/membering Aunt Jemima* approaches Black women's procreation, domestic labor, and sexuality as inextricably entangled and mutually constitutive. If Higbee's kitchen is where Aunt Jemima cooks pancakes enjoyed by all, it is also the site of his sexualized violence, and the conception of her first three daughters. Her "clean, sweet and pure" flour is made in a sanitary napkin mill, guaranteeing its efficacy at guarding white consumers against this omnipresent racial threat posed by (Black) blood and (Black female) sex. Meanwhile, like Black feminist legend Sojourner Truth, she gives birth to thirteen daughters—four by force, eight by choice, and one through an "Aunt Jemima Cake Mix Miracle conception."[50] No stereotypical asexual maternal surrogate or idealized unstinting source of domestic sustenance, Dickerson and Clarke's Aunt Jemima is both worker and commodity, productive and reproductive, asexual matriarch and seductive concubine, domestic worker and endangerment to white domesticity. In short, she is America's Grand Mammy: an iconic, fantastic, and anachronistic character that encompasses the myriad and contradictory forms of Black reproductivity on which the U.S. social formation and racial imaginary has been built.

As an icon of the vexed and multiple aspects of Black reproductivity intrinsic to the production and maintenance of U.S. racial capitalism, *Re/membering Aunt Jemima*'s mythic Grand Mammy is an immanent (and imminent) danger to the very narratives of docile Black subservience, infinite Black nurturance, and national unity via antebellum plantation nostalgia that the brand trademark was created to sustain. The incipient threat is coded in the bodily symbols of her servitude: the "old greasy rag" that she dons over her "half-combed naps" when her daughters are sold away from her; the "brilliantine" grin of rage and vengeance she adopts in the wake of their loss.[51] It erupts without warning in unexpected moments, such as during her appearance at the 1893 World's Columbian Exposition.

> LA MADAMA INTERLOCK-IT-TOGETHERERER: Aunt Jemima flipped more than one million pancakes and gave each one an identity by telling antidotes of how all America had come to love her pancakes.
>
> AUNT JEMIMA: Ole Miss Ann was mighty hard on us niggers. She would take a needle and stick it through my lower lip and pin it to the bodice of my dress and I'd have to go roun' all day with my head drew down that a way and slobberin. It felt like I was goin' crazy. *(All laugh uproariously).*[52]

Dickerson and Clarke replace the apocryphal tales of bucolic plantation life and rollicking antebellum hijinks attributed to Nancy Green with a section of transcript from the 1937 WPA interview with "Auntie" Thomas

Johns, a former slave from Cleburne, Texas.[53] In so doing, they puncture the nostalgic fantasy of benign white paternalism, cheerful Black subservience, and familial affection on which the post-Reconstruction myth of the Black mammy depends. In rupture that is produced, the brutal forms of terrorism that undergirded chattel slavery are exposed; the dependence of white comfort and enjoyment on the mutilation and mortification of Black flesh is laid bare. The narrative center no longer holds.

Black Daughters of the White Imagination

The Grand Mammy of American Myth is not the only "stereotype extraordinaire" depicted in Aunt Jemima's Traveling Menstrual Show. Aunt Jemima's thirteen daughters together constitute a collection of iconic Black women from the past three centuries, from revolutionaries to religious leaders to pageant queens. Each played intermittently and seemingly arbitrarily by any one of four actors, some are drawn directly from the historical record; others are amalgamations of the playwrights' invention. All are "creatures of white imagination," mediated through the raced and gendered discourses that lend the U.S. racial state its coherence.

> Marie, a child born with a rattlesnake in her hand.
> Dorothy, her tragic mulatto chile.
> Pecola, a little melodramatic red baby.
> Dysmorfia, who was half black and half white.
> Anna Julia, a woman who risqued all to learn to read.
> Susie-Faye, Aunt Jemima's earnest child.
> Rebecca, called by the thunder to preach the gospel.
> Bondswoman, a girl with freedom on her mind.
> Sapphire, a girl who could not be tamed by any man.
> The twins, Anita and Aminata,
> Freedom Fighter,
> and the cake-mix miracle baby, Tiny Desiree.[54]

With their iconic names and tongue-in-cheek descriptors, Aunt Jemima's daughters approximate a series of representative figures drawn from Black history and culture, including Marie Laveau, the famed nineteenth-century voudoun practitioner; Dorothy Dandridge, the midcentury actress known for her portrayals of the series of ill-fated mixed-race women known in popular culture as tragic mulattas; Pecola Breedlove, the tragic protagonist of Toni Morrison's 1970 novel, *The Bluest Eye*; Peola Johnson, the iconic "passing" daughter in the famed 1934 race film, *Imitation of Life*; Vanessa Williams, the first Black woman to be crowned Miss America; famed Black feminist intellectual and proponent of racial uplift Anna Julia Cooper; Faye Wattleton, president of the Planned Parenthood Federation of America; traveling Shaker minister Rebecca Walker; Harriet Tubman, fugitive slave and "conductor" on the Underground Railroad; Sapphire, the iconic character on early radio and television's *Amos 'n' Andy Show*; law professor and Clarence Thomas whistleblower Anita Hill; anti–female-circumcision activist Aminata Diop; Black Liberation Army activist and exile Assata Shakur; and Desiree Washington, the woman raped by boxer Mike Tyson.[55]

Taken together, these menstruals/daughters are an accumulation of popular representations, cultural discourses, and apocryphal tales shaped as much by each woman's embeddedness within the structures of white supremacy and Black heteropatriarchy as by her opposition to them. Her first four daughters—"beautiful mixed-up girls"—provide a parodic take on a vast range of literary and popular representations of and narratives surrounding mixed-race women, from tragic mulatta to "hoodoo queen" to passing. Amid the play's lampooning of the tropes of miscegenation, however, another narrative emerges: that of the psychic and structural injury enacted by the desire for whiteness and the violence of antiblackness. Her three "little hammers" are archetypal "race women," carrying heavy burdens, blazing new trails, and uplifting their race, while their "husky sweet sisters" embody the dangerous figure of the angry Black woman, hunted, trapped, and betrayed by the structures of white assimilation that demand their acquiescence. As Black women who challenge Black masculine heteropatriarchy, her penultimate twins, Anita and Aminata, are seized upon to support global and national narratives of Black sexual deviance. But it is Aunt Jemima's final, cake-mix miracle baby, Desiree, who seems to offer the most intriguing enactment of Black reproductivity. Bursting forth from Aunt Jemima's mouth as a tiny copy of her mother, Desiree is born of spirit and self. She emerges not through the norms of heterosexual or biologistic reproduction but through what the Dogon of Mali would dub *nommo*: the power of thought and word to generate new realities.[56]

Eschewing any attempt to represent things as they "really were" or to render these political and cultural icons as heroines, role models, or sympathetic victims, the menstruals perform a satirical mash-up of historical and fantastical Black women figures and archetypes. Unrepentantly anachronistic, improvisational, and irreverent, their renderings provide a dissonant (and, at times, dissident) commentary on the vexed politics of representation regarding Black women. In contradistinction to common interpretations of the play as an attempt to reclaim "the sometimes lost history of black women" in the United States, then—and despite Dickerson and Clarke's description of it as an effort to "write Black female identity into existence on the world stage"—I read *Re/membering Aunt Jemima* as performing a multifaceted critique of the notions around, representations of, and racial-sexual anxieties about Black women; of the myriad functions that these discourses fulfill in the U.S. racial imaginary; and of their material impact in the lives—and deaths—of Black women.[57]

Aunt Jemima as Black Bombshell

Amid the tongue-in-cheek wordplay, caricatured performances, and parodic takes on Black women's history, *Re/membering Aunt Jemima* is a trenchant critique of how the seemingly immaterial politics of representation structure the material conditions of Black life and Black vulnerability to death. By the end of the play, after years of serving Quaker Oats as every possible incarnation of embodied Black reproductivity conjured in the national racial imagination, Aunt Jemima is confined to her pancake box, riddled with cancer, and plagued by diabetes, arthritis, and high blood pressure. She has been stripped of her breasts, uterus, and feet.[58] In a scathing critique of the violence of the "healing" procedures inflicted on her body as well as of the preceding years of malign neglect that necessitated their use, she gives the audience one last vaudevillian performance, sung to the tune of Nina Simone's protest song "Mississippi Goddam."

> IT'S A GODDAMN SHAME
> WHAT THEY DO TO ME
> WHAT WILL IT TAKE
> TO SET ME FREE?
> GODDAMN, GODDAMN!
> DON'T READ MY PAP SMEAR
> FOR A YEAR
> THEY FINALLY TELL ME
> I'M FILLED WITH FEAR
> CANCER'S EATING UP MY WOMB

MOTHER'S EARTH, YOU'LL BE MY TOMB
WHAT THEY DO TO ME, GODDAMN
HYSTERECTOMY, GODDAMN
WHAT THEY DO TO ME, GODDAMN
CLITORIDECTOMY, GODDAMN
WHAT THEY DO TO ME, GODDAMN
MASTECTOMY, GODDAMN
CANCER WRECKTED ME, GODDAMN
CANCER WRECKTED ME, GODDAMN
GODDAMN! GODDAMN! GODDAMN!
GODDAMN! GODDAMN! GODDAMN!
IT'S A GODDAMN SHAME
WHAT THEY DO TO ME
WHAT WILL IT TAKE
TO SET ME FREE?[59]

If racism is, as Ruth Wilson Gilmore defines it, the "state-sanctioned and/or extra-legal production and exploitation of group-differentiated vulnerabilities to premature death, in distinct yet densely interconnected political geographies," then the modes of racialized brutality and terror exercised against Black people mobilizing across the Jim Crow South in pursuit of Black enfranchisement, and the forms of medicalized butchery and neglect enacted on Aunt Jemima's Black, female body, are two nonidentical faces of anti-Black racism.[60] Just as Simone invokes Alabama, Tennessee, and Mississippi as the political geography of anti-Black state and extra-legal terrorism in the civil rights era, Aunt Jemima offers a cartography of gendered and sexualized anti-Black violence on the scale of the female body. At the same time, she relates her own experiences of reproductive health care as an impoverished and abandoned African American woman to a more recognizable trope of violence against the Black female body—clitoridectomy—suggesting that contrary to U.S. narratives of gendered enlightenment, occupying a Black female body anywhere in the world requires an ongoing struggle for basic survival and bodily freedom.

"Poor, fat, black, and crazy," Aunt Jemima remains unassimilable by the saccharine narrative of racial progress that Quaker Oats' Aunt Jemima logo epitomized with her 1989 makeover. Refusing to "dress for success" or "keep up with the changing times" by lightening her skin, taking off her kerchief, and straightening her hair, she is treated like any other recalcitrant welfare queen who rejects the dubious boons of job training and workfare: "Col. Uncle said, 'We should just manumit Aunt Jemima, and run her out of town.' The Quaker Oats man said, 'You got a point there. Let her fend for herself.'"[61] In a chilling reenactment of sixty-six-year-old Eleanor Bumpers's 1984 murder by the New York Police Department, Aunt Jemima is shot dead by the police, who come on Quaker Oats' orders to evict her from her pancake box.

Aunt Jemima's fantastic and mythical life and death offer an opportunity to consider the meaning and limits of historical and contemporary discourses of Black reproduction and Black (un)freedom. Naked and alone, armed only with a kitchen knife, she refuses to be easily evicted from her box or disavowed by postracial efforts at rebranding. In her moment of death, she "hurl[s] herself . . . into the center of the battle" like a postmodern incarnation of the legendary eighteenth-century Jamaican maroon leader Nanny. A "black bombshell" that explodes the very systems of power and meaning that she has enabled, Aunt Jemima's rupture of "law and order, racial hierarchy, and gendered racial difference and docility" reveals the subterranean "power of coerced black female subservience," and demonstrates the political possibilities engendered by a supplemental theory of history in which commodities speak and objects "can and do resist."[62]

The crisis of meaning precipitated by Aunt Jemima's refusal to be erased, assimilated, or dispossessed is short lived, however. Upon her murder by the police, her "microwave miracle daughter" Desiree, having "no compunction about skin peels and pearl earrings," seamlessly takes her place on the box.[63] Rather than disrupting the existing chain of signification—mammy to minstrel to mass commodity—Jemima's microwave miracle of mimetic reproduction reinstantiates the myth of complaisant Black reproductive servitude under the guise of progressive change. Her act of complicity in the name of racial progress can be read as the play's final caution: the call to re/member Aunt Jemima demands more than simply marking her long-standing significance to U.S. cultural politics and racial capitalism. It requires disrupting the material-discursive relations within which she is embedded, in order to make possible the writing of another kind of history.

Liberating Aunt Jemima

This chapter so far has read legal, historical, and dramatic narratives of Aunt Jemima to locate a theory of history that attends to the centrality of

Black reproductivity and the politics of representation in the production and maintenance of U.S. racial capitalism. What remains takes a slightly different tack, turning to assemblage artist Betye Saar's *Liberation of Aunt Jemima* to trace the outlines of the kind of theory of change suggested in the ruptural final stand of Dickerson and Clarke's Aunt Jemima. It is to Saar's work that the remainder of this chapter is devoted, in order to explore how the tools for the reproduction of white mastery and Black commodification also carry within them the potential for the radical restructuring of relations of power and difference.

In 1972 artist Betye Saar was invited to participate in an exhibition at Rainbow Sign, a community arts center in Berkeley, California, known for its gatherings, exhibits, and events showcasing the work of Black cultural producers. Originally an enamel artist and painter, Saar had embraced the techniques of assemblage in the late 1960s, creating three-dimensional boxes and windows constructed of found objects, her own paintings and prints, and family relics and photographs. By the early 1970s, her work had become largely three-dimensional and increasingly explicit in its exploration of race and gender as integral to her personal and political consciousness.[64] During that same period, she became increasingly active in the aesthetic movement some have dubbed "Black Art[s] West": a community of Los Angeles–based Black artists working in the wake of the Watts Rebellion to create art that articulated the political aims and aesthetic tenets of the Black Arts Movement (BAM) in ways that were politically and culturally specific to California.[65] When she was asked by the Rainbow Sign collective to contribute a work of art about her favorite hero or heroine, Saar created what many consider a signature piece of Black feminist art from the Black arts era: *The Liberation of Aunt Jemima* (Figure 3).

The Liberation of Aunt Jemima is a twelve-inch by eight-inch wooden shadow box, just under three inches deep. The inside back wall of the box is papered with row after row of sepia-toned images of the Quaker Oats Company's post-1968, "modernized" Aunt Jemima.[66] Mirrors attached to the inside walls of the box reflect back the smiling brown face, making the image seem to repeat ad infinitum. In the center of the box, Saar has placed a 1930s plastic figurine: a brightly colored caricature of a Black mammy, complete with checkered kerchief, ample bosom, and full red lips stretched over bright white teeth. Originally a memo holder, the mammy has a recessed rectangle cut into her midsection, designed to hold a small notepad where her owner might inscribe fleeting thoughts, predilections, or needs on

Figure 3. Betye Saar, *The Liberation of Aunt Jemima*, 1972. Mixed media assemblage, 11¾ x 8 x 2¾ inches, signed. Collection of University of California, Berkeley Art Museum; purchased with the aid of funds from the National Endowment for the Arts (selected by the Committee for the Acquisition of Afro-American Art). Courtesy of the artist and Roberts Projects, Los Angeles, Calif. Photograph by Benjamin Blackwell.

her synthetic body; the broom that she grasps in one hand is revealed upon closer examination to serve double duty as a pencil. In the place of the memo pad, however, Saar has affixed a stock trade card from the 1880s that depicts another smiling Black mammy, this time with a pale-skinned, open-mouthed baby wedged on one hip. A sheet of linen is draped over the fence in front of this two-dimensional mammy, demarcating the empty space where a business distributing the trade card would have added its own text to advertise its services or wares. Yet the white space on the chromolithograph is obscured—the domestic idyll it depicts ruptured—by a clenched Black Power fist thrusting up from a strip of kente cloth at its base. This iconic symbol of Black liberation is only one indicator that Saar's *Aunt Jemima* is no artistic homage to the docile and jolly mammy of the white racist imaginary but a depiction of her revolutionary alter ego: on one hip, wedged between broom and memo frame, rests a gleaming revolver; in her other hand, with its stock resting amid the cotton bolls and pods strewn across the floor of the box, is an old-fashioned military carbine.

The Liberation of Aunt Jemima was the first of a series of more than twenty assemblages that came to make up Saar's Exploding the Myth series (1972–73).[67] Each assemblage juxtaposed pieces of racist kitsch—Sambo figurines, Aunt Jemima images, posters of so-called pickaninnies eating watermelon—with politicized images of chattel slavery, anti-Black terrorism, and Black liberation struggles. Her use of assemblage to expose and deconstruct what Mary Schmidt Campbell has described as "icons of [anti-Black] racism" demonstrates a close alignment with the broader aims of the Black Arts Movement.[68] The "aesthetic and spiritual sister" of Black Power, the BAM not only emphasized the artistic richness to be found in African and African American subjects, imagery, and traditions but also set as a primary goal "the destroying of those images and myths that have crippled and degraded black people and the institution of new images and myths that will liberate them."[69]

Among the artists who took up the goals of the BAM, if not necessarily all its tenets, Aunt Jemima was a popular theme. Along with Saar, Jeff Donaldson, Joe Overstreet, Murray DePillars, and Jon Onye Lockard each created art that transformed the Quaker Oats Company's infamous icon of cheerful subservience into a visual representation of Black insurgency.[70] Yet Saar's *Aunt Jemima* is unique among these works. Not only is she one of the very few women artists to engage the figure of Aunt Jemima in the early 1970s, but her use of assemblage and incorporation of racist memorabilia;

her feminist engagement with themes of maternity, domesticity, and sexuality; and her intertextual invocation of spiritual iconography make *The Liberation of Aunt Jemima* a generative lens through which to reflect on how the minstrel show character turned mass-market mammy might be reread as part of a Black feminist politic of freedom.

Black Reproductivity and the Mammy in the Box

If the Black mammy is a white supremacist trope of antebellum domestic well-being and Aunt Jemima is a mass-produced mammy—that is, a commoditized representation of Black domestic labor available to urban, white households across the nation—then *The Liberation of Aunt Jemima* combines these two iterations of Black domestic subservience into a single, transhistorical depiction of Black women's labor in the white imagination. From the broom in the memo pad mammy's hand, to the sheet hung out to dry in the foreground of the inset trade card, to the pancake breakfast promised by Aunt Jemima's endlessly repeating smile, Saar's box of nested mammies underscores the ongoing material and discursive centrality of Black women's reproductive labor to the creation and maintenance of white domestic order at home, in the marketplace, and as a nation.

Despite the omnipresent symbology of domestic labor in Saar's assemblage, *The Liberation of Aunt Jemima* is often perceived by critics to depict the moment of political radicalization in which Aunt Jemima repudiates the domestic to pursue her freedom. Saar's inclusion of revolver and carbine is described as the artist's admonition that the goal of liberation will "require [Aunt Jemima] to put down the tools of her trade as a domestic servant and take up the tools for revolutionary transformation."[71] While this opposition of reproductive labor and revolutionary transformation seems an apropos characterization of the art of DePillars, Overstreet, or Lockard, whose Jemimas burst free from or blow up the symbols of their domestic confinement, Saar's mammy stands her ground, holding fast to both her broom and her guns. Rather than illustrating Aunt Jemima's cheerful complaisance or the mammy's complicity with white plantocratic hierarchies, Saar's *Aunt Jemima* resignifies the enslaved domestic as always already a locus of racial and sexual antagonism and contestation. Saar herself describes the figure of the mammy in the box as a "domestic soldier," suggesting that it is not simply outside the realm of the domestic but within it that the battles for Black women's freedom are being fought and that the quotidian performance of reproductive labor has not been antithetical to the labor of revolution but coetaneous with it.[72]

In addition to exposing the domestic as a terrain of raced and gendered struggle, and domestic labor as a radical political practice, *The Liberation of Aunt Jemima* also throws the established relations of enslaved motherhood into crisis. The artist has suggested more than once that the chromolithograph of the Black woman and the light-skinned child embedded in the belly of the gun-toting mammy depicts not a faithful nursemaid carrying the white scion of a slaveholding family but a "mulatto child" in the arms of his enslaved mother.[73] Saar has described her revisionist interpretation of the image of woman and baby as showing the "other side of the coin": the hidden story of enslaved and exploited Black women domestics.[74] Her resignification of the trade card embedded at the center of the assemblage as an image of mother and child rather than enslaved Black nanny and white charge indeed points to several absented presences at the heart of chatteldom. A central contradiction of chattel slavery in the United States was the simultaneous necessity of enslaved reproduction and the impossibility of enslaved motherhood—that is, of claiming one's children as one's own. An attendant dilemma was that even as enslaved maternity was expropriated and disavowed, the romanticized notion of Black surrogate motherhood remained integral to the mythology of a benevolent slave system. By cheerfully abandoning her kinship claim to her offspring in order to provide faithful service and boundless love to her white charges, the mythical mammy sutured the contradiction between the impossibility of enslaved motherhood and the discursive necessity for the slave as surrogate mother of white slaveholders, young and old. Saar's *Aunt Jemima* unravels this suturing of surrogate mother and mother dispossessed. Even as the "mulatto child" in her arms literally recenters Black women's procreation as the necessary condition for the reproduction of U.S. chattel slavery, the resignified image concomitantly asserts the ongoing existence of the very forms of Black kinship upon whose disavowal the trope of the antebellum *familia* of master and slave, mistress and mammy relied.

Yet tellingly, Saar's claim as to the racially ambiguous child's mixed-race parentage complicates the viewer's experience of the piece at least as much as it clarifies her intent. When compared to the original nineteenth-century lithograph, it is difficult to determine if the card in the assemblage has been retouched: Is the child's skin darker? Are his arms thinner? Has his face been relimned to turn a gleeful chortle into an outraged howl? Has the nursemaid/mother's smile been adjusted, so that an ironic sneer appears where a jolly grin once stretched? In the end, it is impossible to determine if anything has been redrawn, let alone to distinguish what has been remade from what was original. Rather, the viewer must contend with the historically and politically vexed character of Black reproductivity: in the context and aftermath of U.S. chattel slavery, the Black reproductive has been deployed both in the service of racial capitalism and as an oppositional practice in the face of dispossession; it has been the signifier of pathological excess and held the promise of incipient heteropatriarchal normativity. In short, the power and possibility of Black reproductivity, like Saar's *Aunt Jemima,* lies in part in its undecidability—its constitutive inability to be reduced to a singular meaning or function.

According to Saar, the trade card mammy's mulatto child "serves as a testimony about how black women were sexually abused or misused."[75] Like Aunt Jemima's daughters (and the Corregidora women I discuss in chapter 3), Saar's Aunt Jemima carries with her the embodied evidence of the sexual domination and expropriation upon which the material and discursive conditions of slavery and subsequent forms of Black unfreedom relied. Yet even as it draws attention to the sexualized violence, coercion, and domination to which Black women have been subjected, *The Liberation of Aunt Jemima* opens itself up to an oppositional reading of Black female sexuality as part of, rather than obstacle to, Aunt Jemima's liberation. From the mammies' broad red smiles, to their red kerchiefs and dresses, to the red edging of the box that gives the sepia-toned background a rouged tint, Saar's assemblage glows red. Read in conjunction with the women's open-mouthed smiles and the mulatto baby wedged jauntily on one hip, *Aunt Jemima* is a virtual display of the collected stereotypes of improper, sexualized Black femininity.[76] As Karla Holloway has observed, the gendered codes of Black propriety—no red dresses; no broad smiles; no public demonstrations of vulnerability—through which Black women have been policed and have, in turn, disciplined themselves and each other are codified responses to "the persistent historical reality that black women's bodies are [sites] of public negotiation and private loss."[77] By appropriating these loaded signifiers of pathologized and criminalized Black female sexuality, Saar's *Aunt Jemima* can be seen as rejecting that "salvific wish" of the Black middle class to mobilize respectability as a shield against sexualized degradation and objectification.[78] Instead, it uses the means through which Black women's bodies have been marked as available for the public consumption and negotiation of racial meaning to make visible ostensibly private struggles for sexual autonomy and against raced and gendered violence at the intimate scales of body and home.

Like Dickerson and Clarke, then, Saar rejects the dichotomous iconography of Black reproductivity as constituted by two opposite poles—the mammy as asexual domestic worker or the jezebel as the embodiment of sexualized violence concealed in the guise of hypersexuality. Instead, just like her assemblage of embedded and overlapping mammies, Saar's portrayal of the Black reproductive female encompasses the sexual and the desexualized, reproductive labor and domestic insurrection, kinship claimed and maternity dispossessed. In this, Saar's Aunt Jemima not only indexes the full range of reproductive tropes that Black women's bodies come to stand for but also illustrates how relations of desire and kinship, struggle and sustenance, labor and property are mutually constituted within the entanglement of discourses, structures, bodies, and practices that constitute the Black reproductive.

The Black Reproductive as Assemblage

For many artists within the West Coast Black arts scene, assemblage was both a method and a metaphor: by transforming the discarded and overlooked into objects of soaring hope or scathing critique, art objects like Los Angeles's Watts Tower interrupted the skyline and the status quo, challenging the cultural and political logics of U.S. racial capitalism in the post–civil rights era.[79] By incorporating the residue of racist commodity culture into her assemblages, however, Saar used the medium to pose an additional challenge; in the case of Aunt Jemima, she used these taboo images and objects to expose and contest popular discourses around Black women's bodies, sexuality, and labor.[80] By imbricating memorabilia of an imaginary idyllic past defined by Black subjugation with the accumulated evidence of white supremacist terror and Black opposition to it, Saar created a series of aesthetic friction points: condensed representations of heightened contradiction intended to expose and explode the racist stereotypes that the pieces put on display. By deliberately invoking degrading stereotypes only to reconfigure them through the lexicon of Black nationalist iconography, Saar engages in what Michael Harris has described as a form of visual signifying, in which racist tropes are "reversed with a difference that exceeds mere mirroring." When Black artists transform degrading icons like Aunt Jemima or Sambo into revolutionary figures, Harris argues, they use aesthetic techniques to destabilize an existing visual sign, "creating a complex visual rhetoric that induces aporia."[81] Harris's notion of visual signifying has resonances with a key argument of this book: that in the context of total dispossession and ongoing unfreedom, the practice of freedom is itself aporetic, an "experience of the impossible."[82]

Interestingly, while Harris applies his concept of visual signifying to the artistic transformations of Aunt Jemima created by Donaldson, Overstreet, DePillars, and Lockard, he describes the effect of Saar's work quite differently, arguing that "Saar's strategy differed from that of the male artists because she tried to *defuse* the stereotypical mammy/Jemima image by recontextualizing it rather than visually transforming it."[83] Harris perceives Saar's *Aunt Jemima* as exposing the intrinsic violence of racist Black kitsch only to defuse it, juxtaposing her approach with the transformative techniques of her masculine compatriots. Yet Saar's armed Aunt Jemima, with her unnerving masklike grimace and Black revolutionary symbology, appears anything but defused. Rather, she has been *weaponized*: the banal instruments of quotidian Black degradation have been recast as agents of Black liberatory violence.

What Harris overlooks in his misreading of Saar's *Aunt Jemima* as an attempt to defuse racial and sexual violence through collocation and juxtaposition is that the historical figure of the Black mammy is, in and of itself, what Gilles Deleuze and Félix Guattari would describe as an assemblage—that is, not a single unified subject but the arrangement of a multiplicity of ideas, objects, bodies, and structures, as well as the relations among them.[84] As historians of women in slavery have noted, while many antebellum households, both large and small, relied on the reproductive labor of Black women as cooks, launderers, cleaners, and childcare providers, these multiple, distinct tasks were rarely performed by a lone individual. Rather, the archetypal mammy portrayed in early nineteenth-century proslavery diaries and novels was more likely an amalgamation of several household workers abstracted into a single, nameless slave.[85] What work could the abstraction dubbed "mammy" do that these living, breathing bondswomen could not? As Deborah Gray White has argued, the mammy's most important role was a discursive one: as the embodied symbol of the patriarchal slaveholding domestic order, she was the "idealized slave" for an idealized society.[86] From her early incarnation in the antebellum South, through her reemergence in post-Reconstruction narratives of reconciliation, to her rebirth under various other names—among them, Aunt Jemima—"mammy" names not only a domestic role but also an idea and a set of practices through which "diverse concepts such as slavery, love, service, [and] motherhood" gain their meaning.[87] In short, she is an assemblage of the dispossessed Black female body, the reproductive labor that body performed, the ideologies and enunciations through which she was constituted as a captive maternal domestic, and the negotiations of intimacy, property, and power within which she was embedded.

Following this line of thought, one might read the Black reproductive itself as a "racializing assemblage": a way of naming the ensemble of racial-sexual imaginaries, social policies, and extralegal systems for the management of and knowledge production around racialized bodies, as well as those bodies themselves and their performances and practices of subjugation and liberation, all of which rely on and materialize the entangled co-constitution of blackness and reproductivity. As Weheliye notes, while born of racial (sexual) violence and often representative of the "modalities in which dehumanization is practiced and lived," racializing assemblages are also productive, generating new meanings, possibilities, and political desires in excess of existing modes of power. It is in this "surplus," this "line of flight," that Black freedom's effaced condition of possibility resides, surfacing along the fissures and gaps created when Black unfreedom meets its limits.[88]

Even as Saar's assemblage of racist kitsch, Black revolutionary symbology, smiling Black subservience, and quotidian domestic insurrection generates the aesthetic friction necessary to fissure the seemingly natural assemblage of Black reproductive subjection, it also produces an unexpected surplus of signification. As a whole, Saar's oeuvre has been described as rhizomatic, "a huge assemblage, all of whose parts are interdependent, intrareferential, and, in a strange way, timeless."[89] Resisting easy chronological periodization, it often is divided instead into binary categories: political work versus mystical work, or boxes versus windows.[90] Yet *The Liberation of Aunt Jemima* demonstrates the limits of such dichotomies. Often invoked as the exemplar of Saar's political work, *Aunt Jemima* has much in common with the shrine-like "ancestral boxes" of the same time period. The open box with tableau inside is reminiscent of the retablos of sacred Spanish and folkloric Latin American art; the mammies' wrapped heads index not only domestic servitude but also spiritual service to the orishas, the West African and diasporic deities. Like Saar's "ritual pieces," *Aunt Jemima*'s box is filled with objects imbued with power, albeit guns rather than gris-gris; the iconic Black Power fist instead of the mojo fetishes of bone, feather, or fur.[91] Read through this lens, Aunt Jemima takes on multiple significations. While she remains the mythic embodiment of the antebellum racial order, a commodified symbol of ongoing Black servitude, and a signifier of the contested political terrain of Black reproductivity, she can be read concomitantly as a "sacred warrior . . . a figure of sacred motherhood, a conjure woman, and a revolutionary warrior."[92]

Moreover, the same box that can be read as a symbol of the mammy's mass commoditization or a ritualized shrine to Black liberation can also be read as a coffin—a mark of the social death that enslaved women not only embodied but also reproduced. Like the box in which Clarke and Dickerson's Aunt Jemima lives and dies, Saar's nested display of racist objects indexes the thoroughgoing processes of objectification and dispossession through which Black women were constituted as and at the limit of the human, even as their bodies, labor, and sexuality were expropriated in the service of racial capitalism. Yet if, as Peter Clothier argues, Saar's assemblage boxes cannot be fully divorced from the mystic windows of the same time period, through which she offered a glimpse into both the spiritual world and the "space of liberation," then Aunt Jemima's box must be read not as *either* a casket *or* a shrine (or, for that matter, as simply a container for mass-produced foodstuff) but as a liminal space, a terrain "between the material world of things and the world of spirit . . . between life and death, restraint and the will to create[,] . . . slavery and freedom."[93] Such a reading calls into question the seemingly stable dichotomies on which many readings of Saar's *Liberation of Aunt Jemima* have unquestioningly relied in favor of the contingent possibilities for freedom that emerge in the liminal points of undecidability between shifting categories of meaning.

Retiring Aunt Jemima

In June 2020, Quaker Oats released a statement announcing the removal of the Aunt Jemima name and image from all products by the end of the year. Citing its "commit[ment] to progress," belief in diversity, and "embrace [of] the full spectrum of humanity," the PepsiCo corporation simultaneously unveiled a new $400 million initiative to increase racial equality and "help create systemic change."[94] Quaker Oats' announcement was part of a national trend of corporate apologies and reevaluations sparked by the national resurgence of the Black Lives Matter movement in protest of the ongoing terrorizing and murder of Black men and women by police and non-Black vigilantes. The brand discontinuation's immediate catalyst, however, was the widespread social media reaction to a viral TikTok video by Black singer-songwriter Kirby Lauryen less than a week earlier. In the thirty-seven-second clip titled "How to Make a Non Racist Breakfast," Kirby, wearing a unitard in the pancake brand's signature red and yellow, hails the viewer: "Baby, you hungry? Let me fix you some breakfast." Opening the refrigerator to reveal a box of Aunt Jemima pancake mix, she narrates the history of the brand icon, invoking both slavery and the fetishization of the Black mammy, even as she gestures to her own natural hair and brown-skinned body. "Not today," she concludes, before dumping the contents of the box into the sink while declaring, "Black lives matter, people—even over breakfast." Within a week, the video had more than 1.8 million viewings and was sparking celebrity tweets and widespread condemnations of Quaker Oats.[95]

The discontinuation of the Aunt Jemima brand after more than 130 years, and the popular and media discourse surrounding it, offers an opportunity to reflect on some of this chapter's primary preoccupations. Much of this chapter's consideration of Aunt Jemima has explored the fraught politics of representation and reproduction that converge in the iconic figure of Aunt Jemima. While her scathing critique departs from the satirical mimesis of Clarke and Dickerson's *Re/membering Aunt Jemima,* Kirby's TikTok performance offers its own resignification of the representational practices that brought the Aunt Jemima brand its success: the notion of a Black woman in the kitchen eager to make breakfast, the juxtaposition between a brightly clad spokeswoman and the nearly matching box in her hand—in Kirby's version, these performed strategies disrupt, rather than reproduce, the seamless narrative of Black female complaisance. Moreover, the video's implicit argument that representations of blackness rooted in histories of captivity, commodification, and fetishized consumption reproduce the conditions for Black physical and social death in slavery's afterlife is directly aligned with this chapter's claims.

Quaker's Oats' announcement, however, cannot be read uncritically as a political victory. Rather, representational shifts like Quaker Oats' exemplify how institutions deploy the discourses and practices of multiculturalism to manage difference and contain contradictions within neoliberal racial capitalism and underscore the inherent limitations of demanding that the administrators and beneficiaries of racial capitalism be the ones to mediate or ameliorate its contradictions.[96] Quaker Oats' promise to maintain the same essence under a new name and packaging illustrates two arguments of this chapter. First, the exploitation, commodification, and co-optation of Black women's reproductive bodies and labor continue to produce economic and affective value even (or especially) when that labor is disavowed or erased. Even as the Aunt Jemima website announced the discontinuation of the Aunt Jemima name and image, Quaker Oats sought to shore up the sentimental ties between commodity and consumer built on more than a century of imagined relations of raced and gendered subservience. Underneath the new packaging, they assured website visitors, loyal customers will find "the same recipe that [they] know and love."[97] The intangible value of brand loyalty accrued through the quotidian reproductive labor of Nancy Green, Anna Short Harrington, and innumerable other Black women who mixed batter, flipped pancakes, and charmed white audiences with tales of cheerful subservience at stores, restaurants, and exhibitions across the country remains sedimented in the commodity form, even as the history of that labor is effaced along with the Aunt Jemima name.

Second, the complex assemblage of dispossessed Black flesh, captive domesticity, and interracial intimacy that makes up the mammy is itself reproducible and reproductive, emerging in new iterations to meet changing historical and political needs. As one name—one incarnation—Aunt Jemima may have at last gotten "off that damn box," but the systems of meaning in which she is embedded remain.[98] Indeed, in an uncanny echo of *Re/membering Aunt Jemima,* media reports of the product rebranding ubiquitously described it as "Quaker Oats retir[ing] Aunt Jemima," illustrating the continuing conflation of the mass commodity and the commodified Black female body.[99]

Among the descendants of the women who worked to portray Aunt Jemima, reaction to the news of the brand's discontinuation has been complicated and heterogenous. The response is perhaps unsurprising, given that Quaker Oats and PepsiCo's declared plan to rectify past wrongs is, simultaneously, a project of historical erasure. In the face of disavowal, and in the absence of reparation—or even, as in the case of Anna Short Harrington's descendants, recognition—what modes of justice can be envisioned or enacted? It is to this question that the next chapter turns.

2

Love and Violence / Maternity and Death

Enslaved Infanticide and Monstrous Motherhood in Toni Morrison's Beloved

> What happens if we assume that the female subject serves as a general case for explicating social death, property relations, and the pained and putative construction of blackness? . . . What possibilities of resignification would then be possible?
>
> —Saidiya V. Hartman, *Scenes of Subjection*

In July 1822, in Brooke County, Virginia, an enslaved woman named Letty was accused of crushing the skull of her newborn infant, wrapping her in a petticoat, and leaving her for dead in the woods behind the slave quarters. While she initially denied the charges, Letty eventually confessed, telling her examiners that "if the child had been one of her own colour, she would not have done as she did." A coroner's inquest concluded she had been "moved and seduced" to kill the infant "by the instigation of the Devil," and Letty was tried immediately and sentenced to death by hanging. At the petition of local citizens, however, her death sentence was commuted to "banishment and sale" outside the state.[1]

In August 1846, in Warren County, Missouri, fifteen-year-old enslaved Nelly was indicted for the murder of her newborn child. After confessing that she had killed the infant because "she was ashamed of . . . becoming pregnant in such a way," Nelly was deemed by a local doctor to have been suffering from a "mental aberration or hallucination" that rendered her unable to "understand the nature . . . of the crime" she had committed. More than one hundred white citizens petitioned the governor of Missouri for clemency, arguing that a public trial would be "exceedingly unpleasant to the sensibilities & delicate feelings of the whole community" and that her conviction would subject her legal owner to the further loss of valuable property. Upon receiving a gubernatorial pardon prior to trial, Nelly was returned to the possession of her late master's widow.[2]

In January 1856, a pregnant Margaret Garner and her family—all enslaved—escaped across the Ohio River in an effort to reach the North. When recaptured, Margaret attempted to kill all four of her children, succeeding only with her toddler, Mary. Returned to their owners on fugitive slave warrants, the Garners were transported downriver; during the voyage, Margaret threw her baby Cilla overboard and jumped in after her. Cilla drowned; Garner was pulled from the water to die of typhoid two years later.[3]

• • •

Ever since Angela Davis first sought to piece together a history of the myriad forms of Black women's opposition to their legalized subjugation from her cell in the Marin County Jail, the study of enslaved women's responses to their captivity has been an integral, and interventionist, part of the revisionist historiography of slavery. Black feminist scholars in particular have explored the breadth of enslaved and fugitive Black women's political resistance: their quotidian acts of theft, truancy, vandalism, and sumptuary excess; their legal challenges for state protection, wages, or custody of their children; their modes of covert socialization and community building; and their written testimonies to the dehumanizing effects of slavery on both enslaved and slaveholder.[4] More recently, alongside this history of nonviolent resistance, a burgeoning field of scholarship on violent resistance and rebellion by captive and enslaved Black women has emerged to challenge presumptions that violent opposition to captivity and chatteldom was largely the purview of men.[5] Amid this multifaceted body of work, however, the history of infanticide by enslaved Black women continues to be notably understudied and highly contested.

While historical and popular studies of slavery have increasingly acknowledged that captive Black mothers in the Americas sometimes killed the infants and children they bore into slavery, the frequency of such acts remains a subject of debate. The rate at which enslaved women were convicted of killing their children vastly exceeds any other category of fatal violence; however, the reasons for this discrepancy are unclear.[6] Within the field of African American history, many scholars of slavery have depicted slave infanticide as an atypical and unlikely scenario whose frequency was exaggerated by paranoid slaveholders prone to ascribe the deaths of frail neonates delivered by undernourished women to the malign neglect or foul play of deviant Black mothers.[7] More recently, a number of feminist historians have cautioned against this wholesale dismissal of infanticide as a historical practice, suggesting that it functioned as a corollary to the more common reproductive practices of resistance by which enslaved women prevented conception and terminated unwanted pregnancies. The frequency with which infanticide occurred, they argue, has been "forgotten" in contemporary research due to "strong taboos in Western culture," historical (mis)perceptions of maternity under slavery, and even scholarly "naïve[té]."[8]

Indeed, the difficulty of determining the frequency with which maternal infanticide took place is a research problem with no easy resolution. Given that enslaved pregnant women continued to engage in arduous field work, were still subjected to physical punishment, and had limited access to adequate nutrition or medical care, it is difficult to distinguish neonatal and infant deaths caused by slavery's structural violence from those precipitated by enslaved women's individual acts. Moreover, the efforts enslaved women took to reduce the incessant and intrusive surveillance and management of their reproductive processes—relying on traditional medicines and treatments, employing the midwifery services of friends and relatives, and maintaining strategic secrecy around their due dates and deliveries—meant that the so-called masters who were primary documentarians of enslaved infant mortality were sometimes left guessing about the actual events leading up to births or deaths. At the same time, because virtually no states offered slaveholders full monetary compensation for slaves seized and put to death as punishment for a capital crime such as murder, there was little incentive for plantation owners to risk a double loss of property—child *and* mother—by reporting suspected infanticides to local legal authorities. Thus, while some sensational cases—like those involving Nelly and Margaret Garner—are extensively documented in court records, the personal papers of local residents, and even the regional media of the time, other incidents of suspicious neonatal or infant death must be gleaned from asides or annotations in slaveholders' farm books, coroners' or doctors' notes, or deeds of sale.

This complexity and unevenness in historical documentation has meant that enslaved infanticide can be described in equally credible sources as "rare" and as occurring "often," as "amply documented," and as leaving "limited documentation."[9] It has also opened such acts to a breadth of characterizations and interpretations, from the fevered suspicions of antebellum southern whites to the cautions and caveats of contemporary producers of slavery's revisionist history. For nineteenth-century slaveholders and twentieth-century historians of slavery alike, the question of maternal infanticide often served as yet another litmus test for Black people's humanity and capacities for self-possession. In the antebellum white South, tales of enslaved infanticide were inseparable from chattel slavery's fundamental discourses of Black incapacity, inhumanity, and sexual and gendered deviance. While southern whites' defense of slavery relied on the notion that all Black people were incapable of caring for themselves, nurturing their children, or planning for their future, Black mothers served as a particular trope of this raced deficiency. As Jeff Forret notes, "To believe the rhetoric [of nineteenth-century southern whites], antebellum black women habitually killed their offspring, ignored enslaved children's basic needs, and treated them without the love and care expected of good, responsible mothers."[10] For some southern whites, reports of enslaved infants' deaths at their mothers' hands confirmed Black mothers' "great carelessness & total inability to take care of themselves."[11] For others, it indicated "an unnatural tendency in the [slave] mother to destroy her offspring."[12] Neglectful or ignorant, unnatural or malicious, Black mothers were deemed unfit mothers for their enslaved children. These enslaved mothers' innate disregard for the children they bore rendered them both materially and discursively available to serve as maternal surrogates for the white families who held their deeds, concomitantly requiring white slaveholders to act in their stead as both possessors and patriarchs.

The transmutation of nineteenth-century discourses of Black maternal barbarity, cruelty, and neglect into popular twentieth-century tropes of Black matriarchs, welfare queens, and crack mothers exemplifies how, in what Sharpe would call the "wake" of slavery, the thoroughgoing negation of Black humanity and ongoing rationalization of Black dispossession still are enacted on and through the Black maternal body. It thus comes as no surprise that many of the progressive, revisionist histories of slavery that formed the foundation for the field of African American history continued to approach the question of enslaved infanticide as an implicit testing ground for Black humanity and either ignored reports of enslaved infanticide altogether or dismissed them as anomalous events blown out of proportion due to whites' racist beliefs in Black deviance.[13] When, for example, renowned historian Eugene Genovese reported that infanticide (and indeed, even abortion) was rare among the enslaved because "the slaves recognized infanticide as murder. They loved their children too much to do away with them," his much-cited and oft-repeated assertion was less a historical fact than a rhetorical maneuver. Refuting what he astutely described as white Southerners' pretense that Black mothers cared little about their children, Genovese sought to supplant popular images of unfeeling Black mothers with those of loving, law-abiding, and pious parents who "courageously resolved to raise [their children] as best they could and entrusted their fate to God."[14] Genovese's idealized depiction of Black parents' love of child and God alike served his goal to humanize and decriminalize enslaved Black people. However, it relies on a historical imagination of the enslaved Black family as shaped by normative conceptions of love and parentage, in which "maternal love and devotion provided a bulwark against slavery's oppressions."[15] In the context of chattel slavery's total dispossession, those socially contingent categories of love, parentage, and motherhood that Genovese's argument takes as given lose their presumed stability and coherence.[16]

More recently, historians of race and medicine have used demographic information to posit that, contrary to the suspicions of southern whites, there was no epidemic of enslaved women intentionally smothering their children or of accidentally suffocating them by "overlaying" them while sleeping. Instead, they argue, these reported incidents were cases of the disproportionately high numbers of sudden infant death syndrome (SIDS) suffered among the enslaved due to the brutal conditions under which they lived and labored.[17] The resulting extensive research on SIDS among enslaved infants has effectively shifted the narrative of raced and gendered (medical) pathology from the individual violence of enslaved Black mothers to the quotidian structural violence of chattel slavery itself, revealing how its death-dealing structures pervaded the nineteenth-century biopolitical imperative of expanding U.S. slavery via natural increase. However, this emphasis on SIDS as the cause of purported accidental or intentional deaths of enslaved infants has also recapitulated a dangerous dichotomy between the "innocent" mothers whom such studies depict as passive victims of slavery's brutal exploitation and the murderous mothers they disavow, who ostensibly killed their innocent children due to ignorance, despair, rage, or misguided ideological zeal. In this epidemiological calculation of innocence versus guilt, there is little room to think critically about the relations of disavowed maternity, intimate violence, and physical and social death that structured enslaved reproduction and constituted the conditions under which enslaved infanticide occurred.

Rather than pinning down the ostensible truth of enslaved infanticide's existence or accruing concrete data about its rarity, then, debates about the frequency of enslaved infanticide obscure at least as much as they reveal. Setting aside these preoccupations with distinguishing victims from perpetrators or calculating rates of occurrence, however, opens up generative analytical and political possibilities. Accordingly, this chapter builds on Darlene Clark Hine's observation that the "number of documented cases [of enslaved infanticide] is less significant than the fact that it occurred at all," by turning away from questions of quantification to attend to enslaved infanticide's signification.[18] I start from the premise that in order to grapple with enslaved infanticide's significance in the context of multigenerational captivity and inalienable dispossession, it is critical to consider the historical and contemporary sequences of signification that have lent such acts meaning or stripped them of coherence, rendered them spectacles or ciphers—or often, both at the same time. After all, it is through this accumulation and evacuation of meaning that contemporary conceptions of Black reproductivity have been sedimented, and it is by tracing these iterations of meaning—from murderous slave to loving mother to medical statistic, and so on—that we can come to see the conditions under which enslaved infanticide and the women who performed such acts have been regarded as both exceptional and inexplicable. Just as important, these overlapping, and at times discordant, ways of making meaning out of a seemingly unthinkable act offers insight into the difficulty of making gendered sense of racialized violence, by which I mean both the use of violence by enslaved Black women and the modes of gendered racial violence that take place on the intimate scales of the body and the home. Grappling with both the significance and the signification of enslaved infanticide, then, offers an important perspective on how the intimate violence of enslaved sexuality and reproduction have been intrinsic not only to U.S. chattel slavery and U.S. racial capitalism but also to the formation of the enslaved maternal subject as disavowed condition of chattel slavery's possibility and imminent threat to its stability.

Motherhood and Madness

In the antebellum South, incidents of enslaved infanticide were rarely perceived as requiring social context, let alone seen as consequences of the captive and dispossessed status of Black women and their children. Historian Harriet Frazier observes that even in the years closely preceding the Civil War, when Missouri newspapers confirmed a number of murders and attempted murders of Black children by suicidal, enslaved mothers, reasons were rarely given. "When the newspaper supplied a reason for such aberrant behavior," Frazier notes, "the cause was never the conditions of involuntary servitude."[19] Generally speaking, most acts of violence by enslaved women were often recorded in farm books and planters' journals or in court transcripts without context or elaboration, rendering them seemingly arbitrary and inexplicable. In cases of infanticide, one explanation appeared with frequency: madness. Whether she was "reputed [to be] Mad," "crazed and frenzied," or suffering from "mental aberration or hallucination," the enslaved woman found to have killed her infant or child was commonly deemed not to have been cognizant, rational, or in control of her actions.[20]

Certainly, the excuse of temporary insanity benefited slaveholders financially by providing a justification for clemency in what would otherwise be capital cases, thus enabling them to recoup the value of a convicted bondswoman through her court-ordered sale and transportation. But it also maintained the discursive and structural coherence of slavery as a social, political, and economic system that relied on wholesale dispossession, sexual and procreative violence, and natal alienation under the guise of racialized paternalism. The repeated finding of madness among women who killed their infants and children born into slavery worked to individualize a sign of broader social disorder by attributing the extreme act of violence to a single, deranged mind rather than acknowledging it as a consequence of the conditions under which enslaved women lived.[21] As an irrational act of madness, each case of infanticide remained unexpected, inexplicable, and exceptional, no matter how rarely or frequently it happened.

This exceptionalizing discourse of maternal madness effectively obscured the material context in which incidents of infanticide occurred, making it difficult to make meaning of contextual factors, even in historical retrospect. Consider, for example, the case of Kate, whose story Jennifer Morgan relates in her history of enslaved women's labor in the early Americas. An enslaved woman imprisoned for murdering "a Negro Child" in the possession of a slaveholder other than her own, Kate was "reputed Mad" for more than a year before her homicidal act. Gleaning Kate's story from the 1746 record of Carolina legislators' debate over the cost of her incarceration, Morgan cannot help but wonder "about Kate and her family, whether her 'madness' was in fact predicated by the sale of her own child to another plantation and whether it was thus her own child that she killed as a result."[22] Morgan's questions, however, remain unanswered, leaving the "unknown causes of [Kate's] madness and the circumstances that led her to murder a child whose relationship to her is unclear . . . buried."[23] In the end, while the legislative record documents Kate's act of violence and the colonial government's efforts to punish and contain such acts, the political and material impetus for Kate's actions remains beyond the historian's reach.

If the historical record cannot be relied on to reveal the true circumstances of or reasons for enslaved infanticides, it often still leaves hints of what plantocratic records and documentarians sought to obscure. For example, while the coroner's inquest determined that the enslaved Letty had acted in the throes of some kind of possession—*moved and seduced by the instigation of the Devil*—the transcripts also reflect Letty's claim that "if the child had been one of her own colour, she wouldn't have done it," offering a clear indictment of the conditions of sexual coercion under which she likely conceived.[24] Similarly, when the young Nelly confesses and explains that she was "ashamed of . . . becoming pregnant *in such a way*," she is declared to be suffering from a form of "Monomania" and mental deficiency.[25] However, given that the petition to the governor for Nelly's pretrial pardon on the grounds of insanity focused largely on concerns that an investigation would be "shocking to the moral sense of the community" and require the testimony of "very respectable ladies who [would] have to be examined as to the facts," it seems likely that the concerned citizens of Warren County were more interested in keeping evidence of Nelly's sexual coercion and impregnation by her late master from becoming part of a trial record than in seeking mercy for a mentally ill teenaged slave.[26] These glimpses into the circumstances of infanticide, only partially overwritten by reports of madness, suggest that the intimate violence of maternal infanticide was entangled with and reflective of the forms of intimate violence on which chattel slavery was built: rape, coerced sexual partnerships, coercive and surveilled reproduction. The violence enacted by these "mad" Black women was an index of the violence to which they were routinely subjected; according to plantocratic logic, if the former violence could be dismissed as irrational, the latter might remain officially illegible.

Even as the explanatory recourse to madness supported existing structures of racial and sexual power in the slaveholding South, it also reflected the epistemologies of race and gender through which nineteenth-century whites—in both the North and the South—made sense of infanticide. Amid nineteenth-century idealizations of motherhood as a natural attribute and defining aspect of womanhood, infanticide appeared as "the antithesis of female nature, a total rejection of maternal ties, duties, and feelings."[27] Given that "the Deed itself [was] contrary to the laws of nature," the women who performed such acts must be mad—or so the reasoning went.[28] The frequency and alacrity with which white southern communities seized upon explanations of temporary insanity or maternal madness to explain local cases of infanticide by enslaved mothers thus reveals a contradiction at the heart of the white heteropatriarchal paternalism on which antebellum slaveholders and their supporters relied for political defense and ethical rationale. Abstract hypotheses and third-hand rumors of enslaved infanticide served to bolster the truism that slavery offered a solution for Black people's incapacity to physically, emotionally, or practically care for their children or themselves; however, when faced with confirmed cases of the "monstrous and unnatural . . . deed," committed by the enslaved women living in their midst and caring for their land, homes, or children, that same deed became dangerously disruptive to slaveholders' domestic spaces and economies.[29] Moreover, while the economic and racial structure of chattel slavery in the United States had relied from its origins on the construction of Black women as the raced and sexed abnormal against which white femininity was defined, and nineteenth-century U.S. slavery increasingly relied on the commodification of enslaved women's reproduction as a mechanism for producing capital and maintaining social control, normative conceptions of maternity as beholden to the material and affective nurturance of life and antithetical to the violent production of death still maintained strong rhetorical purchase in the antebellum period. Under the strain of these conflicting ideological pulls, enslaved infanticide was at once a ubiquitous trope and unimaginable. Maternal madness offered a temporary resolution to this intractable conundrum.

The tendency of those grappling with enslaved infanticide to seek explanatory recourse in "mental aberration" has continued long past the nineteenth century. Several contemporary scholars have argued that the condition from which these "insane" Black mothers were suffering was likely postpartum depression or postpartum psychosis, exacerbated by the violent and traumatizing conditions under which they lived. In states of "psychological depression or . . . distress," such arguments go, enslaved mothers' "love and maternal affection [were] warped" into acts of fatal violence.[30] The resonances between these contemporary analyses and those of nineteenth-century doctors, coroners, and judges is no accident; indeed, the diagnostic origins of postpartum depression and postpartum psychosis can be found in a pair of nineteenth-century perinatal conditions: puerperal melancholia and puerperal mania. Taken together, puerperal melancholia and mania were classified by obstetricians and psychiatrists as puerperal insanity, a not-uncommon, temporary state of mental illness, the greatest danger of which was the possibility it might "take the form of a homicidal mania, threatening the life of the child."[31] While its exact causes remained hypothetical at best, nineteenth-century medical professionals attributed puerperal insanity generally to the "close connection between the sexual organs and the mental state of women" and to the "peculiar state of the nervous system during utero-gestation" specifically.[32] Emerging in the medical lexicon concurrent with the rise of anxieties among nineteenth-century middle-class whites about the proper role and place of women in a rapidly changing world, puerperal insanity was part of a broad retrenchment in the natural, essential, and universal characteristics of femaleness as integral to maintaining the raced and gendered social order. Like other forms of "mental disturbance" deemed exclusive to women and linked to their reproductive organs and capacities, the diagnosis of puerperal insanity relied on an understanding of the nineteenth-century white, middle-class woman as "victim of her fragile nervous system and unpredictable reproductive organs."[33] Like the closely related and more widely studied phenomenon of hysteria (a topic of the next chapter), puerperal insanity offered a medical instantiation of the weakness of the "civilized" female and her vulnerability to disorder in the absence of adequate supervision and surveillance. In the mid-nineteenth century, such diseases of the womb were synecdochic of the dis-ease that improperly contained femaleness could enact on the home and the nation. At the same time, as Hilary Marland astutely argues, among bourgeois whites in the United States and Western Europe, the diagnosis of puerperal insanity offered a form of discursive containment that rearticulated infanticide not as the "antithesis of womanhood" but as an "almost 'normal' side-effect of giving birth" rooted in the essential and natural qualities of white femininity. Even more reassuringly, puerperal insanity was largely temporary, allowing for the reestablishment of full gendered normativity in the not-too-distant future.[34]

My point here is not to dismiss the validity of women and other gestational carriers' experiences of perinatal anxiety, depression, or agitation. It is, however, to observe that while the diagnostic lexicon, criteria, and causes have been updated in the last century, the premise underlying the ascription of enslaved infanticide to maternal mental illness remains rooted in a concept of motherhood as a natural, universal state of being. According to such logic, to kill one's own child, whatever the circumstances, is "not natural" and can only be explained as a symptom or consequence of mental illness.[35] While these kinds of essentializing notions of gendered roles and identities have been problematized ad infinitum over the past half century of feminist and queer scholarship, it bears reiterating that the recourse to universalizing discourses of nature or biology recodes sociopolitical symptoms as medical ones, attaching social conflicts to individual, physical bodies to maintain existing relations of power and difference. That said, there are particular limitations of such an approach for engaging with Black reproductivity in the context of chattel slavery. How could it possibly provide us sufficient analytical tools to make meaning of Nelly's distress at becoming pregnant *in such a way* or to contextualize Letty's fatal distinction between the child she bore and *one of her own colour*? Indeed, what possible insight could this universal telos of motherhood qua womanhood offer into the Black female reproductive body-made-*flesh,* ungendered, both productive and reproductive, worker and commodity, "mother and mother-dispossessed?"[36]

In lieu of such an accounting, the retrospective finding of postpartum depression or psychosis functions as a kind of sleight of hand not unlike that of Genovese and his peers: it seeks to humanize the behaviors and motivations of enslaved Black women by incorporating them into a category created to delineate the boundaries of heteronormative white, middle-class femininity. By recasting the "monstrous and unnatural" act of infanticide as a "'normal' side effect" of motherhood, these historiographic diagnoses attempt to relocate the enslaved Black mother from the realm of the monstrous or barbaric to that of normative gendered femaleness. In its search for medical explanations, however, this ethical repudiation of the racialized category of murderous-mother-as-monster sacrifices important ground: it forestalls deeper consideration of the conditions under which the monstrous and unthinkable can be imagined as well as acted upon—what *partus sequitur ventrem* identifies as "the condition of the mother."

Motherhood and the Republic

In many ways, the case of Margaret Garner—while often invoked as exemplary of antebellum infanticide—is an exception to the trends of individualization, depoliticization, and mystification that characterized most cases of enslaved infanticide. Garner's attempt to kill her four children and herself, and the subsequent fugitive slave trial through which her fate was decided, happened amid a highly contentious, widely studied, and thoroughly historicized national debate in the aftermath of the Fugitive Slave Law of 1850. As such, her case was immediately politicized. For a brief window of time, it was among the most documented and discussed incidents of its kind, debated in political venues and media sources as exemplary of the Fugitive Slave Law's bloody and brutal consequences. Yet, as a number of scholars have noted, the proliferation of discourses surrounding the Garner case largely functioned to amplify existing narratives, arguments, and ideologies within the proslavery and abolitionist movements, rendering Garner and her children "symbolic property" in a national contest over the meaning of her actions.[37]

It comes as no surprise that the members of the white plantocracy and their proslavery allies in Ohio portrayed Garner as a "crazed and frenzied negress" and her actions as "brutal and unnatural."[38] However, white abolitionists also seized upon the case as a sensational and effective tool of antislavery propaganda.[39] Garner became an abolitionist icon, lauded as a national hero and compared to Roman republicans and icons of the American Revolution. "Patrick Henry spoke the words—'Give me liberty or give me death,'" one letter to the editor commented. "Margaret did the deed."[40] By depicting her as a hero of the republic, white abolitionists were able to challenge the status quo of slavery while simultaneously upholding the U.S. nation-state. In this narrative, Little Mary's death became a sacrifice necessary in order for the nation, corrupted as it was by slavery, to achieve the liberal ideals of individual freedom and universal natural rights on which it was ostensibly founded.

Abolitionist portrayals of Garner as liberal hero of the free republic, however, were hindered by the constitutive limits of liberal individualism. First, as feminist and antiracist scholars of political philosophy have amply demonstrated, the notion of individual freedom based in natural rights is inextricable from the idealization of white masculinity and relies on the exclusion of all women and nonwhite men for its coherence and value.[41] Moreover, just as the properly defined subject-citizen of the liberal republic was white, male, and landed, so was the proper sphere of political activity for such subjects public. The stark intimacy of Garner's act of violence—the family home; the blood-spattered bedroom; the children, husband, and mother who bore witness—stymied efforts to seamlessly insert her into the existing tropes of public, patriotic heroism. Garner, then, posed a problem: her value as a symbol relied on disregarding how her blackness, femaleness, and enslaved status foreclosed her from true sovereign subjecthood and overlooking what her entire life, from birth to escape to recapture to death, laid bare: that the political philosophy of liberal universalism and racial terror are not simply compatible but "cheerfully complicit."[42]

To suture the structural contradictions revealed by their attempts to reincorporate her into the national body politic, antislavery advocates and reporters who made the Garner case their temporary cause célèbre marshalled nineteenth-century tropes of republican motherhood. From nationalist narratives of the mother's duty to ensure the future of the U.S. republic through proper scientific childrearing; to sentimental tropes of mother and child that drew on Christian archetypes to lend moral support to social reforms; to the pages of ladies' journals and magazines that defined the inherent duties of womanhood to lie not in (masculine) independence, self-control, or rationality but in (feminine) piety, purity, domesticity, and subservience, mid-nineteenth-century idealizations of motherhood were closely entangled with ideas regarding the moral and political future of the nation. Thus, even as abolitionist and women's suffrage advocate Lucy Stone described Garner as manifesting the heroic spirit of "our ancestors to whom we erected the monument at Bunker Hill—the spirit that would rather let us all go back to God than back to slavery"—she cast her actions in the sentimental language of Christian motherhood.

> If in her deep maternal love, [Garner] felt the impulse to send her child back to God . . . that desire had its root in the deepest feelings of our nature—implanted in black and white by our common Father. With my own teeth would I tear open my veins and let the earth drink my blood, rather than wear the chains of slavery. How then could I blame her for wishing her child to find freedom with God and the angels, where no chains are?[43]

Stone describes Garner's act of violence as a form of republican motherhood: a patriotic sacrifice for her child's freedom and the soul of the nation. At the same time, she draws on Christian motifs of motherhood familiar to her audience from popular sentimentalist narratives of redemptive maternal love in the face of a child's tragic death. With this elision of republican and Christian motherhood, Garner's gender-bending heroism is recast as evidence of the Christian piety and feminine sacrifice that constituted "true womanhood."[44]

Of course, Garner was no more an exemplar of nineteenth-century "true womanhood" or republican motherhood than she was a national hero of the white, liberal republic. The forms of domesticity, religiosity, maternity, and sexuality under which she lived as a dispossessed captive had no equivalencies in the "patriarchalized female gender" of the middle-class white, northern women whose ideals were invoked to explain her actions. But the strategic elision of white motherhood in the U.S. North with enslaved Black maternity in the antebellum South was less a case of fact or aspiration than utility: part of Garner's symbolic value to abolitionists rested in her availability for empathetic surrogation by the white Northerners who formed the true audience for abolitionist commentaries. Through the dubious exercise of putting themselves in Garner's place, rapt and empathetic readers could shift their perspective and, in the process, the target of their condemnation.[45] Reimagined as the actions of a tragic heroine and sacrificing mother, the perceived aberrance of maternal infanticide—its unimaginability within contemporary conceptions of feminine gentility—no longer proved the enslaved Black mother monstrous but instead evidenced the depraved character and extreme consequences of slavery.

From antebellum abolitionists to scholars of African American history, scions of the plantocracy to public health researchers, the quest to explain—or at a minimum, quantify—acts of enslaved infanticide has remained closely entangled with the question of slave humanity. What critical and political possibilities might emerge if, rather than repudiating, looking away from, or seeking to recast the monstrosity of the infanticidal slave mother, we instead were to heed Spillers's exhortation to *claim* the insurgent ground her existence signals? As Michelle Oberman has argued, infanticide is "deeply embedded in and responsive to the societies in which it occurs," reflecting the social and political management of violence, reproduction, and motherhood within a social formation.[46] To meditate on the social and political meaning of enslaved infanticide through the lens of the enslaved mother in the *flesh*, then, is to perceive it as part of a broader struggle over bodily autonomy and material and psychic freedom in the context of slavery's overweening penetration and domination of the intimate scales of the body and the home. Such an approach recognizes violence as "a self-legitimating sphere of social discourse and transaction"—that is, a form of power that is produced and deployed through discourses and practices and is capable of generating meaning and producing subjects through its enactment.[47] It understands enslaved women's reproductivity as inextricable from the violence of slavery in the United States, constitutive of enslaved Black people's gendered commodification and racial dispossession, and integral to the processes by which the enslaved challenged the conditions of their objectification. In short, it regards enslaved infanticide as a reflection of and response to the multiple intimate violences of enslaved sexuality and reproduction that enabled and sustained chattel slavery. Following this avenue of thought requires that we eschew efforts to quantify, disavow, naturalize, or exceptionalize the fatal violence of infanticidal mothers so that we might instead speculate on the fraught meanings of love and violence, maternity and death, intimacy, domination, and—most ambitiously—freedom in the context of chattel slavery. The remainder of this chapter engages in this mode of generative speculation, moving from the questions of "how often," or even of "why," to ask instead: *What does it mean?*

Beloved and the Narration of Violence

While the romanticized figure of the abject and despairing infanticidal mother persisted in abolitionist sentimental fiction throughout the antebellum era, most real incidents of enslaved infanticide faded from historical view as soon as inquests were completed or captives were transported. Margaret Garner's case, on the other hand, proved such an effective symbol for antebellum abolitionists that she became an archetype in her own right, with versions of her story appearing in poetry, prose, and printed imagery for much of the mid-nineteenth century. Yet in the wake of chattel slavery's legal abolition, her story quickly disappeared in plain sight, garnering scant scholarly or popular attention until it reentered the popular imagination more than a century later via Toni Morrison's Pulitzer Prize–winning novel, *Beloved.* The novel's origin story has been told and retold: how Morrison, then an editor at Random House, came across an 1856 newspaper clipping on the Garner case during her collaboration on *The Black Book,* an ambitious volume of more than five hundred images and ephemera on "the Black experience"; how a decade later, the haunting story of a slave mother killing her infant daughter became the catalyst and point of origin for her first novel after leaving Random House; how Morrison eschewed further research or fact-finding missions so that the story she told would be her own, not Garner's. The result was a phantasmal tale of the profoundly material afterlife of chattel slavery that uses an "unspeakable" infanticidal act as the catalyst for a meditation on the meaning of love, death, memory, kinship, and freedom for the socially dead and the nominally free. The imagined return of the vengeful and betrayed ghost of a murdered baby girl to her former home in post-Reconstruction Cincinnati serves as a narrative point of origin from which to trace the lasting impact that slavery and the attempts of the enslaved to free themselves have had on a community of former slaves and their descendants—both living and dead. Morrison's evocative tale of the forgotten and angry ghost, Beloved, and the community left divided by her killing is an allegory for the disavowed, ghostly presence of African chattel slavery's raced and gendered terror that continues to haunt the United States.

Beloved was a literary sensation, not only winning the 1988 Pulitzer Prize and the American Book Award in fiction but also garnering Morrison international acclaim as a key figure in the constellation of late twentieth-century American authors. Canonized within academic and popular circles, the novel has become virtually ubiquitous in college classrooms, has generated a nearly endless body of critical work and a film version, and has found its place on numerous lists of twentieth-century "best novels" and all-time "must-reads." At the same time, *Beloved*'s three decades of literary preeminence have precipitated renewed scholarly and popular interest in the historical figure of Margaret Garner. From innumerable encyclopedia entries, to museum exhibits, to a commissioned opera based on Garner's life and penned by Morrison, to a nearly endless series of historical and cultural texts that each promise to tell "the true story" of Margaret Garner that *Beloved* refuses to provide, Garner's infanticidal act has become nearly as iconic an example of U.S. slavery's violent consequences as Nat Turner's rebellion and as vexed in its repeated retelling in search of "truth."[48] From infamous cautionary tale to effaced historical footnote to apocryphal story of antebellum slavery, and from minoritized literature to canonized text to cultural phenomenon, Garner's desperate act of infanticide and Morrison's novel together instantiate the dialectics of spectacle and cipher, signification and unspeakability, ubiquity and exceptionalism, that structure social discourse around enslaved infanticide.

What follows takes to heart Allen Feldman's call "to locate narrative in violence by locating violence through narration" by employing Morrison's own meditation on enslaved infanticide as a theoretical framework within which to consider the intimate violence of chattel slavery as it was reproduced through blood and bone, in body and home.[49] I attend to this sublated history of intimate violence and enslaved reproductivity in accordance with Black feminist precepts that attending to slavery's "intimate worlds . . . does not merely add to what we know, it changes what we know and how we know it."[50] That said, *Beloved* cannot be read as a simple retrieval of the voice of the silenced Margaret Garner or of the innumerable other enslaved mothers who responded to slavery's intimate violence in kind. Rather, it offers what Jacques Derrida would have called a *supplement* to the history of enslaved infanticide: a repetition with a difference that calls into question both the truth claims of previous versions and the very possibility of a single, "true" history.[51] A *supplement* such as this has generative potential for things other than the "real story." As Avery Gordon has persuasively argued, while "avowedly fiction," *Beloved* opens the doors to another politic—one that "stretches at the limit of our imagination and at the limit of what is representable in the time of the now, to us, as the social world we inhabit."[52] To follow the traces of the dispossessed and monstrous enslaved mother and the disavowed and unthinkable history of enslaved infanticide through the pages of Morrison's narrative is to construct an itinerary by which to track this other politic, in the belief that doing so might make some small but critical room to imagine alternative modes of living and dying in slavery and its afterlife.[53]

I Was a Man Now

When former fugitive slave mother Sethe attempts to explain to her uncomprehending lover and old friend Paul D the conditions under which she killed her daughter, she knows that "circle she was making around the room, him, the subject, would remain one. That she could never close in, pin it down, for anybody who had to ask. If they didn't get it right off, she could never explain."[54] Indeed, much time is spent in *Beloved* on the ineffable and inexplicable character of Sethe's infanticidal act. For the Black community of Cincinnati that shuns her, the daughter that fears her, the lover who condemns her, Sethe's act of maternal violence cannot be assimilated—not into the dogged structuring logics of Black survival in the wake of chattel slavery; not by Denver, who loses her hearing rather than face the enormity of her mother's actions; and not by Paul D, who cannot accept what Sethe has done, or its implications. While the white infanticidal mother disrupts the boundaries of "proper" heteronormative womanhood and motherhood, the enslaved infanticidal mother also impedes efforts to incorporate the enslaved and their descendants as proper subjects of humanity. Nor does infanticide easily fit within the accepted methods by which the enslaved opposed their captivity. Neither a mode of everyday resistance as is commonly ascribed to enslaved women nor the kind of explicitly articulated act of political rebellion associated with the "heroic [masculine] slave," the killing of enslaved children by their mothers straddles the limits of public and private, opposition and abjection, structure and feeling.[55]

Paul D responds to Sethe's attempt to explain by calling her humanity into question: "You got two feet, Sethe, not four," he reminds her (194). His rebuke is as much about the sexual as the bestial; even as he speaks, he is uncertain whether his utterance is driven by the memory of "the calves of his youth" that the enslaved men of the Sweet Home plantation had taken for sexual pleasure or by the thought of Beloved herself, who—skirts hoisted and flanks exposed, with her head turned "over her shoulder the way turtles had"—had brought forth his own shame when she demanded that he "touch [her] on the inside part" and call her by her name (137).

To make sense of Paul D's entangled invocation of sexuality, bestiality, humanity, and violence, it helps to turn to a different narrative of slavery: the memoirs of Frederick Douglass, whose life writing has come to serve as the "prototypical black master text" of chattel slavery.[56] In each of his three autobiographies, Douglass relates how he puts an end to the "brutification to which slavery had subjected [him]" via his man-to-man struggle with the slave breaker Edward Covey. He marks this transformation from "brute" to "manly independence" as crucial to his spiritual—and, eventually, formal—liberation.

> I was *nothing* before; I WAS A MAN NOW. It recalled to life my crushed self-respect and my self-confidence, and inspired me with a renewed determination to be A FREEMAN. A man, without force, is without the essential dignity of humanity. . . . I was no longer a servile coward, trembling under the frown of a brother worm of the dust, but my long-cowed spirit was roused to an attitude of manly independence. I had reached the point, at which I was *not afraid to die*.[57]

Douglass's tale of psychic liberation through epic one-on-one struggle has become an archetypal narrative of the resistance of the oppressed to racial domination. Juxtaposing "independence" with wormlike "nothing[ness]," he counters the tropes of bestiality used to justify the containment of and brutality toward Black bodies with an articulation of his humanity, dignity, and self-determination. At the same time, by risking his life to secure his freedom, Douglass offers a powerful revision to the Hegelian dialectic of master and slave, transforming "Hegel's metanarrative of power into a metanarrative of emancipation."[58]

To describe the processes of desire and recognition through which the individual achieves self-consciousness, Hegel offers the allegory of a life-and-death struggle between two elements, in which one element, recognizing the absolute sovereign power of death, yields to enslavement rather than perishing. As Susan Buck-Morss and others have noted, Hegel's philosophical musings reflect their very material context amid the Atlantic slave trade and the Haitian Revolution, just as his metaphor of trading life for freedom has its counterpart in a juridical system within which slavery often functioned as a perpetually suspended death sentence that remained conditional on the slave's total acquiescence.[59] In essence, Hegel's dialectic serves as the phenomenological master narrative of the slave's social death, while Douglass's account of his battle with Covey serves as its negation: the refusal to embody the perfect submission that was the necessary precondition for the Black captive's continued existence as a physically living, socially dead slave.[60]

Yet in Douglass's tale of his transformation from slave to freeman, brute to universal free subject, his rhetorical slippage from "the essential dignity of humanity" to his "sense of [his] own manhood" posits manhood as the essential modality through which full self-consciousness can be achieved and nothingness overcome. By employing "manhood to signal the personal and social integrity of the free black male," Douglass constructs his narrative of Black liberation on the foundations of heteropatriarchy, producing an elision between the sovereign, free subject and masculine power.[61]

This opposition between free manhood and enslaved bestiality has a resonance in the character of Paul D, for whom individual sovereignty and masculinity are also inseparable. "The last of the Sweet Home men," Paul D considers himself a rarity: a slave who was also a man. Anointed as such by the master of the Kentucky farm on which he was enslaved, he and the four men with whom he lived and worked were "allowed, encouraged to correct Garner, even defy him. To invent ways of doing things; to see what was needed and attack it without permission. To buy a mother, choose a horse or a wife, handle guns, even learn reading if they wanted to" (147).[62] It is only after Garner's death that Paul D realizes the truth: "They were only Sweet Home men at Sweet Home.... One step off that ground and they were trespassers among the human race. Watchdogs without teeth; steer bulls without horns; gelded workhorses whose neigh and whinny could not be translated into a language responsible humans spoke" (147–48). For Paul D, the descent from humanity is both contemporaneous and synonymous with emasculation. Like Douglass, he ascribes to a Manichean logic in which freedom, humanity, and manhood exist in contradistinction to slavery, animality, and nothingness, rendering the feminine the engendered lack left in masculinity's absence. It is this calculus that underpins Paul D's accounting of Sethe's feet: while Douglass's choice of death over slavery proves his distance from the beasts of burden alongside whom he worked, Sethe's infanticidal act merely positions her as indistinct from the calves to whom Sweet Home men turned as proxies for women.

Paul D's resort to the bestial when faced with Sethe's actions underscores the extent to which enslaved infanticide exceeds accepted parameters for making gendered sense of Black political subjectivity under slavery. As I have argued elsewhere, in African American political thought, the centuries-old dialectic between freedom and death traditionally has been articulated in implicitly gendered terms.[63] Such gendered dichotomies persevere; while the enslaved Black male's oppositional political subjectivity is often represented through his willingness to risk death for freedom, the captive female is just as frequently mobilized as an exemplar of enslaved abjection or cautionary tale of the slave's misguided participation in her own subjugation. Indeed, it is through just such an imagined dichotomy that Paul D and his fellow prisoners survive on the chain gang and that Paul D hammers his way back from trembling brokenness to manhood.

> Singing love songs to Mr. Death, they smashed his head. More than the rest, they killed the flirt whom folks called Life for leading them on. Making them think the next sunrise would be worth it; that another stroke of time would do it at last. Only when she was dead would they be safe. The successful ones—the ones who had been there enough years to have maimed, mutilated, even buried her—kept watch over the others who were still in her cock-teasing hug. (128)

If Death is a man with whom the enslaved and incarcerated men do battle for their freedom, then Life is the emasculating betrayer who seduces them into continued subjugation. In this gendered dualism, the ideal of masculine liberation can be articulated only in juxtaposition to feminized subjugation or complicity, against which free masculinity achieves its definition.

As Hazel Carby astutely observes, this masculinist conceptualization of Black political agency and enslaved oppositional consciousness has roots in nineteenth-century narratives of slave empowerment, in which "the spectrum of representation of the female slave" ranged from "active collaborator," to "passionate whore," to "hapless, cringing victim."[64] It is, therefore, worth noting that the same text in which Douglass's account of his battle with Covey is transformed into the metanarrative of free Black masculine humanity, the story of Aunt Hester's whipping—Douglass's oft-analyzed primal scene of slavery—also undergoes significant revision. In *My Bondage and My Freedom*'s turgid retelling of Douglass's initiation into chatteldom, Aunt Hester is transformed into a beautiful and young "slave-girl," Esther.[65] While her victimization still stands as surrogate for the wide-scale, systemic brutality and terrorism of slavery, Esther herself has become an archetype from abolitionist propaganda and fiction of the era: the helpless victim of the sexual predations of a rapacious master. Douglass paints for his readers a sensational and sensual picture of Esther's half-naked female body—bared to the waist, her arms tightly covering her bare breasts; her "plump and tender" shoulders, exposed for the first time to the "vigorous" and penetrating cut of the cowskin that the master wields with deliberation and delight. This erotic spectacle of Esther's feminized and brutalized Black body is an example of what Spillers has dubbed "pornotroping," in which "the captive body" is at once a "source of an irresistible, destructive sensuality," an objectified "thing," a "physical and biological expression of 'otherness,'" and the embodiment of "general powerlessness."[66] The phonography of the scene is no longer what Moten has aptly described as a wordless shriek; it is not the "passionate utterance" that constitutes the "mutual negative positioning of master and slave," no sonic "improvis[ation]" through which the coherence of each category and the relation between them is thrown—however briefly—into crisis.[67] Rather, Esther's "piteous cries," her pleas for "*mercy*," and her avowals of repentance—"*I won't do so no more!*"—approximate the "perfect submission" by which the slave is defined.[68]

In Douglass's transition from *Narrative* to metanarrative, and from Aunt Hester to Esther, the female slave's political subjectivity is foreclosed, as her sexualized femininity and her subjugation become inextricably intertwined.

Described in dispassionate tones devoid of the childhood terror and horror Douglass confesses in his original *Narrative,* Esther's bloody and beaten flesh is no longer the location of an "impossible substitutive motherhood" but the site of the "simultaneous sexualization and brutalization of the (female) slave," to which Douglass the narrator is omniscient witness.[69] Her wretched articulations and sensuous embodiment of "sheer physical powerlessness" spectacularize her distance from subjecthood and codify her sensual otherness—not only from her master but also from Douglass himself. Her "castrated female body"—the quintessential signifier of nothingness—becomes the ground on which Douglass comes to recognize his own subjugation and, eventually, transcend it by claiming the free subjectivity of universal manhood.[70]

It bears remembering that in the production of history, in Gayatri Chakravorty Spivak's words, "the track of sexual difference is doubly effaced."[71] That is, to follow Spivak, the enslaved male as a subject of history, and indeed, the very possibility of a history of the slave at all, "is produced on (I intend the copulative metaphor—philosophically and sexually) the dissimulation of [the enslaved female's] discontinuity, on the repeated emptying of her meaning as instrument."[72] I quote Spivak here—double entendre and all—to underscore two critical points: first, that the manifestation of the enslaved male as historical subject and the production of a history of slavery are inextricably linked to and structured by the enslaved female *under erasure*; and second, that the absented presence of the enslaved female as historical subject is both rooted in and reflective of the illegibility of sexual violence and maternal dispossession as constitutive elements of chattel slavery through which the enslaved were both subjugated and subjectivated.[73] Rather than lamenting these constitutive erasures, it behooves us to consider the generative potential of following the unassimilable trace of the infanticidal enslaved mother. Doing so might well open up new ways of understanding the structuring role that Black reproductivity—that is, sexualized violence, dispossessed maternity, and disrupted domesticity—has played in the foundation and maintenance of Black unfreedom, as well as its undoing.

Love and Violence, Maternity and Death

Following the unassimilable trace of the infanticidal enslaved mother requires returning to the question with which this chapter begins: "What happens if we assume that the female subject serves as a general case for explicating social death, property relations, and the pained and putative construction of blackness? . . . What possibilities of resignification would then be possible?" If, as Saidiya Hartman argues, considering the enslaved female as the general case for Black social death allows us to consider "the role of property relations . . . and racial subjugation in the constitution of gender and sexuality," then it also enables a more trenchant exploration of the deployment of gender and sexuality as technologies of subjection that structured the relations of property and race under slavery. An interested reading of *Beloved* locates one possible answer by reframing Hartman's original query to posit the enslaved maternal subject as not only the case exemplar of social death but also its structuring condition. To be sure, such an attempt relies on the specific workings of chattel slavery in the United States, where natural increase and a booming domestic trade in Black captives made enslaved reproductivity "critical to the reproduction of property and black subjection," even as the possibility of Black motherhood was disavowed and the Black maternal subject was dispossessed.[74] In that context, her concomitant necessity and dispossession, centrality and alienation, have made the enslaved Black mother the "founding term" of the "human and social enactment" that was chattel slavery, as well as in the postemancipation afterlife of ongoing Black unfreedom.[75]

Sethe's own mother was a "saltwater" African who "threw away . . . without names" all the others to whom she gave birth, each conceived through rape by European captors (74). Despite being her only living child, Sethe never knows her ma'am's name. She recognizes her only by the hat she wears while she works the rice fields and by the punishing imprints of slavery on her body: the permanent smile where the bit left its mark; the brand on her ribs for an unknown infraction. Sethe's elusive ma'am is a personification of the power of "natal alienation": the structural disruption and delegitimation of past, present, and future kinship networks that define and enable the slave's social death.[76] After her ma'am is killed, Sethe is left with just one memory.

> She picked me up and carried me behind the smokehouse. Back there she opened up her dress front and lifted her breast and pointed under it. Right on her rib was a circle and a cross burnt right in the skin. She said, "This is your ma'am. This." And she pointed. . . . "Yes, Ma'am," I said. "But how will you know me? Mark me, too," I said. "Mark the mark on me, too." (72–73)

With her plaintive request to be marked too, the young Sethe seeks a form of relationality that exceeds the bounds of natal alienation; she does not understand that she already carries the mark of her enslaved mother. Through the legal code of *partus sequitur ventrem,* the status of person as property was a matrilineal inheritance, handed from mother to child in the place of any other parental claim. From the moment of her birth, then, Sethe has been marked by her ma'am, "*handed by* her . . . in ways [s]he cannot escape."[77]

The simultaneous biological necessity and social alienation of enslaved mothers rendered them not simply units of labor or dominated subjects but a unique form of property: a fetishized bio-commodity. Under the legal code of *partus,* the conditions for chatteldom were reproduced literally on and through the enslaved maternal body, rendering the "maternal function . . . indistinguishable from the condition of enslavement and its reproduction."[78] When Sethe's ma'am disrobes behind the smokehouse to stand before her daughter *in the flesh,* her urgent exhortation—*This is your ma'am. This*—is a fragile bulwark against the forces of natal alienation. At the same time, however, her refrain attests to the violent "ungendering" through which the enslaved mother is reduced to her status as a nexus of production and reproduction, a cipher whose social meaning can be deciphered only through the brand that marks her flesh.

Motherhood and the Flesh

When she hears the young Sethe's request to be marked, her ma'am slaps her. It is a response that Sethe doesn't understand until she carries her own mark: a back choked with scars in the shape of a tree. The marks borne by Sethe and her ma'am are the physical manifestations of the processes of "total objectification" through which the captive Black body is rendered enslaved *flesh.*[79] From the chokecherry tree on Sethe's back, to the brand on her mother's ribs, to the "scars from the belt . . . thick as rope" around Ella's waist, this "seared, divided, ripped-apartness" of the flesh demarcates the zero degree of social conceptualization that constitutes the Black captive as slave. It is this total objectification that Patterson alludes to in his elaboration of the "absolute" power of the master and the "total domination" of the slave characteristic of social death.[80]

As I suggested in the previous chapter, this visceral corporeality of "mutilated flesh" is part of what Patterson's abstracted consideration of the "idiom of power" fails to fully grapple with.[81] More significant, however, Patterson's schema cannot account for the inextricable articulation of such modalities of power with slavery's intimate violences of forced sex, coerced procreation, and ruptured kinship: the structured alienation of Sethe's ma'am from the only child she bore who was not the outcome of rape; the sexual assault behind the barn that preceded Sethe's whipping; the memories Underground Railroad conductor Ella carries of an adolescence spent as the sexual captive of the father and son she dubs "the lowest yet" (305). This combination of "*internalized* violation" and "*externalized* acts of torture and prostration" produces the capacity for the degradation that Morrison describes as slavery's ultimate form of power: "that anybody white could take your whole self for anything that came to mind. Not just work, kill, or maim you, but dirty you.... Dirty you so bad you forgot who you were and couldn't think it up" (295).[82] Through this coexistence of the intimate and the spectacular, this co-constitution of the racial and sexual, the enslaved mother is dispossessed, ungendered, reduced to flesh, even as slavery is reproduced as an economic system and a set of social relations.

No scene in *Beloved* makes this conjuncture of intimacy and violence as clear as Sethe's description of the sexual assault she experiences at the hands of slaveholders while escaping Sweet Home: "two boys with mossy teeth, one sucking on my breast the other holding me down, their book-reading teacher watching and writing it up" (83). With their act of sexualized racial violence and the whipping that follows, schoolteacher and his nephews reduce Sethe to "seared, divided" flesh, even as the nephews' grasping hands and sucking mouths render her "captured sexualit[y]" a "physical and biological expression of otherness," to be studied and documented in schoolteacher's notebook.[83] But it is neither the sexual violation nor the brutal cut of the whip that most preoccupies Sethe when she tells Paul D what happened.

> "After I left you, those boys came in there and took my milk. That's what they came in there for. Held me down and took it...."
> "They used cowhide on you?"
> "And they took my milk."
> "They beat you and you was pregnant?"
> "And they took my milk!" (19–20)

While Paul D is riveted by the brutal whipping that ripped open Sethe's back and scarred her flesh, Sethe is focused on the seizure of breast milk from her pregnant, nursing body. In their brief interchange, the sear of ripping cowhide vies with the feel of pawing hands and mossy teeth; broken and bloodied skin clashes with bruised and leaking breast. Slavery's mingling of blood and sex is not unfamiliar to either former slave; indeed, Paul D's rape by white chain gang guards offers its own evidence of how frequently sexual violence was used as a tool of racial terror and domination. But Sethe's unswerving emphasis on her stolen milk demands that Paul D—and the reader—also acknowledge the assault as an act of reproductive violence. "I had to get my milk to my baby girl," she explains to Paul D.

> Nobody was going to nurse her like me. Nobody was going to get it to her fast enough, or take it away when she'd had enough and didn't know it. Nobody knew that she couldn't pass her air if you held her up on your shoulder, only if she was lying on my knees. Nobody knew that but me and nobody had her milk but me. (19)

When schoolteacher's nephews steal the milk intended to nourish her fugitive child, they rupture the networks of intimacy, knowledge, and nurturance that constituted the bond of kinship between Sethe and her already crawling baby girl. With their violent theft, they demonstrate the ease with which the ostensible bodily signifier of maternal nurturance—breast milk—can be made into a tool of slavery. Suckling at her breast, a new generation of white would-be masters comes to understand the limitless expropriability of Black reproductivity and the permeability of Black domesticity and kinship to the brutal terror of white mastery. In a social formation within which white wives, free white offspring, and Black chattel were all legally part of the slaveholding *familia,* the notion of family was inextricable from the structures of white supremacy and Black dispossession that relied on the forcible and often brutal supersession of Black kinship networks and familial relations to those of their white captors.[84] In this sense, *pace* Spillers, slavery was not where Black kinship *lost* its meaning but where it gained a new one, founded in its ability to be "invaded at any given and arbitrary moment by property relations."[85] It is this meaning of family that Sethe's ma'am and Baby Suggs lived and died knowing: one in which the sites of Black reproductivity—the breast, the body, the home—were characterized not by privacy, sanctity, or intimacy but by contingency, vulnerability, and violence. The white boys' sexual assault can thus be read as one manifestation of the processes of "endocolonization"—the spectacular and quotidian exercise of domination enacted through the "command of domestic spaces and bodies"—that was the precondition for the reproduction of slavery as an economic system and a set of domestic relations.[86]

To focus on the particularities of reproductive violence in the context of chattel slavery is not to grant special status to reproductive violence as somehow more violating than the other modes of domination with which it was articulated. Nor is it to bemoan Black females' lack of access to the dubious protections and privileges of the domestic sphere as the terrain of proper (white) femininity; indeed, the gendered language and imagery historically deployed to valorize reprosexuality and to construct and police the boundaries of the "private" have most frequently operated to bolster racial heteropatriarchy. It is, however, to insist that if we do not attend to such specificities, then, like Paul D, we fail to apprehend fully the constitutive role that the violent invasion, domination, and expropriation of Black reproductive places and practices played in chattel slavery or the ways in which Black reproductivity was deployed as a mode of racial terror and control.

Alternatively, attending to reproductive violence in U.S. slavery yields three related insights: First, the racial sexual grammar of slavery that I have previously referred to as pornotroping operated not only through public spectacles of blood and sex, mutilated flesh and violated bodies, but also through ongoing, quotidian, intimate violence to the body and home. Second, given that the intimate scales of body and home are crucial places for the production, negotiation, and transformation of race and gender, their thoroughgoing endocolonization demonstrates yet again that slavery was never simply a racial project but was always a state-sanctioned and extralegal project of unmaking and remaking what we think of as gender.[87] Third, and finally, as a formation within which categories of race and gender were fabricated, transfigured, and put under erasure, U.S. chattel slavery relied on the violent control and biopolitical management of the technologies of reproduction, including procreation, domestic labor and leisure, and sexual bodies, acts, and desires. Exploring the inextricable entanglement of enslaved reproductivity with the other matrices of violence upon which chattel slavery relied thus offers unique insight into the terror of enslaved domesticity and the collocation of love and violence, maternity and death, that were the context for captive Black reproductivity and enslaved infanticide.

The Violence of the Domestic

Throughout *Beloved,* we witness how slavery's thoroughgoing practices of endocolonization produce the terror and contingency of Black domesticity in slavery and its afterlife. Through a recursive narrative that slips between past and present, North and South, slavery and postemancipation, Morrison tells the story of two homes. The first is a home of "rememory": the Kentucky farm, Sweet Home, from which Sethe fled but can never fully escape (43). It is through Sethe's memories of Sweet Home that the reader first comes face-to-face with the contradictions of chattel slavery.

> There was Sweet Home rolling, rolling, rolling out before her eyes, and although there was not a leaf on the place that did not make her want to scream, it rolled itself out before her in shameless beauty. It never looked as terrible as it was and it made her wonder if hell was a pretty place too. Fire and brimstone alright, but hidden in lacy groves. Boys hanging from the most beautiful sycamores in the world. It shamed her—remembering the wonderful soughing trees rather than the boys. Try as she might to make it otherwise, the sycamores beat out the children every time and she could not forgive her memory for that. (7)

The name of the Garner farm—Sweet Home—is indicative of the fraught construction of the domestic under slavery. Simultaneously pastoral idyll and staging ground for spectacular terror, the ghostly "rememory" of mutilated Black boys suspended from lacy sycamore trees surfaces as testimony not only to the extraordinary brutality of lynching that the "lacy groves" of southern gentility both relied on and concealed but also to the quotidian intimate violence through which the pastoral domestic of the antebellum plantocracy was created and maintained. It is that everyday process of dispossession and displacement that the beautiful sycamores of Sweet Home offer neither sanctuary from nor amelioration of; they instead serve as means of demarcating the protected spaces of white domesticity while channeling violence toward the Black bodies and homes in which the lives of the enslaved were reproduced.

This strategic use of the gendered rhetorics of domesticity and family to obliterate the boundaries of Black bodies and homes and render them vulnerable to more penetrating modes of domination is not unique to Sweet Home, or to antebellum slavery.[88] As scholars of state violence have argued, the idealized symbolisms of mother, family, or God have long been leveraged to "deterritorialize" the "quotidian sanctuaries" of subjugated peoples and to delegitimate norms or expectations of safety, sanctity, or privacy.[89] This process of delegitimation through deterritorialization of intimate and domestic spaces can be seen in the paramilitary invasions of churches and homes in Northern Ireland, the kidnappings of Indigenous children during the Dirty Wars, and Israel's use of home seizures and olive grove demolitions in its occupation of Palestine. The bodies and homes of enslaved Black people, however, were both delegitimated through their violation and *produced* by it. That is, it was not simply the violence enacted against her flesh that produced the slave subject but the slave's *multiscalar vulnerability* to violence. The body's availability for penetration or flagellation, the accessibility of the home to invasion, the ease with which family and kinship structures were dislocated in the interests of capital—these qualities defined the slave as a nonsovereign subject, as and at the limit of the common law and "natural rights" that produced and defined the nineteenth-century liberal human.

The second home in *Beloved,* 124 Bluestone Road, stands as a testament that Black domesticity's vulnerability to white supremacy's invasion and domination is not attenuated by emancipation. Located on the outskirts of post-Reconstruction Cincinnati more than a decade after the legal end of slavery, 124 Bluestone Road is where Sethe and her daughter, Denver, live surrounded by the recriminations of the past, in a house "palsied by the . . . fury" of Sethe's murdered baby girl (6). In the world of the novel, the isolated home is both unique and iconic. Its haunted walls and rooms remind us that, as Baby Suggs notes, there's "not a house in the country ain't packed to its rafters with some dead Negro's grief," precisely because American domesticity is built on the foundations of Black physical and social death (6). But even more than the Black grief that permeates its walls, 124 is marked by its absence of safety. It is this lack of safety that Paul D experiences from his first moment in the door, that wears out Baby Suggs's great, beating heart, and that strikes Denver deaf when she is faced with what her mother has done. The home's lack of safety is described by many characters in the novel, and in many ways: as "white people . . . [who] don't know when to stop"; as "rememory" that is always there waiting for you; but, most often, as that which cannot be stopped from coming in the yard whenever it wants (122–23, 43–44, 211, 242). It is this constitutive permeability of the domestic and inalienability of Black dispossession that is rendered into law through the Fugitive Slave Act; this constant availability to disruption—whether by white bloodlust or the voracious presence of an angry baby ghost—haunts the house on Bluestone Road and the people who live in it. Like 124, whether captive or emancipated, Black bodies and homes cannot be protected from violence because their very definition is that which has no such protections.

It is this very impossibility of protecting the domestic from the state and civil systems of violence in which it is antagonistically embedded that Paul D must also face when he discovers what Sethe has done. Despite his best efforts, he has been unable to make 124 Bluestone Road "safe" because, as Sethe has already come to accept, there is no way to keep the outside out and the inside in. Nor, he concludes, is there a way to contain Sethe within conventional understandings of domesticity.

> This here Sethe talked about love like any other woman; talked about baby clothes like any other woman; but what she meant could cleave the bone. This here Sethe talked about safety with a handsaw. This here new Sethe didn't know where the world stopped and she began. (193)

Sethe subjects the myth of the domestic to the scrutiny of the enslaved and recognizes that for the slave, there is no finite boundary between the "world" of raced and gendered violence and her body, children, or home; for her, intimacy, family, and domesticity are inextricable from state and local structures of racialized and sexualized brutality and terror. There is no version of enslaved motherhood that is not a structuring relation of Black dispossession, no form of Black kinship that is not vulnerable to the forces of state and extralegal violence. It is in the context of that impossible reality, that set of contradictions, that Sethe kills her crawling-already baby girl.

The Slave Mother's Claim

In the instant in which Sethe looks up, sees schoolteacher's hat, and goes to the shed behind 124 Bluestone Road to kill her children, she acknowledges that there is no domestic ritual or legal code that can keep her children or herself safe from the comingling of domesticity and violence, kinship and dispossession, species life and social death, that shapes captive Black reproductivity. With shovel and handsaw, she performs an iteration with a difference that simultaneously exposes and defies this intimate violence on which slavery is built. It was, Sethe recalls,

> simple: she was squatting in the garden and when she saw them coming and recognized schoolteacher's hat, she heard wings. . . . And if she thought anything, it was No. No. Nono. Nonono. Simple. She just flew. Collected every bit of life she had made, all the parts of her that were precious and fine and beautiful, and carried, pushed, dragged them through the veil, out, away, over there where no one could hurt them. Over there. Outside this place, where they would be safe. (192)

In that split second, Sethe assesses slavery's concatenation of intimacy and violence, motherhood and social death, and arrives at one simple answer—no. With her infanticidal act, she attempts to make her family safe from the consequences of chatteldom—the alienation and the brutal dispossession, the dirtiness that cannot be washed off. For the fugitive slave mother, those moments in the shed proffer another opportunity for escape, another chance to gather her children and carry, push, drag them to safety. Contrary to Paul D's admonition, Sethe's decision was not a choice between right and wrong, or life and death—or, for that matter, a choice at all. "If I hadn't killed her," she argues, "she would have died and that is something I could not bear to happen to her" (236). In this context, Sethe's "simple" no serves as a rejection of *partus sequitur ventrem*'s "'condition' of the mother," under which her sole maternal role is to reproduce, indeed, to multiply, her own social death in the bodies of her children. It refutes the calculus of slavery under capitalism that reduces her to the means through which her children are produced as someone else's property. The sound of wings that fills her ears, the short flight to the shed, the blood-soaked thrust through the veil: all are part of a performative undoing of the symbolic contract in which freedom is traded for mere existence, as well as its underlying presumption that the transmutation of human into commodity is preferable to physical death.

Read through the echo of Sethe's "no," her act of infanticide thus takes on a meaning that exceeds explanations of psychosis or SIDS, malign neglect or maternal ignorance, one in which "more important than what Sethe had done was what she claimed" (193). In the face of *partus*'s natal alienation, Sethe finds a way to articulate a claim of kinship in the limited terms available to her. She refuses her structural dispossession by claiming those who are also dispossessed, insisting that "when I tell you you mine, I also mean I'm yours" (239). After all, what is kinship but a form of mutual possession, one that exceeds the claims of property and law? Her act of "too thick," violent love exposes and repudiates the plantocratic rhetoric of *familia* as another word for endocolonization and rejects the master's authority to enforce his own claim of property rights. When she kills her child rather than relinquish her to schoolteacher, she makes a maternal claim that necessitates a rearticulation of maternity that exceeds the captive flesh, enacting a performative rupture of the social and legal conjoining of enslaved motherhood and social death.

If, as I argued in the previous chapter, Black reproductivity is an assemblage—a material-discursive nexus of power and meaning in, on, and through which the sometimes contradictory demands of white supremacy, capitalism, and patriarchy are negotiated—then the enslaved mother was both the product of these contradictions and their spatial resolution. It was through the Black "mother-dispossessed" that social death converged with species life to transmute biological reproduction into the production of the socially dead and where the simultaneous processes of gendering and degendering met the violent logic of property relations to produce sexualized violence, coercive reproduction, and forced labor.[90] At the same time, in the antebellum United States, the always already dispossessed enslaved Black mother was the effaced condition of possibility for the reproduction of chattel slavery as an economic and social system, the radical absence that enabled the material/discursive production of slavery as a self-reproducing system of laws, codes, and meanings. Her subjection marked a point of aporia in the logic of slavery, functioning as its "positive condition of possibility" while simultaneously holding the potential to implode the system of meaning and capital with which she was unwillingly imbricated.[91]

Infanticidal mothers' capacity to turn the violence through which they were produced as socially dead against the system that negated them was born out of this embeddedness among often-conflicting vectors of power and knowledge production. Objects of property through which both human capital and domestic social order were reproduced, without claims to their own lives or to the lives of those to whom they gave birth, infanticidal mothers performed an articulation of will by the ostensibly will-less and the lodging of a claim by the legally dispossessed. Whether motivated by "too thick" love, a rejection of the conditions under which they became pregnant, or a determined refusal to reproduce the conditions of chatteldom, they posed a radical challenge not only to slavery's racial and sexual order but also to that order's means of reproducing itself. By deploying the contradictions through which the enslaved mother's status as nonsovereign subject was produced—love and violence, maternity and death—enslaved, infanticidal mothers exercised their capacities to provoke both a "crisis in meaning" and a "crisis in authority," a violent disruption of the coherence and the authority of the formation within which they were embedded and from which they were foreclosed.[92]

The enslaved mother's infanticidal act can thus be read as the emergence of that which has been put under erasure: a subjectivity in excess of the modes of subjection within which she is embedded and through which she and her children have been made slaves. She is the radical alterity of chattel slavery's dispossession, which "outruns and counters the conditions of its emergence," temporarily transfiguring social and subject formations.[93] The material and discursive crisis that she enacts exemplifies the contingent, contradictory, and impossible practice of Black freedom that can be located, however transiently, at the heart of Black unfreedom. With her "monstrous and unnatural deed," then, the infanticidal enslaved mother signifies one example of the political potentials of "*claiming* the monstrosity (of a female with the potential to 'name')." As she reconfigures normative conceptions of kinship and violence, of maternal love and social death, she occupies the "insurgent ground" that exists outside the "traditional symbolics" of gender, making possible new modes of being.[94]

Monsters, Mothers, and Melancholy

Of course, the tricky part of crises is that while they are full of potential, their outcomes are never guaranteed. The violent disruption of the logics and structures of slavery initiated by the enslaved mother's infanticidal act is an instance of insurgent potential, not a promise of political transcendence. Nelly is returned to her rapist's widow, while Letty is sold and transported out of state. The Fugitive Slave Law is upheld; Margaret Garner is sent downriver to die. And the return of Beloved barricades Sethe inside 124 Bluestone Road, stuck in a melancholic unfreedom spawned from past violence revisited; trapped by recriminations, thwarted desires, unspeakable thoughts.

Rather than reading this as Morrison's statement on the futility of Garner's actions, it is useful to remember that *Beloved* was published in the midst of a national melancholic fugue. The 1980s marked a turning point in state strategies to resolve the global hegemonic crisis in capitalism—both as mode of production and as mode of life—that reached its apex in 1968. The neoslave narrative emerged to the forefront as a literary genre at the precise moment of a global ideological, political, and economic shift that marked the increasing consolidation of violence in the hands of the state.[95] The eighties were the moment when the New Right appropriated the rhetoric of the civil rights movement, using "the content of our character" to justify deliberate national amnesia around centuries of state-sanctioned violence. The "law and order" shell game exemplified by the first War on Drugs, the rising rate of Black incarceration, and the malign neglect of the Atlanta child murders proved once again that the condition for Black subjection remained Black subjugation, rather than freedom, and that the material and ideological terrain on which such struggles for a state monopoly on violence were waged remained Black women's bodies.[96]

Judith Butler argues that within the hegemonic state, melancholia must be seen as "a political nascent text," an affective indictment of a social formation in which certain losses may not be grieved.[97] Following this logic, Beloved's return is the embodiment of Sethe's melancholia—Sethe's grief and anger at surviving in a world in which she cannot mourn her dead daughter because she was never hers to love. But on a different scale, Beloved's return marks a larger and longer melancholy, a radical indictment of a national refusal to adequately acknowledge, mourn, testify to, the originary violence of African chattel slavery and the Middle Passage. When Beloved passes on through the veil of death, she finds herself in the body of a slave ship, in the deep waters into which Africans threw themselves rather than be enslaved. When she returns, her ghostly presence stands as silent testimony to the systemic abduction, enslavement, and exploitation that built America but must be erased in order to maintain it. Like Beloved herself, the history of slavery and the Middle Passage is disremembered. A superseded ghost that cannot be exorcised with the liturgy of liberty or the holy water of the American Dream, it has a claim but is not claimed.

"You think she sure 'nough your sister?" Paul D asks Denver after Beloved's disappearance. "At times," Denver replies. "At times I think she was—more" (314). Sharon Holland notes that Beloved bears a striking resemblance to the white creatures known as *bakulu* in lower Zaire: "deceased ancestors who become white creatures . . . who inhabit the villages of the dead located under river beds or lake bottoms [and surface] from this underworld to mingle with the living."[98] But if the pale and slender girl in the fancy white dress who arrives at 124 Bluestone Road and can barely keep her head on her neck or her teeth from dropping out of her mouth is a *bakulu,* she is also an invocation of Oshun, orisha of the fresh waters, lover of sweets, wearer of white. And by the time she departs, she is once again something more. Trapped together in the spiteful house, soaked in the grief and anger of the dead and the dispossessed, Beloved expands, ripens, even as Sethe shrinks to a childlike shadow of herself. By the end of the novel, Beloved has metamorphosed into a naked, pregnant woman, larger than life, "thunder-black and glistening," with "vines of hair twisted all over her head" and a dazzling smile. Her shining black skin, burgeoning belly, and "fish for hair" mark her as Yemaya, mother of the oceans, avenger of the betrayed and solace for those lost beneath the sea (308). From ghost child to returned ancestor, daughter to mother, Oshun to Yemaya, Beloved is transformed into the apotheosis of the monstrous Black mother, whose very presence ruptures the fabric of space and time, bringing dead loved ones and forgotten memories with her. No longer a supplicant to the mother who "left" her across the veil, she is the embodied demand for a justice long denied and a reckoning interminably deferred. And just as the intimate violence of chatteldom invaded the lives and bodies of the enslaved, she disrupts the "order and quietude of everyday life" with the violent "chaos of the needy dead" (xix).

To Break the Back of Words

This chapter has focused on one facet of Black reproductivity: enslaved procreation and dispossessed maternity. Employing enslaved infanticide as a critical lever, the previous pages take two different approaches to opening up new avenues for conceptualizing the relationship between Black reproductivity, chattel slavery, and intimate violence. First, it revisited the historiography of infanticide to demonstrate how its significance has been minimized through an adherence to some of the same preoccupations that undergirded chattel slavery—most notably, the parsing of distinctions between human and inhuman or innocent and guilty, and the scientific and numerical rationalization of populations—even as the historical application of categories of meaning used to define and contain white heterofemininity have functioned to obscure the conditions of intimate violence that produced the enslaved infanticidal mother, rendering her actions inexplicable. This critical engagement with the historical significance of enslaved infanticide sought to provoke reflection on the centrality of intimate violence and enslaved reproduction to the structures of chattel slavery.

Second, the subsequent reading of *Beloved* proffered a Black feminist theory of the history of enslaved infanticide that centers the enslaved Black mother as not just a case exemplar of social death but its enabling and structuring condition. Just as the condition of the enslaved mother—her legal dispossession and natal alienation—is the necessary condition for the reproduction of chattel slavery, the captive's vulnerability to violence on the intimate and domestic scales remains the condition for the reproduction of both slavery as a system and antebellum domesticity. This reading of enslaved maternity and domesticity suggests that rather than losing their meaning through slavery's ungendering, domesticity's and kinship's inextricable imbrication with terrorizing violence, brutal dispossession, and continuous expropriation are the constituent elements of the process of ungendering through which the enslaved female is reduced to flesh. As I have argued throughout, then, the act of infanticide by the enslaved mother is both a response to and a reflection of the intimate violences that constitute chattel slavery.

At the same time, this reading of Morrison's *Beloved* points to the structuring contradictions of enslaved Black reproduction as they are embodied by the figure of the enslaved mother, dispossessed. Through Sethe's infanticidal act, we glimpse how the claims of Black maternity might have the capacity to produce a crisis of meaning and authority at the heart of chattel slavery, creating the conditions for a contingent, contradictory, and aporetic possibility of Black freedom at the heart of Black unfreedom. As the practice of this impossible claim, enslaved infanticide is the rupturing crisis that lays bare the inextricability of intimacy, domesticity, and kinship from violence, dispossession, and expropriation. The political potential of this *monstrous* act lies not in its ethical value or unquestioned social good but in the "insurgent ground" that is opened up by looking toward, rather than away from, the specter of the monstrous Black mother. Among those radical possibilities are new ways of unraveling the raced and gendered dichotomies of public and private, human and inhuman, life and death, on which the death-dealing hierarchies of power and difference that structure our atomized, vulnerable, and nominally free lives rely.

As one example of this, this chapter closes with a last scene from *Beloved*, one that offers yet another approach to the claims of kinship in the face of ongoing Black dispossession and gestures to a contingent, ephemeral, and unspeakable practice of freedom. As Denver watches her mother slowly being destroyed by her private battle with Beloved, she realizes that "it was she who would have to step off the edge of the world and die because if she didn't, they all would" (281). For Denver, the daughter who lived, this step off the edge of the world toward a different kind of death requires her to step out into the community that surrounds her, to give up her autonomous self-identity and to attempt another, collective kind of being. The women of her community respond, assembling outside the house in a performance of public intimacy in the face of intimate violence. In their public performance of a kinship that exceeds the imperatives of blood or sex, Denver and the women who come to her aid initiate another powerful crisis of meaning, one that breaks the back of words, that plumbs the depths of the Middle Passage and returns to land to be reborn. By refusing the false lure of natal alienation disguised as liberal individualism, these former slaves and children of slaves turn against their own subjection with the faith that a collective being has the power to create a break in the material and discursive systems that have offered them life only at the cost of their freedom. They articulate a desire to live differently, to live within contradiction, in an alliance that bridges the gap between public and private, slavery and freedom, the living and the dead. In so doing, they initiate a practice of freedom that is rooted in intimate collectivity and ethical responsibility to and for each other.

Banished by the women of the community, Beloved leaves traces of the alienation that structured her existence in her slowly disappearing footprints; the loneliness that drew her back through the veil lingers on the wind in the eaves. But eventually, Morrison tells us, even her trace is gone. Forgotten in favor of a different kind of safety and another form of kinship, she once again becomes the absented presence—unnamed, disavowed, and disremembered. Her sublation into a story "not . . . to pass on" is concomitantly an opening that enables Sethe, her family, and her community to imagine a different kind of future: one that is no longer founded in holding the abiding past at bay (323–24).

To imagine possible modes of being in slavery's afterlife that escape or exceed the biopolitical imperatives of slavery while acknowledging the cost of opening these avenues is to recognize that, in the wake of emancipation, the already double-edged quality of Black procreation becomes no less vexed. As the lure of kinship collides with old imperatives to bear generations and the compulsion to bear witness meets the limits of that which can be remembered and testified to, the question of Black reproductivity in slavery's afterlife takes on new resonances. It is to these resonances that I turn in the next chapter.

3

Hysterical Bodies as Embodied History

Corregidora's *Genealogy of Resistance*

> An account, I tell you, of descent from ancestors. Of longing. To know. Where/who/how. The how we know: Sex. Is how we all got here. The where and the who are what too often escapes me. That African woman I speak of—my great-great-grandmother—was in all likelihood a slave. There is a story, a tale. And I am the one who speaks it.
>
> —M. NourbeSe Philip, "A Genealogy of Resistance"

> the body returns
> in the breath of a saxophone
>   of a trumpet
>   or a piano
>
> —Mohamed Kacimi, "The Body of Memory"

Bodily Exposures

In 1831 *The History of Mary Prince: A West Indian Slave, Related by Herself* was released to a curious British public. Prince's sensational and controversial memoir of her enslavement in Bermuda, the Turks Islands, and Antigua and her plight as a destitute free woman in England was the first narrative by an enslaved woman from the West Indies to be published in Britain and was reissued three times in a single year.[1] With the third edition, a new appendix joined the already extensive supplementary materials with which Thomas Pringle, the secretary of the London Anti-Slavery Society and editor of Prince's *History,* had framed the memoir. In response to numerous "benevolent" inquiries into "the existence of marks of severe punishment on Mary Prince's body," Pringle included a letter to the Birmingham Ladies' Society for the Relief of Negro Slaves drafted by his wife, Margaret. In it, Mrs. Pringle offers a final, further, testimonial to Prince's victimhood, and to her veracity: "The whole back part of her body is distinctly scarred, and, as it were, *chequered,* with the vestiges of severe floggings," Mrs. Pringle avers. This "full and authentic evidence," she assures her readers, was gathered through not one but two separate "inspection[s] of Mary's body" and was witnessed by three female compatriots in the British abolitionist community.[2]

The Pringles' and their compatriots' interest in and examination of "the marks of former ill-usage on Mary Prince's person" reveal much about the mechanisms by which her formerly enslaved body was made legible by her white sponsors for the readers of her *History* (*HMP,* 130). As scholars of slave narratives have long argued, the texts' inclusion of representations of the former slave's body and of white sponsors' written testimonials were inextricably linked. Indeed, Dwight McBride notes, the reliance within abolitionist political discourse both on white substantiation and on the displayed body of the former slave attest to the insatiable desire by white audiences for an approximation of "the real original authentic slave experience" from which their whiteness protected them.[3] These approximations of the "irretrievable experience" of slavery were not simply sought after but essential: given the tenuous and contradictory status of fugitive and free Black persons under the law, for former captives to "tell the truth" of slavery required not just the imprimatur of white narrative authentication but the revelation of the scarred Black body—what Saidiya Hartman has described as "making the body speak."[4] In this sense, the scars on Prince's body were not only icons of the physical brutality of slavery but an index of its discursive violence as well: within a system in which Black testimony alone could never claim the status of truth, Prince's body became "the last authentic, irreducible, material sign of the truth of her narrative. Her scarred Black body—unlike language and rhetoric—cannot but tell the truth. . . . *Prince's body quite literally assumes evidentiary status.*"[5]

Squeezed in amid the various supplements and appendices attached to Prince's narrative, Margaret Pringle's affidavit as to the state of Prince's body might seem to be an afterthought. These appendages to Prince's *History,* however, provide valuable insight into the terms and stakes of the two-year legal, political, and cultural battle over the autobiography, which included two libel cases, a petition before Parliament, and numerous letters and articles published in media sources in both Britain and the West Indies.[6] The controversy over Prince's narrative raised pressing questions regarding British colonialism and the abolition of slavery throughout the empire and exposed the ongoing conflict over how—and by whom—the lives of enslaved women in the West Indies would be remembered and retold. As such, Prince's *History* and the discourses surrounding it exemplify how the display of the wounded, scarred, and brutalized Black body has served to simultaneously approximate and conceal the Black reproductive body's entailment in "the intertwining of sexual access and labor, of production and reproduction," which Adrienne Davis has dubbed the "sexual political economy" of slavery.[7]

The ideological struggle surrounding Prince's *History* was articulated primarily through a racialized and sexualized discourse that linked the question of Prince's veracity to concerns about her morality. In his lengthy supplement to Prince's memoir, Pringle spends several pages dissecting the numerous accusations made by her former master, John A. Wood, in response to her soon-to-be-published narrative and pending emancipation petition. In his October 1830 letter to the secretary of the governor of Antigua, Wood describes Prince as a "loose," quarrelsome, and immoral woman who refused to stay home at night or to be faithful to the husband he had induced her to take in hopes of steadying her "troublesome character" (*HMP,* 100–101). Seizing upon the period's conventions and rhetorics of "true womanhood," he seeks to impugn Prince's claims by condemning her as "a sexually wayward woman whose immoral license cannot be held in place by the affective bonds of conventional 'womanly' sentiment."[8] Just over a year later, Wood's allegations found new life when *Blackwood's Edinburgh Magazine* published a scathing indictment of Pringle and Prince by *Glasgow Courier* editor James Macqueen, in which he characterized the *History* as fraudulent and Prince as a "dissolute character" known to trade sex for money, whose incessant promiscuity and tendency toward violence had caused endless tribulations for the Woods.[9] The agent for the Jamaican planters' lobby and vehement anti-abolitionist took his accusations of sexual immorality one step further, implying that the reasons for Pringle's role as Prince's "knight errant" could be found not in his sense of moral obligation but in their frequent "secret closetings and labours" together. By associating so closely with his licentious washerwoman, Macqueen suggested, Pringle had removed his own family and home outside the boundaries of appropriate, white middle-class domesticity: by "nestl[ing] amidst all kinds of colonial immorality and uncleanness . . . everything that is groveling, despicable, and low, in the vices of semi-barbarians," Pringle and his female family members had abandoned "delicacy, modesty, and morality," and with them, all claims to truth (*HMP,* 136–39).

It is telling that Pringle's defense of Prince in the pages of his supplement uses similar language to that of Macqueen's accusation, lauding his new servant's "*decency* and *propriety* of conduct—and her *delicacy,* even in trifling minutiae" (*HMP,* 115). By responding in the same lexicon that Wood, Macqueen, and their fellow proslavery advocates had leveraged to impugn her, Pringle demonstrated his recognition that attacks on the freewoman's femininity and morals posed a significant threat both to Prince's *History* and to the society that had published it. Like the white abolitionist groups that had flocked to Margaret Garner's case two decades later, the London Anti-Slavery Society had garnered much of its public support through the strategic portrayal of enslaved women as pure and helpless victims of the brutalities of slavery. In the pages of the society's *Anti-Slavery Reporter,* enslaved Black women became icons of proper womanhood, as signaled by their exemplary Christian piety, sexual purity, and feminine domesticity. Even more than their religious constancy or proclivity for domestic life, the terrain on which enslaved women's moral authority and truthfulness were evaluated was their sexuality; thus any suggestion of sexual activity tarnished the image both of the martyred slave woman and of the society that had appointed itself her protector, rendering her testimony valueless.[10]

Allegations of enslaved women's sexual activity carried the threat of invalidating their testimony regardless of the relations of coercion, violence, and unfreedom within which enslaved sexuality was embedded. This collapsing of all sexual practices "under the single sign of an immorality that cannot be named" relied on the dialectic of willfulness and will-lessness through which enslaved Black women's sexuality was construed by pro- and antislavery advocates alike.[11] Edlie Wong observes:

> Antislavery print culture portrayed enslaved women . . . as the helpless victims of rapacious planters and their corrupt judiciary, while colonialist propaganda insisted on the enslaved women's willful license and immoral agency. Advocates on either side of the "West India Question" made competing claims on behalf of enslaved West Indian women who were cast as either utterly willful (and *not* in need of humanitarian aid and protection) or will-less (and *in* need of humanitarian aid and protection).[12]

While often presented as antithetical, these divergent constructions of enslaved women's agency were, in practice, dependent on each other. As

Hartman aptly notes, the legal discourse that constructed the slave as an object without will rendered her rape impossible: because she was juridically incapable of giving her consent, she had no legal will against which to be forced. "As the enslaved is legally unable to give consent or offer resistance," Hartman explicates, "she is presumed to be always willing."[13] The very absence of will that defined her as a slave was thus transmuted into "a monstrous willfulness" rooted in her "immoderate and overabundant sexuality, bestial appetites and capacities," and depraved failure of domesticity.[14] Concomitantly, the sexual coercion and sexualized violence to which she was subjected and by which she was made a slave was not just rendered illegible as a form of "unredressed or negligible injury" but was resignified as evidence of her Black criminality, deviance, and immorality.[15] In short, the very processes of sexual expropriation, commodification, and consumption through which she was engendered as slave, Black, and woman foreclosed her recognition as a speaking subject of her own truth.

In this context, the depiction of Prince's exposed body in the appendices to her *History* holds a double-valanced significance: on the one hand, her brutalized and scarred body establishes her narrative authority and putative subjectivity through its wounds and scars; on the other hand, her "slave body *is* the sexual body": a materialization of gendered Black excess and seductive deviance that threatens not only the validity of her narrative but also the British empire as a whole.[16] Prince and the abolitionists who transcribed and edited her narrative thus faced a representational conundrum: while Prince's marks of bodily injury evidenced the truth of her tale, her unmarked bodily purity was the precondition for such evidence to be offered and accepted. *The History of Mary Prince* negotiates this double bind of morality and veracity, violence and will, through the strategic invocation of Prince's body. By exposing her scarred body both literally and in the text, Prince and her publishers deploy a tactic of hypervisibility in order to conceal that which must remain unseen. Excising or encoding virtually all allusions to experiences of sexual coercion, Prince's *History* instead elaborates at length tales of flogging, torture, caging, and deprivation more easily recognized as bodily violence by its intended audience of white, middle-class abolitionists.[17] In this context, the exhibition of her scars to Mrs. Pringle and her compatriots—and its textual reiteration for all readers of the third edition—is simultaneously an act of exposure and of concealment, a sleight of hand that maintains the veracity of Prince's narrative by acceding to the logic that renders enslaved women either innocent victims of ostensibly nonsexual violence or immoral agents of sexual licentiousness.

While the rhetorical strategies differ, the strategic deployment and concealment of enslaved women's sexuality was integral to the political function of virtually all nineteenth-century slave narratives. As I argued in chapter 2, nineteenth-century narratives of heroic, and manly, slaves often reduced enslaved women to gendered tropes ranging from impotent victim to depraved jezebel or duplicitous collaborators—a set of archetypes from which Black masculine narrators could distinguish themselves in order to establish narrative and political sovereignty as self-possessed agents of their own freedom. Yet, as Prince's *History* reveals, narratives by bondswomen also strategically navigated tricky raced and gendered terrain in their attempt to articulate an empathetic enslaved humanity; while they did so differently, such narratives were no less beholden to dominant tropes of enslaved femininity in their negotiation of the raced and gendered contradictions of the peculiar institution. If the political efficacy of the slave narrative depended on its literary deployment of the enslaved or fugitive Black body as an "authentic" form of irrefutable evidence and a site for the emergence of verified/verifiable testimony, its affective potency lay in its scripted spectacle of the suffering slave as an object of empathy for white readers.[18] Given this, enslaved women's narratives relied on the iconic power of the physically marked and wounded slave body not only to expose the "real" experiences and core humanity of Black subjects but also to conceal other complex forms of sexualized violence and practices of nonconsent in which the enslaved body—and, in particular, the enslaved female body—was embedded and through which it was constituted. Through this strategic maneuver, these counterdiscourses to Black subjugation often unintentionally reiterated an existing calculus in which certain forms of physical violence, coerced labor, or physical punishment were verifiable, authentic, and deserving of empathy, while other, sexualized modes of violence, labor, and resistance remained unspeakable within existing lexicons of power.[19]

If the preceding chapter focused its attention on the intimate violence of enslaved reproduction and domesticity, this chapter turns its attention to the reproductive work of sexual labor and domination within chattel slavery. I start from the premise that enactments of sexual desire, forms of sexualized violence, and systems of commoditized sexual labor were vital and interconnected elements of the reproductive work of slavery. By this I mean both that within a slave society, sexual labor was an integral part of the quotidian reproduction of a slave society—that is, no less central to the day-to-day sustenance of slaveholding life than serving as nursemaid, body servant, or cook—and also that the rhetorics and practices of sexual domination, expropriation, and commodification were crucial to the reproduction of the material and discursive conditions for slavery as an economic and ideological system.[20] Given this, what follows seeks to revise the relationship in alterity that Prince's *History* illustrates so clearly between legible forms of racialized and gendered domination and illegible forms of sexualized violence, labor, and coercion.

At the same time that Mary Prince's *History* illustrates the structural limitations of an emancipatory narrative strategy that distinguishes between valid and invalid forms of bodily injury through the occlusion of the sexual, it also raises two questions: First, given the centrality of the sexual as a vital form of labor, mode of domination, and technology of subjection through which slavery in the Americas reproduced itself, how might we follow its illegible and illegitimate trace through the history of chattel slavery and its afterlife? And second, if the injured and laboring Black body has been a vital terrain for the production of Black legal and literary subjectivity, then how might the deployment of the body as evidence of sexualized domination open up new alternatives or expose incipient dangers of narrative embodiment as an oppositional strategy?

In short, how might the narrative of slavery read differently when it centers the sexual body? Gayl Jones's 1975 neoslave narrative, *Corregidora,* provides a provocative framework through which to explore these questions. Covering a twenty-two-year period from 1947 to 1969, *Corregidora* tells the story of blues singer Ursa Corregidora, whose grandmother and great-grandmother were the captive concubines of a Portuguese slaveholder and "whoremonger" from whom the women took their name.[21] Part of the fourth generation of the "Corregidora women" who fled Brazil and their former master by moving first to Louisiana and then to Kentucky, Ursa has been raised with a familial imperative to remember and pass on the story of Corregidora. Like those of her great-grandmother, grandmother, and mother before her, Ursa's raced and gendered body is the terrain on which the conflict between past and present, love and hate, sex and violence are played out; she must not only bear witness to the experiences of her great-grandmother and grandmother as enslaved and unfree prostitutes and concubines in nineteenth-century Brazil but also bear daughters to carry the story to the next generation. When a tumble down a flight of stairs during a fight with her husband, Mutt, results in a miscarriage and hysterectomy, Ursa's life is thrown into crisis. As Jones's tale zig-zags back and forth from the multivocal memories of Brazilian slavery and postemancipation unfreedom to the contemporary relations of desire and violence in which Ursa finds herself enmeshed, both Ursa and the reader are repeatedly confronted with the necessity and impossibility of testifying to her foremothers' past, and the always imminent danger of being subsumed by it. The following reading of *Corregidora* takes Ursa's crisis as a generative entry point from which to interrogate the conditions of possibility for, and structuring limitations of, the strategic political deployment of the logics of Black reproductivity as a response to slavery's sexual violence and dispossession. From the Corregidora women's use of their bodies to (re)produce a genealogy of sexual violence and subjugation, to the irruption of the hysterical, mulatta body as both symptom of sexualized trauma and precondition for modern conceptions of sexuality, *Corregidora* illuminates both the radical potential and the pitfalls of a model of embodied testimony for grappling with the disavowed sexual register of chattel slavery and its afterlife.

Bodies of Evidence

When Ursa Corregidora seeks to understand who her grandmother and great-grandmother were, beyond their status as Corregidora('s) women, she confronts the processes of sexual commodification under slavery that reduced her ancestors not merely to bodily property but to dismembered, sexualized body parts available for the enjoyment, exchange, and profit of the master.[22] Her attempt to grapple with the violent expropriation of the Corregidora women's reproductive and productive labor requires her to parse the workings of a sexual economy that consigned Black females "to the marketplace of the flesh" through modes of "commodification so thoroughgoing that the daughters labor even now under the outcome."[23] "And you with the coffee-bean face, what were you?" Ursa asks. In her answer—"You were sacrificed. They knew you only by the signs of your sex. . . . They ate your genitals"—Ursa recognizes that Dorita's genitals were both a nexus of power and knowledge and a site of commodity consumption (59).

Readers first come to know Ursa's great-grandmother, Dorita, through her skin, the color of a coffee bean, and her genitals, dubbed his "*little gold piece*" by Old Man Corregidora (10). Described in terms of the coffee and gold on which Brazil's slave-labor mining economy, colonial plantation system, and eventual slave empire were built, Dorita's depiction as a dismembered set of commodities embodies the complex relationship between the land-based expropriable resources whose production demanded the incessant importation of a captive African labor force—sugar, gold, and coffee—and the enslaved human capital upon whose subjugated labor, both productive and reproductive, Brazil's wealth relied.[24] Discursively constituted as the sum of usable parts, her commodification indexes the processes by which the slave trade transformed captive Africans into racialized commodities, their use value anatomized in their strong hands, muscular limbs, and unmarked (and thus obedient) backs and shoulders.[25] At the same time, by naming Dorita—and, specifically, her genitals—his little gold piece, Corregidora underscores the exchange value of her gendered reproductive and intimate labor and his ownership of her as female chattel, a sexual commodity, "his pussy."[26] Within a system in which traders "*paid attention only to the genitals,*" her unfettered availability for unpaid sexual labor is integral to her status as an enslaved Black woman (54).

As an enslaved sex worker—a concubine and prostitute—Dorita is located at the collision point of race, gender, and civil status, where the nineteenth-century racial state's heteropatriarchal ideals of female sexuality collided with capitalist guarantees of the free subject's inherent and juridical right to possess property in the form of other people. The state delineation between endogamous marriage and extralegal (hetero)sexual relations of concubinage served to regulate both the distribution of property and mixing of races through two disparate constructions of female sexuality, and thus of women's subjectivity and civil standing. On the one hand, the state deployed rhetorics of masculine honor and feminine chastity to control the bodies, sexuality, and property of elite white women—vessels of family honor and racial purity—by mandating endogamous, heterosexual marriage. On the other hand, commonsense understandings of poor white women and women of Indigenous or African descent as always already dishonored excluded them from such dubious protections and provided more socially mobile and economically privileged men with the means to enter and exit such relationships at will and with no legal, economic, or religious consequences.[27] Within a settler slave society such as Brazil's, structured around the commodity exchange of raced and gendered bodies, the capacity of the "free" concubine—white or Black, *mulata* or *cruila*—to exercise even limited control over the sexual use of her body was thus simultaneously dependent on her legal difference from enslaved women and limited by the gendered form of dishonor that she held in common with them.[28]

The articulation of patriarchy and capitalism that shaped relations of both concubinage and marriage in nineteenth-century Brazil take on considerably more complexity in the context of enslaved concubinage. The slave, by, definition, was subject to the master's total and absolute enjoyment; she was "included in the order of personal goods and chattels, without will, without a juridic personality."[29] Indeed, under Brazilian law, the slave did "not possess a right to property, to freedom, to honor or to reputation"; her sole right was to "the preservation and sustainment" of her body.[30] Her existence as a subject under the law depended on the understanding of her as a "commodity that could be bought and sold," as property available to the master for whatever productive and reproductive purposes he desired.[31] Neither white vessels of honor to be defended through regulated marriage codes nor free, dishonored subjects prosecuted for their sexual misdeeds by the Catholic Church and Brazilian state, enslaved females constituted a particular category of woman-as-commodity, characterized by unlimited bodily availability to sexual domination.

In this context, and given the extensive monetary and political wealth garnered by the imperial state and its elites from the continuation of African chattel slavery and various forms of traffic in women of all races, it is perhaps unsurprising that the conflicting and ambiguous Portuguese legal codes that criminalized concubinage and mandated emancipation for slaves who were forced by their masters to perform tasks that were "illegal or immoral" were considered largely irrelevant and were seldom enforced in cases of enslaved sex workers.[32] Nor were enslaved women protected from rape or pandering under the Portuguese codes—inherited from Roman law—that prohibited all but the "moderate" punishment of slaves. Contrary to the state's rhetoric of compassion and humanity, laws such as Brazil's functioned to limit the legal definition of a master's crimes to those actions "resulting from the authoritative power over [slaves] and from [the masters'] right to punish," delimiting slaves' status as legal subjects with access to the state's protection to cases of excessive punitive violence by masters.[33] Despite the centrality of sexuality to slavery's technologies of intimidation and discipline, however, the intimate acts of sexualized violence that constituted the quotidian experience of the enslaved concubine or prostitute were deemed not punishment but cases of a master's right to the free use and enjoyment of his property. Having legally experienced no punishment, foreclosed from the limited civil status of wounded juridical subjectivity, and exempted from legal codes granting prosecutors "the right to press charges when slaves are physically injured," the enslaved sex worker was understood to have experienced no injury to her honor or her personhood and thus had no claim to legal subjecthood.[34] Subject to illegible and inarticulable forms of violence and to atomizing and anatomizing modes of commodification, then, she is the product of the system of violence that names her but that she cannot name.

It is in the face of these multiple and layered erasures that the Corregidora women deploy their bodies as both evidence of and sites from which to testify to sexualized injury. Within a system in which the rights of the enslaved are limited to bodily preservation and sustainment, the Corregidora women seize the lever of power available to them. As Ursa tells her second husband, Tadpole, family legend holds that at Brazil's emancipation, all slave papers were burned, "so it would be like they never had it" (9). In response, the Corregidora women take on an embodied transgenerational mission: to bear children onto whom they can pass their history in the face of its total erasure. "*The important thing is making generations,*" Ursa's great-grandmother, grandmother, and mother tell her repeatedly. "*They can burn the papers but they can't burn conscious, Ursa. And that's what makes the evidence. And that's what makes the verdict*" (22).

The Corregidora women's retelling of the time-worn tale of the Brazilian Ministry of Finance burning all documentation of slavery and the slave trade has a double valance in the context of *Corregidora*'s narrative of the psychic and embodied afterlife of enslaved sex work. On the scale of the nation-state, it can be read as an allegory for the structural and individual racialized brutality that built Brazil but was disavowed through a genre of nationalist historiography that romanticized Brazil's "gentler" paternalistic slavery as the origin story for contemporary state narratives of multicultural democracy.[35] In the more intimate register of the body, however, the evidence that the Corregidora women seek is of the sexualized violence and gendered bodily commodification that neither legal slave codes nor post–Golden Act histories could recognize or articulate. In this sense, the burning of the archive of slavery is a historical instantiation of ongoing occlusions of chattel slavery's embeddedness in and reliance on the quotidian technologies of sexuality. In short, the absence of evidence that the Corregidora women decry predates the archive's incineration; the documents that burned to ash never told the version of history that Dorita and her daughter seek to pass on.

A Genealogy of the Body

By *making generations* and passing on the story of the old Portuguese, Corregidora, the women produce a "counterdiscourse of the black body" that challenges their multiscalar erasure by both the archive and its destruction.[36] Deprived as slaves of the right to bear witness or give testimony, they deploy their bodies and those of their offspring as living archives for histories that cannot be burned, rewritten, or whitewashed. Recognizing that "for [Black descendants of slaves] to reconstitute their humanity, they must return to the site of that violence—their own captive bodies," the Corregidora women provide living evidence of disavowed wounds.[37] Their collective project constitutes what M. NourbeSe Philip names "a genealogy of resistance" that is at once an accounting of "descent from ancestors," a tracing of "longing," and a project of "knowing."[38] The account that the Corregidora women construct, however, is a genealogy both in the traditional sense of "an account of descent from ancestors" and in the Foucauldian sense of genealogy as that which plumbs the affective, the quotidian, and the ephemeral to "record the singularity of events . . . in what we feel is without history."[39] As what Foucault, following Friedrich Nietzsche, defines as *herkunft*—a genealogy of descent—the Corregidora women's project of making generations to bear witness to slavery's violent and effaced history deploys their twisting and twisted lineage to "disturb what was previously considered immobile" and "fragment what was thought unified": the multiculturalist history of Brazil's slaveholding past that recodes sexual domination as the necessary precondition for contemporary racial peace.[40]

For the Corregidora women, their bodies become the legible texts for a resistant genealogy written in lines of flesh and of blood, produced through violence and inscribed in pain, a "*scar that's left to bear witness*" (72). Like scars, the remnants of slavery remain in and on their bodies as a sedimented history of injuries inflicted and covered over. They collect in Great Gram's "*palms like sunburnt gold.*"

> *Her hands had lines all over them. It was as if the words were helping her, as if the words repeated again and again could be a substitute for*

> *memory, were somehow more than memory. . . . Once when she was talking, she started rubbing my thighs with her hands, and I could feel the sweat on my legs. . . . Sweat inside her hands.* (11–12)

Ursa's memory of Great Gram's lined hands is generative on multiple levels. First, Dorita's hands, like her genitals, are associated with the gold that enslaved Africans mined in Minas Gerais, associating both of these bodily sites with the broader system of slave labor that produced the vast sources of capital on which Brazil's slave economy was built. Moreover, the palms of the hands were favored in the punishment tactics of Brazilian slaveholders, who made frequent use of the *palmatória,* a perforated wooden paddle capable of producing large welts on the palms of the hands.[41] Embodied signifiers of the history of slavery that exceeds words—sweat and blood, labor and violence—and is, instead, carved in lines into the body, they are also reminders that the story must also be told in words: lines to be memorized, repeated, passed on. In Great Gram's hands, story and body merge to produce something that is equal parts evidence and testimony. Tellingly, when Ursa questions the truth of Great Gram's story, Dorita's response is a slap—a literal transfer of pain and violence from her palm to her great-granddaughter's face. "*I'm leaving evidence. And you got to leave evidence, too,*" she admonishes Ursa (14).[42]

Yet, as Foucault reminds us, *herkunft* is always a vexed genealogical project, its deployment of descent all too available to be appropriated by the eugenic logics of biological inheritance. For it is not only the "conscious" of their counternarrative of their history but also its literal embodiment that the Corregidora women are determined to pass on through their embodied genealogy. By "making generations," they seek the embodied transmission of the past across generations and through bloodlines. Within the cultural vernaculars of societies built on slavery and hierarchized by race, blood is a symbol of genetic and social inheritance, a metaphorical vehicle for the transfer of historical social and civil status across generations from body to body, justifying and organizing both slavery and continuing structures of white supremacy. At the same time, for the Corregidora women, blood is the transmitter of historical memory, the living evidence of the miscegenetic and incestual violence through which they were constituted. Thus, when Great Gram admonishes Ursa to keep the shared history of the Corregidora women "*as visible as our blood*" (72), her words contain a double meaning, invoking the significance of blood as a visceral marker of bodily injury and gesturing to the near-century of coerced sex and enslaved reproduction that reaches its conclusion in Ursa's mixed-race body—a living archive in which her family's past is both stored and displayed.

"Was your mama mulatto?" Mutt asks Ursa. "I'm darker than her," Ursa responds, simultaneously alluding to her dark-skinned father and revealing the ambivalence that surrounds her embodied relationship to the Corregidora past (59). Despite her claims of difference, her body and her blood seem to somehow betray her. "I'd always thought I was different," she recalls. "*Their* daughter, but somehow different. Maybe less Corregidora. But . . . I had it. What my mother and my mother's mother before her had. The mulatto women" (60). Ursa's naming herself a "mulatto woman" both invokes and inverts the long-standing racist fantasies of the tragic mulatta, in which the mysteries of the blood determine a woman's identity and her destiny.[43] Her "veins are centuries meeting" and her "mixed blood" is "stained" by the Corregidora history (46); however, in contradistinction to the paranoic white supremacist discourses on miscegenation in which the stain of *blackness* is imagined to contaminate all that it touches, Ursa's blood ostensibly carries the stain of *whiteness*: the bodily evidence of rape, sexual coercion, and the attendant degrading narratives of the ceaseless sexual availability and seductiveness of Black women.[44] Her very body indexes an imagined blood inheritance, a lineage she simultaneously embraces and struggles to reject. Seductive yet sterile, she renders literal the racist fantasies of the nineteenth century that depicted mulattas to be as infertile as their equine namesakes.[45]

When Ursa jokes to her first husband, Mutt, that she has a birthmark between her legs, she constructs her genitals as the visible signifier of her status as a Corregidora woman: a symbolic site for the collocation of body and psyche, sex and blood, past, present, and future.[46] Her genitalia marks the convergence of what Foucault has named the "analytics of sexuality and the symbolics of blood" through which biopolitical racism is produced: her "pussy" holds as its historical referent the sexualized contact and violent conflict between Corregidora and "his women" out of which she was born; her vaginal canal signals her inherited/imperative destiny to "make generations."[47] For Ursa, her genitals are, indeed, the mark of her birth: her pussy is Mutt's "little gold piece" just as her Great Gram's was Corregidora's; like Dorita, she is known by the signs of her sex (60). Like her grandmother's "cunt," "*slapped . . . till it was bluer than black,*" the birthmark between Ursa's legs indexes her embeddedness in the structures of sexualized violence that are the legacy of the Corregidora women, and chattel slavery more generally (54). Unlike Gram, whose "cunt" carries bruises as discoloring and disfiguring reminders of what the women experienced, Ursa's very genitals are the transgenerational mark of dismemberment, objectification, and coercion—the wound that, literally, will not bleed.

Hysterical Bodies, Embodied History

Ursa's barren body, carrying "*barbed wire where a womb should be,*" is both the ultimate betrayal and the culmination of the Corregidora women's genealogy (76). "We were supposed to pass it down like that from generation to generation so we'd never forget," she tells Tadpole bitterly. "Yeah, and where's the next generation?" (9). She cannot forget, nor forgive, the violence of her lover that has rendered her incapable of making generations; nor can she separate it from the transgenerational sexualized violence passed down by her foremothers. The silence in Ursa's womb echoes her mother's "*swollen belly with no child inside*"; both women reproduce Gram's and Great Gram's past in lieu of their own future (100–101). At the same time, her mother's empty womb and her own injured and excised uterus echo the "wombsickness," or hysteria, experienced by Dorita and her daughter during their years as Corregidora's captives.

> I thought of the girl who had to sleep with her master and mistress. Her father, the master. Her daughter's father. The father of her daughter's daughter. How many generations? Days that were pages of hysteria. Their survival depended on suppressed hysteria. (59)

For the Corregidora woman, hysteria is both symptom of and salvation from the sexualized violence of enslaved and unfree concubinage. The trope of the hysterical female indexes diverse and conflicting meanings that have sedimented around the concept of hysteria in the past four thousand years, drawing on a complex and contradictory discourse of "misogyny, pathology, death, religion," colonialism, and white supremacy.[48] While Ursa calls for the ostensible "cures" for hysteria ("*Sperm to bruise me. Wash it away. Vinegar and water*") to remedy the "*curdled milk*" of her nonreproductive uterus, she recasts them as "bruis[ing]"—visibly injurious (76). If Ursa's damaged womb, like her foremothers' "bluer than black" cunts, is bodily evidence of a continuing history of sexualized racial violence, then how might we make sense of the promised "cure" that brings not healing but renewed violence? That is, how might a reading of *Corregidora* that attends to the histories of gendered and sexualized violence both indexed by and enacted through medical, psychoanalytic, and metaphorical discourses of hysteria not only make legible the alternative forms of meaning-making around sexualized racial violence narrated within the text but also enable renewed attention to the role of race in the production of modern discourses around deviant feminine reprosexuality including, but not limited to, hysteria?[49] And, in turn, what insights might that offer into the possibilities and limits of strategies of narrative embodiment in which the Black female body becomes a living archive, bodily evidence of chattel slavery's sexualized racial violence?

Hysteria, Trauma, and the Medical Making of Gender

A significant body of literary criticism has addressed how *Corregidora* functions as a traumatic narrative—an approach that seems particularly apropos for a text whose central concerns, like the phenomenon of trauma itself, emerge at the intersection of body and psyche.[50] As a medical and theoretical discourse, however, the history of trauma is concomitantly a history of the reproduction and maintenance of gender difference through a simultaneous invocation and disavowal of hysteria as a feminized condition. In what follows, I seek to conceptualize *Corregidora* not as a narrative of hysteria *rather than* of trauma, nor as a narrative of hysteria *as well as* trauma, but as a narrative convergence of the hysterical and the traumatic that enables and requires an interrogation of how the processes of modern raced and gendered subjection in general, and the construction of the enslaved sex worker in particular, might rely on the narrative foreclosure of sexualized violence as well as the sublation of racial logics within discourses of gender differentiation.

Psychologically defined as "the response to an unexpected or overwhelming violent event or events that are not fully grasped as they occur, but return later in repeated flashbacks, nightmares, and other repetitive phenomena," trauma has also come to be understood by theorists of history and memory as "a symptom of history," embodied in the complex set of testimonial practices—oral and written, extraordinary and everyday—through which individuals or groups seek to face the violence of their past and the unimaginability of their own survival.[51] A performed and performative repetition necessitated by an incessant struggle both to confront the relentless return of past violence in the present and to come to terms with the incomprehensibility of one's own survival, trauma produces an affective archive through body and psyche, making history possible where understanding and experience are not.[52]

Not unlike the Brazilian and U.S. slave laws discussed earlier in this chapter, however, contemporary trauma theory has its roots in conceptions of injury that elided sexualized violence and constructed the female body as a place of negligible injury. From the early German, French, and British writings on "railway spine," "traumatic neuroses," and "shell shock," to the emergence of the contemporary medical diagnosis of post-traumatic stress disorder (PTSD) as a means of naming, and thus delimiting, the symptoms of returning Vietnam War veterans, trauma was defined as the consequence of shocking and injurious events in public places—railway cars, the factory floor, the battlefield—that were seen to be largely the domain of men. As Paul Lerner and Mark Micale have argued, diagnoses of trauma emerged in turn-of-the-century Europe in contradistinction to diagnoses of male hysteria, which connoted a sensitive nature or malingering subterfuge rather than empirically measurable injury.[53] The conditions of trauma's emergence as a medical discourse, then, were both its implicit categorization as a *masculine* disorder and its explicit distinction from the existing medical conceptions of hysteria, with its millennia-old history as a (if not *the*) malady of womanhood.

Hysteria—a disease of the wandering, or starving, womb; a result of women's sexual continence or of their hypersexuality; a sign of their failure to engage in the necessary reproductive tasks of heterosexual married sex and biological reproduction or a consequence of overtaxing their reproductive system—was uniformly understood as a problem whose solution lay in the social and physiological fortification of "proper" femininity. Treated through the inhalation or ingestion of noxious formulas, vaginal fumigation with various substances believed to lure the uterus back to its proper location, physical stimuli from ice-water baths to genital massage, and/or bodily incarceration or containment, hysteria became one of the primary vehicles through which women's sexual and reproductive processes were pathologized, medicalized, and regulated.[54]

If the late nineteenth-century publication of Jean-Martin Charcot's *Leçons du mardi à la Salpêtrière* (named for his weekly presentations of hypnotized hysterics to students and colleagues at the famed Parisian hospital) cracked the door of the discursive shift from womb to brain to psyche that Charcot's student Freud soon threw open, it did little to initiate a degendering of hysteria. Despite innumerable studies of "male hysterics," hysteria remained, as it had always been, a gendered and sexualized diagnosis, "invariably represented as feminine through the figures of medical and historical speech."[55] Indeed, in the shift in focus from womb to psyche, hysteria's function as a sociocultural category through which ideas of femininity were produced, promulgated, and policed was not attenuated but was reproduced. Indeed, it was only through his study of male hysterics that Charcot came to create the new diagnostic category, "*hystérie traumatique,*" or traumatic hysteria, to discuss the onset of hysteria among (male) patients who had experienced physical or psychic shock.[56] Despite frequent references to past experiences of sexualized violence in both his case notes on female patients and the narratives that accompanied the photographic collections of his weekly *leçons,* Charcot and students never diagnosed such patients as suffering from traumatic hysteria. Indeed, the continued disparity in medical discourse between (feminine) hysteria and (masculine) trauma marked the convergence of the illegibility of sexualized violence and the imagination of the (white) female body as a locus of emotional instability, sexual deviance, and mysterious disorder.

In their 1895 *Studies on Hysteria,* Sigmund Freud and his coauthor, Josef Breuer, suggested for the first time that, just as in Charcot's diagnostic category of (male) traumatic hysteria, female hysteria's origins were most likely to be external. "Our investigations reveal," they asserted, "precipitating causes which can only be described as psychical traumas," past events that had been erased, elided, or suppressed. Arguing that "*hysterics suffer mainly from reminiscences,*" Freud and Breuer redefined hysteria as an act of "conversion": the uncontrollable embodied repetition of an initial traumatic event.[57] Additionally, they agreed, the vast majority of such traumas seemed to be sexual in nature.

Within the next five years, however, Freud's analysis of the female hysteric underwent a formative transformation. Increasingly suspicious of his inability to elicit a full confession from his ostensibly hysterical patients and thus successfully prove the existence of an originating event of sexual trauma, Freud came to doubt the truth of both his patients' memories and his own theory. It was this doubt that heralded his increased attention to childhood sexuality; the resulting reformulation of hysteria as originating in the repressed Oedipal desire of young girls; and the publication of the case study of Dora, Freud's most famous "failure," in which the analyst's seeming compulsion was to frame all of the seventeen-year-old girl's behavior, dreams, and impulses as signs of a deviant and/or repressed sexuality capable of emerging only in hysteria rather than as a result of her traumatic sexual experiences several years earlier.[58]

When trauma reemerges in Freud's later work as "traumatic neurosis," it is not only divorced from his analysis of hysteria but in many ways is also opposed to it. If trauma is exhibited through the compulsive repetition of the original event in the effort to truly come to terms with it, hysteria is the uncontrolled production of the fantastic in order to repress the "truth" of childhood desire. It is in this theoretical divorce of trauma and hysteria that a literal uncoupling of masculine and feminine is repeated and reified, and it is out of this tradition that much of the contemporary work on trauma has emerged.[59]

The logic by which hysteria and trauma were constituted as differently gendered maladies can best be understood as one in which the etiology of one diagnosis relied on the ontology of the other: women were hysterical because they were women, while men were traumatized because they were not hysterical. The creation of the hysteric through the mystification of the conditions of her production has marked resonances with the production of the enslaved Black female as the inhuman site of negligible injury. How, then, might a conjunctural reading of the histories of these two categories, each inextricably enmeshed with the effaced history of sexualized violence enacted on the female body, enable an understanding of hysteria as a raced and gendered practice of counternarrative by which the history of sexualized domination is materialized in body and psyche?

Pages of Hysteria

With her invocation of suppressed hysteria, Ursa enacts a multiform refiguration of hysteria's meaning for her own purposes. In the context of enslaved and unfree concubinage, "hysteria" certainly sheds its connotation of bourgeois white womanhood, subject to the vicissitudes of so-called overcivilization.[60] Concomitantly, the term exceeds revisionist interpretations by 1980s feminist scholars as the exemplar of women's subjugation, the embodied subjectivity of womanhood in revolt, or the early articulations of a kind of proto-feminism—a set of theories that held in common with their precursors the assumption of a largely white and middle-class subject.[61]

The Corregidora women's claim to "generations," "days," "*pages* of hysteria" work to resituate the trope of the female hysteric within the continuing history of racialized and sexualized violence against Black bodies in the Americas, exposing and reconfiguring the complex interaction between modernity's production of the deviant sexual and reproductive female body and of the "inhuman human" Black body.[62] On the one hand, *Corregidora* posits the deployment and regulation of Black sexuality as crucial to the production and maintenance of racial subjugation both during chattel slavery and in its wake. The novel's correlation of hysteria with sexual trauma and sexualized violence with visible injury goes beyond positing a legitimate wounded subjectivity for enslaved and unfree Black women. In a radical reordering, it argues that "all them beatings and killings wasn't nothing but sex circuses," or in other words, it makes a case for the centrality of sexuality in all of slavery's practices of racial terror and brutality (125).

On the other hand, *Corregidora*'s narrative of Black female hysteria points to the deeply interconnected roles that the "hysterization of [white] women's bodies" and the sexualized objectification of enslaved and racially subjugated Black women's bodies played in the production of modernity. In the first volume of *The History of Sexuality,* Foucault lists the "hysterization of women's bodies" as one of the four primary means by which sexuality is deployed in the production of biopower. He describes this "hysterization" as

> a threefold process by which the feminine body was analyzed—qualified and disqualified—as being thoroughly saturated with sexuality, whereby it was integrated into the sphere of medical practices, by reason of a pathology intrinsic to it; whereby, finally, it was placed in organic communication with the social body (whose regulated fecundity it was supposed to ensure).[63]

What Foucault fails to mention is how deeply indebted modern discourse on the hysteric was to preexisting conceptions of Black women. Nineteenth-century scientific discourse relied heavily on the production of an analogous relationship between race and gender—and particularly, white women and Black people. As Robyn Wiegman has observed, such analogies

> simultaneously differentiated and linked two of the nineteenth century's primary forms of social difference, instantiating and perpetuating the visible economies of race and gender by locating their

> signification on bodies that could not claim the disembodied abstraction of those both white and male.[64]

With this in mind, the hysterization of white women's bodies—Charcot's spectacles of barking, spinning, and babbling hysterical women in the Salpêtrière—can also be said to be a practice of racialization: a redeployment of the discursive strategies by which Black women were constructed as pathological and uncontainable hypersexual creatures devoid of higher reasoning. Through this convergence of meanings, hysteria came to be seen as "the eruption of the lower, the animal, signifying a sexuality that is antisocial, even criminal"; thus the sexed body became both signifier and root cause of women's psychic pathology and status as deviant subject.[65]

Tellingly, Freud's early collaborator on the study of hysteria, Breuer, also invoked familiar racialized and sexualized biological parlance to describe the female hysteric. Hysterics, Breuer noted, "are the flower of mankind, as sterile, no doubt, but as beautiful as double flowers."[66] As Elaine Showalter has noted, his observation and case notes depict the hysteric as "seductive and attractive, but incapable of maternity or creativity," and go even further to suggest that the hysteric's sterility and her intense abnormal flowering go together.[67] Certainly, the double flower, with its seemingly infinite production of the bloom within the bloom and inability to reproduce itself from seed, resuscitates foundational premises of hysterical reproductive abnormality that psychology had ostensibly left behind. At the same time, however, Breuer's floral metaphor mirrors contemporaneous conceptions of the mulatta as genetic aberration: beautiful, seductive, and sterile. Indeed, by wedding the hysteric's sexual appeal with her presumed sterility, Breuer reiterates a whitened version of that which the mulatta exemplifies: what Spillers has described as the "iconographic equation" between "black-female-as-whore" and "black-female-vagina-less."[68]

Breuer's reliance on an idiom of reproduction exemplifies how, out of the "overlappings, interactions, and echoes" of discourses of blood and sex, both modern racism and psychoanalysis emerge to "reinscribe the thematic of sexuality in the system of law."[69] Within this legal and social narrative, the enslaved Black concubine-cum-hysteric emerges as a constitutive absence. As the legal subject whose negligible injury marks her as outside the bounds of recognizable humanity and whose pathological sexuality "fix[es] the frontier of woman," she is decontextualized from the relations of power and violence in which she is enmeshed, rendered ahistorical, abstract, and evacuated of legal and social significance other than as deviancy in need of regulation.[70]

From Ursa to Dorita, Jones traces a hysterical lineage, establishing the connection between historically and geographically specific forms of violence against the female body, enacted through racialized sexual and reproductive practices and norms. By centering the hysterical female body within the text, Jones locates sexualized violence at the core of African chattel slavery. And in her simultaneous identification with and transformation of the trope of the female hysteric, she redefines hysteria as an embodied production of history capable of addressing the inextricability of race and sexuality in producing the limits of the human.

Embodying Justice

To read the hysterical presence in *Corregidora* as a *historical* symptom—that is, as a form of embodied testimony to historical sexualized trauma—requires returning to the conjoined theoretical roots of hysteria and trauma. Such a reading demands an understanding of hysterical trauma as simultaneously mobile and rooted; for while it functions transhistorically, it does so in the specific geography of the raced and gendered body. Hearing her mother recount the story of Corregidora, Ursa marvels that "it was as if their memory, the memory of all the Corregidora women, was her memory too, as strong with her as her own private memory, or almost as strong" (129). In some ways, it is, Mama suggests: "Corregidora is responsible for that part of my life," she tells Ursa. "If Corregidora hadn't happened . . . part of my life never would have happened" (111). In arguing this, Mama acknowledges the pull of what Marianne Hirsch has dubbed "postmemory." She assumes her mother and grandmother's memories as if they were her own, bearing witness to "traumatic memories that preceded her birth but nevertheless define her life's narrative."[71] The trauma to which Mama testifies is both individual (the captivity, rape, and abuse that Dorita and her daughter suffered at Corregidora's hands) and collective (the incessant production and reproduction of the Black female as both a void of subjectivity and a surfeit of sexuality).[72] The history of Corregidora, as told by the Corregidora women, "exceed[s] individual bounds" to engender transgenerational communities of memory.[73]

In its hysterical reenactment, however, traumatic history is spatialized on the scale of the body.[74] While hysteria breaches the boundaries of history, it does so by rendering the female body a synecdochic surrogate for national and transnational structures of domination. The female hysteric, whose "wandering womb" and "hysterogenic zones" signify the inextricability of body and psyche, is not just a witness to but also an *embodiment of* the past sexual trauma. Her "body is transformed into a theater for forgotten scenes" that can be represented only through her compulsive re-presentation of them.[75] In their own hysteria, Great Gram and Gram, too, ceaselessly reiterate the foreclosed historical trauma through which they were engendered. In order to testify to "what was done," they render themselves living evidence of that which exceeds them; they bear witness not only to the rape of female slaves but also to the engendering of a slave subject who could not be raped; not only to incest but also to the total natal alienation that constitutes social death.

The Corregidora women reproduce history as well as reconfigure it; in their version, the past "[is] now," the mythic Palmares is almost within sight, and that which was done can still be vindicated (126). As Mama and Ursa, in turn, join the ranks of Corregidora women and concubine daughters, they each create their own embodied mimetic testimony to the legacy of chattel slavery in Brazil that defies its postemancipation erasure. For them, however, the reemergence of the past in the present holds little promise for redemption; rather, it marks the persistent physical and epistemic violence through which the Black female as less-than-subject is continually reproduced. Being born neither slave nor sex worker does not protect Mama from being seen as a "bitch" and a "whore" or help Ursa emerge from the shadow space between being some man's piece of gold and his piece of shit (165). In the final pages of the novel, Ursa wonders,

> Was what Corregidora had done to *her,* to *them,* any worse than what Mutt had done to me, than we had done to each other, than what Mama had done to Daddy, or what he had done to her in return, making her walk down the street looking like a whore? (184)

Ursa's musings can be read as recognition of the continued salience of preemancipation constructions of Black female sexuality, of their capacity to be reproduced, transformed, and redeployed in new historical and geographical contexts.

It was precisely such persistence and variability, the difficulty of locating the originary violence or eradicating it, that led an exasperated Freud to abandon his theory that hysteria originated in trauma altogether. Not only was it virtually impossible to ever fully unearth the elusive memory at the root of the hysterical symptoms, he complained in 1897, but in his sessions with hysterics, it was "impossible to distinguish between truth and emotionally-charged fiction."[76] As Hélène Cixous and Catherine Clément observe, Freud's frustration reflects his own need to uncover what he perceived to be the truth. "Pursuing a real cause," they reflect, "he sought to discover a true story. When this discovery became impossible . . . a definitive corner was turned."[77] The truth that Freud desired seemed to him incommensurable with the kind of changeability and impossibility he repeatedly ran aground upon.

When she first hears the stories of her own family's suppressed hysteria, five-year-old Ursa's reaction mirrors Freud's.

> *"You telling the truth, Great Gram?"*
> *She slapped me.*
> *"When I tell you something don't you ever ask if I'm lying. Because they didn't want to leave no evidence of what they done. And I'm leaving evidence."* (14)

Great Gram responds to Ursa's request for the truth with an assertion not of veracity but of necessity. Like Freud, Dorita and her daughter know that the truth can be hard to pin down and impossible to prove, and that "*it's hard to always remember what you were feeling when you ain't feeling it exactly that way no more*" (79). But unlike Freud, they will not allow the impossibility of fully representing the truth to supersede their ethical obligation to bear witness.

In the case of historical trauma, Dori Laub has suggested, testimony will always fail: "There are never enough words or the right words, there is never enough time or the right time, and never enough listening or the right listening to articulate the story that cannot be fully captured in *thought, memory,* and *speech.*" If the ultimate end of African chattel slavery was the production of blackness as "the absolute bio-political . . . limit," the "zero degree of social conceptualization," then its success was measured through the extent of social death, the philosophical annihilation of the very possibility "of being heard, of being recognized as a subject, of being answered."[78] If to leave evidence is to rehabilitate the possibility of (wounded) subjectivity, then testimony is made possible only through the failure of social death. To bear witness to the full extent of dehumanization would appear to be philosophically impossible; the records were always already burnt.[79]

The futility of attempting to bear full witness is even more evident for Mama and Ursa, who have only Great Gram's and Gram's memories upon which to rely. "*They'd look at her. They'd tell theirs and they'd look at her to bear them witness,*" Ursa recalls, "*but what could she say? She could only tell me what they'd told her.*" Yet Mama, unlike the five-year-old Ursa, knows that her task in witnessing is not to know the truth but to demand justice. Mama articulates the question that all the Corregidora women need answered: not "Is it true?" but "*How can it be?*" (102).

It is the haunting power of this question, and the quest for justice that it signifies, that prevents Ursa and her mother from doing as Ursa's biological father, Martin, and Mutt demand: to forget what Gram and Great Gram went through. To forget, Jones seems to suggest, would require effacing how their own lives continue to be shaped by racism and patriarchy. Forgetting would not only constitute a "freedom that is fundamentally a betrayal of the past" but also require affecting a freedom that belies their lived experience in the present.[80] Forgetting is as impossible for them as representing the true history of chattel slavery and enslaved concubinage.

When viewed through the lens of hysteria, what appears to be an epistemic web of impossibilities in which the Corregidora women are ensnared can instead be seen as a point of profound radical possibility. For, as Elin Diamond has suggested, the very characteristics that have made hysteria "the trope par excellence for the ruination of truth-making" also enable its reappropriation as "a disruption of traditional epistemological methods of seeing/knowing."[81] Like Freud's hysterics, the Corregidora women do not offer a transparent re-presentation of unmediated experience; rather, by merging biological reproduction and narrative reiteration, they perform what Luce Irigaray has dubbed *mimétisme,* the practice of "mak[ing] 'visible,' by an effect of playful repetition, that which was supposed to remain invisible."[82] In this conjoined process of biological reproduction and hysterical reiteration, the Corregidora women repeatedly enact a "mimesis without truth," destabilizing the terms through which their own bodies are deployed and their own narrative is enunciated.[83] As each reiterates a collective past that can never be fully known, they make visible a necessary impossibility: a Black female subjectivity that encompasses both injury and agency. If, as Derrida has argued, "aporetic experiences are the experiences, as improbable as they are necessary, of justice," then through their repetitive re-presentation of the past, the Corregidora women constitute their own justice—one that emerges from an aporetic engagement with the impossible.[84]

Possession and the Past

In his writing on historical trauma, Laub recounts how Holocaust resistors worked relentlessly against the Nazi evisceration of subjectivity and history, chronicling, salvaging, and safeguarding evidence through the written word.[85] In *Corregidora,* however, the written records repeatedly betray, whether through the burning of the archives of slavery in Brazil or the destruction of the courthouse records deeding land to Tadpole's family. Faced with the unreliability of written media constructed to serve whites, the Corregidora women choose instead to encode their testimony in the flesh. Their strategy is necessarily double-edged, a simultaneous experience of claiming the past and of being claimed by it, of *possessing* and *possession.*

There is an extensive body of work on trauma as a relation of possession. According to Cathy Caruth, for example, trauma is both the "repeated possession of the one who experiences it" and "a history that [the traumatized] cannot entirely possess."[86] Alternatively, hysteria has long been tied to demonic possession, most famously in the *Malleus Maleficarum* (Witches' Hammer) of 1494.[87] In *Corregidora,* the double sense connoted in theories of trauma and hysteria—possession as both a relation of property and the spiritual inhabiting of a subject by something other than herself—are inextricable.

Soon after marrying Tadpole, Ursa dreams of giving birth to Old Man Corregidora, only to have him immediately penetrate her sexually. His act brands her as the daughter of the daughter of the concubine daughter, one of four generations of women tied to the old man by manifold forms of reproductive violence and coercion. Although she has never met him, Corregidora is always inside her; they were, as he puts it, united at birth (76–77). Ursa's dream certainly recalls Freud and Breuer's description of hysteria's originating trauma as "a foreign body which long after its entry must continue to be regarded as an agent that is still at work."[88] At the same time, it underscores two crucial—and intertwined—aspects of African chattel slavery: the determining role of hereditary status in transforming captive Africans into slaves and the centrality of sexual availability in defining enslaved females as chattel. As a Corregidora woman, Ursa carries the mark of Corregidora; like Freud and Breuer's mysterious foreign body, the "old man still howls inside [her]," branding her as both a product of and available for sexualized racial violence (46).

Ceaselessly told and retold, Great Gram and Gram's stories of the old man impregnate Ursa's childhood memories, carrying out the work of making history. "*They squeezed Corregidora into me,*" she remembers (103). "Procreation," Tadpole remarks. "That could also be a slave-breeder's way of thinking." Ursa disagrees, arguing that political intent—"if it's for you or somebody else, your life or theirs"—makes all the difference (22–23). Over the course of the novel, however, the confusion only grows regarding for whom the Corregidora women have been (re)producing history. While the Corregidora women deploy their own, refigured form of hysteria in order to testify to their subjection through raced and gendered subjugation, they can do so only by reproducing the discourses that they seek to oppose: the hysterization of women's bodies and the constitution of Black humanity and Black injury as concomitant legal categories. The categories they seek to unmake are reinstantiated even as they are challenged: the Black female body becomes both object and artifact of sexualized racial violence and deviant sexuality; Corregidora is at once the violating master/father and the stunted offspring. Ursa's words and dreams connect her childhood indoctrination to the processes of forcible sex, enslaved prostitution, and coerced reproduction practiced under slavery; full up with the story of Corregidora, she has little room to do more than survive.

In her own work on the spectacle of the enslaved body as witnessed and narrated by white abolitionists, Hartman has addressed a concern not unrelated to my own. "Beyond evidence of slavery's crime," she asks,

> what does this exposure of the suffering body of the bondsman yield? Does this not reinforce the "thingly" quality of the captive by reducing the body to evidence in the very effort to establish the humanity of the enslaved? Does it not reproduce the hyperembodiness of the powerless?[89]

The dynamics at work in the kind of paternalistic and/or vicarious displays of white abolitionist empathy that Hartman seeks to destabilize certainly differ in many, if not most, respects from those at work in the intraracial, transgenerational testimony depicted in *Corregidora.* Nonetheless, both are exemplary of how counterhegemonic discourses have relied on the body to furnish evidence of Black humanity and Black subjugation. To give bodily evidence necessarily demands a reiteration of the Black body's objectification—its reproduction as an object of violence and scrutiny.

By making generations, the Corregidora women seek to leave evidence. Their bodies and the bodies of their offspring become dynamic repositories capable of rearticulating, however incompletely, past injuries. Yet the cost is a high one: in order to produce female descendants capable of bearing witness, Great Gram and Gram must pick up where Corregidora left off, transforming their female descendants into concubine daughters, possessed vessels for the continuation of Corregidora's legacy, living evidence to the objectification of slavery. The distinction between objectified and objectifier is incontrovertibly blurred; it is a process from which no one escapes intact.

A Split Second of Hate and Love

The last of the Corregidora women, Ursa is also the first to identify the trap inherent in a strategy of reproducible embodied testimony. While it is her hysterectomy that renders her physically incapable of making generations, it is her career as a blues singer that offers both Ursa and the reader a window into alternative forms of bearing witness. In refutation of "*a life always spoken, and only spoken,*" Ursa "*give[s] witness the only way [she] can*" to her grandmother and great-grandmother's stories, trying to explain in song that which she can neither reproduce biological evidence of nor testify to in words (103, 54).

Through the blues, Ursa seeks to produce yet another iteration of the narrative of Corregidora. "I wanted a song that would touch me," she muses, "touch my life *and* theirs. A Portuguese song, but not a Portuguese song. A new world song. A song branded with the new world" (59). In Ursa's revised form of witnessing, it is not the body but the song that carries the brand of slavery in the Americas; it is her voice, not her palms, that transfer the sweat of generations of labor. When she sings the blues, Ursa acknowledges that even the living archive of the body cannot contain the truth of slavery. She thus deploys her body less as incontrovertible evidence than as one aspect of a broader performance of testimony. As a thread woven through *Corregidora* from beginning to end, the blues signals an alternative approach to reproducing history that emerges from the interstices of desire and violence to interrogate the political, economic, and sexual overdetermination of Black female subjectivity. Within the novel, the world of the blues provides a cultural terrain in which the central issues of enslaved and unfree concubinage—sexual commodification alongside sexual agency, the intersection of productive and reproductive labor, and the construction of political subjectivity—can be confronted and transfigured.

As a scene of ideological contestation and political articulation, the blues are marked by ambivalence—a characteristic of which Jones is well aware. In her critical study of the role of oral tradition in African American literature, she explains the blues with a quote from Ralph Ellison's *Shadow and Act,* in which he defines them as

> an impulse to keep the painful details and episodes of a brutal experience alive in one's aching consciousness, to finger its jagged grain, and to transcend it, not by the consolation of philosophy, but by squeezing from it a near-tragic, near-comic lyricism.[90]

With the capacity to squeeze pleasure from pain, to transcend the unbearable by embracing it, Ellison's and Jones's blues constitute a kind of performed jouissance.[91] They originate in an impulse, a desire to both grasp the brutality of the past and transform it—not into pleasure but *through* it. And while they are closely concerned with past and present injury, they also signal the possibility for radical change in the future. Indeed, Houston Baker has argued, "even as they speak of paralyzing absence and ineradicable desire, their instrumental rhythms suggest change, movement, action, continuance, unlimited and unending possibility."[92] For female blues singers, however, the radical potential for change emerges not only in language and rhythm but also in the embodied performance.

When she sings the blues, Ursa mediates a set of conflicting discourses around Black female sexuality, subjugation, and political agency. In recent years, Black feminist scholars have produced well-supported and convincing arguments as to how the blues provided Black women an opportunity to represent themselves as female sexual subjects rather than as objects of masculine desire.[93] In *Corregidora*, however, singing the blues constitutes a murky zone between sexual agency and sexual commodification. Ursa's first husband, Mutt, repeatedly argues that to be a blues singer is equivalent to being a whore.[94]

> When you get there, Urs, just go over to one a they tables for me, and . . . kinda lean down so you show a little bit of them titties, and then just ask one of em what he wont. If you don't know what he's gonna say, I do. "Piece a ass please." "Piece a whose ass?" "Yours, good-lookin woman." (165)

It is, in part, her open transgression of the categories of public and private that renders the Black female blues singer available to reinterpellation as sex worker. For Mutt, when Ursa's sexualized body goes beyond the private scale of the home to the public space of the blues club, it becomes the literal object of exchange; he sees little difference between her singing on stage and the auctions at which both her and his great-grandmothers were sold as slaves.

While Mutt's description of Ursa as "a piece a ass" for sale certainly illustrates the patriarchal resentment that accompanies his inability to claim her exclusively as *his* object of property, it also illuminates a repeated slippage between sex and blues, prostitution and performing, that runs throughout the novel. If one keeps in mind Jones's Ellison-influenced definition of the blues, then it is in the shifting parallels between the affective labor of singing the blues and sexual labor of her grandmother and great-grandmother that the potential for a radical transformation of relations of domination emerges. For what Ursa produces in her performance—what Mutt seeks to prevent her from reproducing in his absence—is a moment of jouissance, with all its attendant connotations of pain and pleasure, sex and death. Indeed, it is this performative aspect of Ursa's performances—her capacity to produce in her audience just such an experience of jouissance—that Mutt resents. He understands that by choosing a form of gendered labor through which she can bear witness, she has also chosen one that relies on female sexuality.

By blurring the distinction between work that performs Black female sexuality and sex work, Jones highlights how, by taking "sensuality and sexuality out of the private sphere and into the public sphere," the female blues singer negotiates between sexual agency and sexual commodification. Yet just as important, the performance of the blues has long served as a vehicle through which Black women can become, at least momentarily, "the primary subject[s] of [their] own invention."[95] As Ursa clearly understands, what she does is both a form of labor and a performance of sexuality; however, the blues are also a performative practice through which she constitutes herself as a political subject. While she feels an ethical necessity to re-present the history of her foremothers, she does so not through flesh and word but in melody and measure, pain and pleasure, through a musical genre in which, as Angela Davis has noted, "the protagonists . . . are seldom wives and never mothers."[96] When she sings, she is both blues woman and concubine daughter, capable of reconfiguring the narrative of sexual exploitation with which she has been raised by performing her own agency and objectification as deeply intertwined rather than antagonistic trajectories through which she defines herself as a raced and gendered subject.

"You have the kind of voice that can hurt you," Ursa's boss, Max, observes, "hurt you and make you still want to listen" (96). When Ursa sings the blues, her voice, like her body, indexes a history of violence. "It sounds like you been through something," her neighbor Cat tells her (44). Poised at the precipice between singing and screaming, her voice narrates a story of "pleasure mixed in the pain"; her performances demand that the audience bear witness to what she believes Mutt has done to her and, by extension, what generations of men have done to the Corregidora women (50). And yet, when she sings what she cannot explain, Ursa does not simply seek to legitimate herself as a subject by making her injury legible for all. Instead, she constructs a sensory experience of sexuality and violence, woven together to mirror the complex conjoining of "*hate and desire*" that she suspects shaped Great Gram and Gram's existence as Corregidora's concubines (102). Through her "new world song," she seeks to imagine and give voice to the collision of desire and subjugation within a context in which Black female desire was not only legally irrelevant but also philosophically unimaginable. What emerges from her performance is—like Black female sexuality itself—both absent and excessive, an instance of impossibility with the potential to expose and challenge the discursive conditions under which the Black female sexual subject has been rendered unrepresentable.

In an intriguing reversal of the dynamic through which the blues serve as a vehicle for Black female sexuality to emerge from the private scales of body and home into the more public ones of community, city, and even region, it is through a blues-inflected return to the scale of the body that both Ursa and Mutt are able to revisit and reconfigure their individual and mutual relationships to past traumas. More than two decades after Ursa's fall and their split, the two encounter each other at the club in which Ursa sings. In the same hotel in which they once lived together, she performs fellatio on him. In an instant that is equally composed of pain and pleasure, sex and violence, Ursa realizes what it is that Dorita had done before fleeing Corregidora forever.

> In a split second of hate and love I knew what it was, and I think he might have known too. A moment of pleasure and excruciating pain at the same time, a moment of broken skin but not sexlessness,

> a moment just before sexlessness, a moment that stops before it breaks the skin: "I could kill you." (184)

The sexual standoff ends not with Mutt's death or castration but with his orgasm, a perfect moment of jouissance in which *eros* and *thanatos*—desire and death—converge to produce an aporetic instant of radical (im)possibility.

In that "split second," Ursa and Mutt are rendered profoundly, if not painfully, aware of themselves both as individual subjects and as surrogates for a transgenerational collective history of trauma to which they must somehow bear witness without being consumed. "It was like I didn't know how much was me and Mutt and how much was Great Gram and Corregidora—like Mama when she started talking like Great Gram," Ursa recalls (184). At the same time that she replicates the performance of hysterical mimesis for which she was trained since birth, Ursa makes a choice not to fully embody her foremothers. Holding Mutt's ankles, and life, in her hands, she makes a choice: she rejects Dorita and Corregidora's "moment of broken skin but not sexlessness" for "a moment that stops before it breaks the skin" instead (184).

Ursa's "split second" serves as a point of psychic and ideological crisis out of which new forms of connection—a new relation to the past, present, and future—become possible. In the last paragraph, after Ursa's "split second" decision, Jones concludes the novel with a poignant, antiphonal blues riff.

> "I don't want a kind of woman that hurt you," he said.
>
> "Then you don't want me."
>
> "I don't want a kind of woman that hurt you."
>
> "Then you don't want me."
>
> "I don't want a kind of woman that hurt you."
>
> "Then you don't want me."
>
> He shook me till I fell against him crying. "I don't want a kind of man that'll hurt me neither," I said.
>
> He held me tight. (185)

In Ursa and Mutt's moment of jouissance, Ursa defines herself as both part of and exceeding the history of Corregidora—and, by extension, the sexualized racial violence and unfreedom that has shaped Black female subjectivity and sexuality in the Americas. Her moment of simultaneous identification and difference—in short, of disidentification—with her foremothers was an instance not of transcendence but of possible transfiguration enacted by claiming the Black female body as a place of both historical subjugation, objectification, and violence and (im)possible sexual and political agency. For both Mutt and Ursa, it opens the possibility of revised forms of sexual and emotional intimacy that are not grounded in the inevitability of hurt.

By ending with an exploration of how Ursa negotiates an alternative approach to embodying her family's collective history of trauma, my goal is not to suggest a linear progression from her foremothers' "primitive" or "regressive" hysterical reproduction to her own performative jouissance. Indeed, to do so would be to replicate precisely the raced and gendered approaches to hysteria theory that I have sought to interrogate here. In place of such a temptingly neat—albeit deceptively redemptive—conclusion, I offer instead Monique David-Ménard's intriguing observation that the hysterogenic body and the erotogenic body—or, as she names it, "*le corps de jouissance*"—are one and the same, embodied signifiers of that which remains in excess of the possible, the articulable, and the narrativizable.[97] If we were to follow David-Ménard's argument to its logical end, would it not suggest that Ursa's blues-inflected jouissance and the hysterical *mimétisme* of Great Gram, Gram, and Mama are differantially related iterations in the repeated effort to claim one's past as one's own?

Embodying the Past, Desiring the Future

Reduced to commodified, dismembered objects within a material-discursive system produced and maintained through sexualized racial violence, the Corregidora women struggle to redeploy their bodies in a transgenerational struggle to provide evidence and bear witness. Their political project escapes easy categorization; as both unfree objects of violence and agential subjects of history, their unceasing opposition to their historical subjugation and its subsequent erasure finds its greatest potential in its reiterative articulation of the unrepresentable, the impossible, and the unforgettable. By seizing the means within their reach to testify to their historical subjectivity in the context of raced and gendered subjugation and commodification, however, the women must simultaneously contend with the limits of subjectivation; for, like all forms of reproduction and reiteration, the narration of the self is never only the discursive process through which the subject is produced but is also the means by which she is contained, regulated, and disciplined. It is only through their strategic embodiment of this contradiction, their embrace of mimétisme as both a kind of performative agency and an articulation of past injury, a sexual act that necessarily reiterates an act of sexualized violence, that the Corregidora women can revise the terms by which they have been rendered objects of negligible injury or wounded subjects to produce the conditions of their own possibility.

Unlike Mary Prince's scarred back, the Corregidora women's raced and gendered bodies come to stand for the sublated history of intimate violence and coerced labor through which the structures of slavery in the Americas were reproduced. As Ursa comes to realize, however, neither the knowing nor the telling of her family's history produces resolution. Indeed, the Corregidora women's embodied testimonies to slavery's miscegenetic past create new contradictions and spark new crises. It is to the implications of and possibilities that emerge in the face of such crises of meaning and authority that the next chapter turns. I do so through a Black reproductive reading of the United States' disavowed founding narrative of miscegenation—the story of Thomas Jefferson and Sally Hemings.

4

Our Founding (M)Other

Sally Hemings and the Problem of Miscegenation

> The doubleness (blackness) of blackness is given as the aftermath of a determined, durative, fleshly, sexual encounter: the symbolic is cast in reference to the materiality of the miscegenative natal occasion. . . . But the deep-down love, the bone-deep love, convergence of death and love, memory and narrative (that's what recognition is), that accompanies the miscegenative origin of black/American identity is exceeded by another love: that of/for freedom.
>
> —Fred Moten, *In the Break*

> She was transgressing boundaries, crossing borders, spinning on margins, traveling between dualities of Manichean space, rigidly bifurcated into light/dark, good/bad, white/Black. No longer immediately identifiable . . . she could thus enter the white world, albeit on a false passport, not merely passing, but trespassing. . . . Accepting the risk of self-annihilation was the only way to survive.
>
> —Cheryl Harris, "Whiteness as Property"

It was the fall of 1802 when the first written reports appeared in Virginia's *Richmond Recorder* claiming that the third president of the United States, Thomas Jefferson, was in a sexual relationship with the enslaved half sister of his late wife. "It is well known that the man *whom it delighteth the people to honor,* keeps, and for many years past has kept, as his concubine, one of his own slaves. Her name is SALLY," gleefully reported columnist and Jefferson critic James Thomson Callender.[1] Callender may not have been the first to utter such an accusation—one can certainly imagine such a rumor winding its way through Washington salons and Virginia boudoirs—but his published column remains the recorded and archived catalyst for a two-hundred-year ideological struggle revolving around the slaveholding drafter of the Declaration of Independence and the young slave woman dubbed

"Dusky Sally." Captured on film and allegorized in poetry, the subject of preteen novels and college classroom debates, the tale of the Founding Father and his enslaved Black concubine became a disavowed yet oft-repeated national rumor.

Nearly two hundred years later, on November 1, 1998, *Nature* magazine, the popular publisher of scientific scholarship, released the long-awaited official results of a study that genetically linked Thomas Jefferson to Eston Hemings Jefferson, the youngest son of Sally Hemings. In an article published in that week's issue, a group of scientists led by retired University of Virginia pathologist Eugene Foster argued that the Y-chromosomal DNA found in common among Eston's descendants and the recognized progeny of Jefferson's paternal line proved that Eston's biological father was one of a handful of genetically related men with regular and open access to Jefferson's home plantation, Monticello, and its denizens.[2] This empirical evidence gave greater credence to existing undervalued historical data correlating the birth dates of each of Hemings's children with visits by Jefferson to Monticello some nine and a half months prior and to the oral histories narrated by Jefferson's former slaves and their descendants, leading most to conclude that Thomas Jefferson had almost certainly fathered at least one, if not all, of Sally Hemings's enslaved children.[3]

In the years immediately following the DNA revelation, thousands of pages of political commentary, historiographic analysis, and newspaper reportage have been devoted to the question of what Jefferson's affair with a woman he legally owned reveals about the man whose political legacy includes many of the nation's core political ideologies and structures. Many Jefferson historians have emphasized how the academic and popular debate surrounding the Hemings/Jefferson relationship offers a window into how Jefferson—and by extension, the nation for which he stands as synecdochal symbol—negotiated the seeming contradiction between liberal ideals of natural rights and the malign realities of eighteenth-century white supremacy.[4] Other scholars have emphasized instead its implications for African Americans, perceiving the DNA evidence as instantiating "ties [of Black people] to the founding of the nation" and legitimating "[Black] birthright claims."[5]

I, too, am intrigued by the view from this historical window. However, I start my inquiry from a different vantage point to ask instead what insights become possible if our horizon of inquiry is neither the much-documented tangle of contradiction that constitutes Jefferson as revered Founding Father nor the long-delayed recuperation of African American citizens into the nation's historical and political origin story but the trace of Sally Hemings, disavowed, maligned, and mythologized. In other words, if we were to read the now-legendary story of Sally Hemings and Thomas Jefferson through the lens of the Black reproductive as the disavowed origin story of the U.S. nation-state, how might it help us parse the complex grammar of historical and contemporary Black subjugation as inextricable from the fraught and imbricated intimacies of desire, property, and kinship created in the context of chattel slavery?

From historians to talk-show hosts and from Monticello Association members to Hemings's descendants, the proliferation of discourses around the sexual relationship between Sally Hemings and Thomas Jefferson underscores the political stakes of delineating the meaning of interracial (hetero)sexuality in the context of African chattel slavery.[6] They were bound together by a doomed love that transcended the societal norms of the day; or, Jefferson was guilty of an ongoing act of rape and their offspring were the product of that violent sexual coercion; or, their relationship was a mutual calculation of reciprocal benefit, in which Hemings provided her master sexual satisfaction in exchange for a set of otherwise unachievable protections and privileges, including the eventual legal and de facto freeing of their children. Rooted in widely divergent ideologies and leveraged in the service of multiple—and at times diametrically opposed—political projects, these conflicting versions of the narrative each underscore its ongoing symbolic significance as a national origin story founded in relations of mastery and miscegenation.

The two-hundred-year conversation about the existence, role, and significance of Sally Hemings is illustrative of how miscegenation has been a crucial terrain for the production, naming, and containment of racial/gender difference in the context of chattel slavery and its afterlife, even as the topos of miscegenative sexuality engenders, endangers, and recodifies U.S. racial-sexual common sense. The long disavowal and subsequent celebration of Hemings and her descendants demonstrate how, even as miscegenation's risk to racial purity endangers the racial body national, it also rationalizes projects of racial segregation and eugenic purity as the acceptable exception to the United States' multiculturalist narrative of itself as a nation founded on Jeffersonian liberalism. Moreover, the years of historiographic and political conflict surrounding Hemings's existence, significance, and legacy offer a window into how oft-articulated concerns with purity, legitimacy, and contamination that permeate debates over processes of academic and cultural knowledge production might be understood as a related—and indeed imbricated—kind of miscegenetic anxiety. Situated as it is at the discursive conjunction of miscegenative reprosexuality and illegitimate knowledge production, the sublated history of Hemings calls into question the racial, legal, and historical boundaries of Black and white as well as the epistemological segregational hierarchies between fact and fiction. In so doing, it offers insight into the production of knowledge about racialized reproductivity within U.S. chattel slavery, the imbrication of sexual desire and racial mastery, and the conditions of (im)possibility for the articulation and recognition of free Black subjectivity within the United States.

Sally Hemings; or, The Problem of Miscegenation

Against the Perversion of History

After the DNA revelation, scores of historians, genealogical statisticians, and media pundits alike declared the two-hundred-year mystery solved. From newspapers to academic journals, at scholarly conferences and on television talk shows, it was agreed: the oft-told tale of Tom & Sally was no longer legend but proven historical fact. Rather than offering resolution, however, the facticity of the relationship opened up new terrains of ideological struggle. While reporters, entertainers, and even visitors to Monticello connected the results of the Jefferson/Hemings DNA analysis to the incriminating DNA test that had just recently confirmed President William Jefferson Clinton's sexual affair with White House intern Monica Lewinsky, the concerns of Jefferson scholars and memorialists extended beyond electoral politics to encompass the production of knowledge and the racial purity of the nation and its legacy.[7]

To follow the new scientific evidence where it seemed to lead not only required the more conservative of Jefferson historians and political theorists to revisit existing frameworks for analyzing his writings on slavery and miscegenation but also demanded that they critically interrogate the racialized hierarchies of valuation upon which their past evaluation of competing historical truth claims had relied. If the implications of the DNA findings were correct, then as feminist and African Americanist historians of slavery had long argued, the normalized protocols of institutionalized early American historiography that rated document-based knowledge production above oral history and used the testimony of white family members to negate the oral traditions of former slaves and their descendants were unreliable.[8]

In the face of this epistemological challenge, a renegade cadre of Jeffersonian scholars and memorialists decried such interpretations of the study—and the attendant overturning of the scholarly order of things—as undermining established scholarly standards in the interests of "political correctness . . . , multiculturalism, and post-modernism." Giving scholarly credence to the claim that Jefferson fathered Eston Hemings not only "denigrated" the Founding Father, they warned, but also colluded with the "enemies of the Enlightenment" to attack the "Jeffersonian principles of individualism, reason, science, and private property."[9] Or, to put it differently, to take seriously the possibility of Jefferson's miscegenetic practices would extend beyond figuratively—if not literally—blackening their esteemed hero to contaminate and delegitimate the very foundations of Western knowledge production.[10]

The rhetorical correlation of the Hemings/Jefferson story with a racialized threat to national and historical purity did not originate with the 1998 DNA revelations. As the mid-twentieth-century Black freedom movement opened up increased discussion of the racist elisions, erasures, and fallacies of the established historical record, the story of Sally Hemings garnered increased attention in both academic texts and popular Black periodicals. Not unlike the nineteenth-century newspaper drolls who warned that news of Jefferson's "Dusky Sally" would embolden enslaved Black "Quafhee[s]" everywhere to snatch a white wife in exchange, white Jefferson scholars decried all references to the "Hemings myth" as an illegitimate incursion into established historical fact and methods, motivated by what noted Jefferson biographer Dumas Malone described as "Negroes' pathetic wish for a little pride and their subtle ways of confounding the white folks."[11] For the majority of the 1970s historical establishment, this perceived ingress of blackness endangered both established racial hierarchies and the epistemological foundations of the Enlightenment tradition.

Unsurprisingly, this racial threat of blackness was imagined and articulated in sexualized terms. Nowhere was this more evident than in the response to revisionist historian Fawn Brodie's 1975 psychobiography of Jefferson, in which she used a combination of archival research, oral history, and psychoanalytic theory to argue that the rumored relationship between Hemings and Jefferson not only had a basis in historical fact but also was a lifelong love affair. Julian Boyd, editor of the thirty-three-volume collected Jefferson Papers, dismissed Brodie's account as an ahistorical political panacea,

> soothing to those who so eagerly embrace the concept of collective guilt, who project out views of the rights of women and blacks into the past, and who cast the new abolitionism, the new sectionalism, and the new attitudes toward sexual liberation into molds manufactured in our own time and in our own image.[12]

The appeal of such an approach, Boyd acceded, was understandable, "but it assuredly is not scholarship."[13] The nascent body of research on Hemings and Jefferson initiated by Brodie and extended by Annette Gordon-Reed's 1998 *Thomas Jefferson and Sally Hemings: An American Controversy* was described by the white lions of the field in the lexicon of miscegenation as a "perversion of the doctrine of equality," an alluring form of illegitimate scholarship pursued by ambitious Black upstarts and embraced by misguided white progressives. Like the body of an enslaved concubine herself, this body of dangerous and profane knowledge production threatened to "drag an extraordinary man"—and the Western intellectual tradition he iconized—"down to the common level" with its illicit embrace.[14]

All Jefferson's Children

While the memorialists' vehement rejection of the DNA study and its implications reiterated old rhetorics that linked historical revision with the threat of sexualized racial contamination, the interactions between Jefferson's descendants via his free white wife and those descended from his enslaved Black concubine reenacted long-standing social antagonisms around race, sex, and property on the scales of the body, home, and nation. The ensuing public conflict between the two groups over Jefferson's name and access to his home demonstrated how the imperatives of racial purity, essential to and reinforced by long-standing claims to whiteness as property, operated in vexed relation to liberal narratives of the multicultural nation as family. In the subsequent battle, the competing discourses drew on racial capitalism's instantiation of whiteness as property, on the one hand, and multicultural neoliberalism's strategic incorporation of difference, on the other.

For many Black and white observers and participants, the reunion of the descendants of Sally Hemings with those of Thomas and Martha Wayles Jefferson became a perfect metaphor for the path toward national racial reconciliation between those whose ancestors had been enslaved and those whose forefathers had been slaveholders. At White House commemorations of Jefferson's "complex legacy," during tear-filled family gatherings on the Oprah Winfrey show, and in the pages of coffee-table books celebrating the shared legacy of "Jefferson's children" as "the story of one American family," the reunification of Jefferson's progeny, Black and white, became an allegory for new-millennial approaches for managing relations of racialized power and difference within the imagined national family.[15]

Within this national morality tale, the ideal of racial reconciliation was actualized through the grammar of normative heteropatriarchy. According to the reprosexual logic of the patriarchal family, in which the regulation of patrilineal descent via procreation constitutes the raison d'être for monogamous marriage, the possible existence of eight children born to Hemings by Jefferson validated and naturalized the relationship between master and slave. Touted as Jefferson's "slave wife," Sally Hemings was cast as Martha Wayles Jefferson's unfree counterpart. The two women's rumored similarity in appearance and shared genealogy were invoked frequently to reinforce an imagined equivalency between them that leveraged what Roderick Ferguson has described as the universalization of heteronormativity, effacing chattel slavery's reliance on differentiating practices of objectification, coercion, and consumption.[16] Within this framework, the story of Tom, Sally, Martha, and their progeny became a metaphor for the liberal multicultural nation, in which the romanticized fidelity, relations of reproduction, and "possessive individualism" that characterize both the white heteropatriarchal family and the modern liberal nation-state were imagined to transcend the raced and gendered relations of power and difference through which both family and nation are articulated.[17]

As Ferguson argues, however, relations of property under modern racial capitalism operate in tandem with race, gender, and sexuality to proliferate discourses, subjects, and social formations in excess of normative heteropatriarchy.[18] In contradistinction to the celebratory narrative of family reunion and racial reconciliation depicted in the national media, the largely white members of the Monticello Association—the private, nonprofit organization of recognized descendants of Thomas Jefferson—voted overwhelmingly not to recognize Hemings's progeny as descendants of Thomas Jefferson, to deny them membership in the association, and to delimit their access to association gatherings held on the grounds of Monticello. Monticello Association members' subsequent defense of their exclusive claim to Jefferson produced an alternative—albeit no less problematic—discourse that resisted incorporation into the liberal multiculturalist narrative of racial reconciliation via the chattel/marital bed.

While the resulting public battle ostensibly centered on burial rights in the Jefferson family graveyard, owned and controlled by the association, the less tangible—but no less material—stakes were what Cheryl Harris has described as the "volatile and unstable form of property" that is whiteness itself.[19] As recognized descendants of Thomas Jefferson, members of the Monticello Association were inheritors not only of his white racial status but also of his political legacy as a key figure in the U.S. Enlightenment, in which whiteness came to define and demarcate those subjects with access to sovereign rights and reason. By seeking acknowledgment as part of the Jeffersonian family, Sally Hemings's descendants put forth a competing claim upon the inherited whiteness previously monopolized by the recognized descendants of Thomas and Martha Wayles Jefferson. Moreover, the demand to be included in the Monticello graveyard by those whose ancestors made up the majority of Monticello's domestic and artisanal labor pool drew attention to the enslaved, coerced, and expropriated Black labor that sustained Jefferson and his white family members, thus working to demystify the commodity fetish that is whiteness.

At least as significantly, however, within the logic of hypodescent, to claim whiteness is necessarily and concomitantly "an assertion that one is free of any taint of black blood"—the very taint that the Hemings descendants embodied.[20] This miscegenetic taint could not be exorcised, even through the spatial imposition of racial purity: at the suggested creation of a new, segregated graveyard for all those descended from Monticello slaves, association members vehemently protested, warning that through diverse stratagems, "the *line* between the graveyards would *blur,* and it would become just a graveyard of Jefferson's descendants, both real and imagined."[21] By barring Hemings's descendants from the organization and its burial grounds, then, Monticello Association members sought to legitimate and protect their multigenerational investment in whiteness from the incursions of blackness by exercising private property's characteristic right to exclusion.[22] In the process, they illustrated the extent to which liberal multiculturalism is subtended by the continuing imperatives of white supremacy.

A Slave or Just a Slave for Love?

In the wake of the 1998 DNA results, one question about the affair was repeatedly raised, though it remained conspicuously unanswered.

> *What about the nature of the relationship?* Was it consensual or coercive? love or rape? or a mutual arrangement that provided both parties with something they wanted (Jefferson with physical gratification and Hemings with privileged status and the promise of emancipation for her children)?[23]

This impulse to categorize, and thus contain, the relationship between Hemings and Jefferson as one of consensual love, forcible rape, or reciprocally beneficial concubinage imagines antebellum relations of desire and power to be constituted through a set of mutually exclusive dichotomies: coercion versus consent, lust versus love, violence versus seduction. As I have argued throughout this book, such limited and limiting raced and gendered dyads have long been integral to conceptions of American cultural politics. While the relations of submission and subjection, desire and repulsion, that made up the material-discursive structures of chattel slavery cannot be so easily parsed into recognizable polarities, our continuing inclination to do so demonstrates the continued thrall in which we are held by those Manichean categories of meaning on which American raced and gendered logics of subjugation and dominance have long relied.

Whether seen as impossible or subversive, anachronistic or exculpatory, the possibility of Hemings and Jefferson's interracial love is represented by both proponents and skeptics as a would-be liberal humanist force, aligned with the ideals of personal sovereignty, universal natural rights, and untrammeled free will, and against systems of coercion, unequal rights, and bodily subjugation. As the consummation of liberalism's ideals, interracial love is imagined to have at least the potential to mitigate slavery, bringing "blacks and whites together, blurr[ing] the distinctions between them, and . . . clos[ing] the gap between the free and the enslaved"; in its most utopian manifestation, it is envisioned as "the great leveler," through which the humanity of both the slave and the master can be reaffirmed.[24] Under this rubric, only one question is imagined to remain: "Whether it was—how do I say this?—consensual sex. Whether she was a slave or just a slave for love."[25]

If interracial love is envisioned as wielding liberal humanism's alchemic power to produce humans from what slavery had rendered property, then

Hemings's rape—and by extension, the rape of enslaved women as an institutionalized practice of slavery—comes to serve as an apocryphal tale of slavery's historic violation of Black bodies, labor, and honor. As a metaphor for chattel slavery in general, rape has come to fulfill a discursive function as the iconic representation of slavery's physical and psychological degradation precisely because it is normatively gendered and sexualized as feminine. Yet this invocation of rape as the exceptional trope of gendered violence simultaneously disavows the extent to which, as I have argued throughout this book, the (re)production of the slave always relied on the violent production and deployment of the grammars of gender and sexuality for its coherence and continuity, even as the historic "erasure and disavowal of sexual violence engendered Black femaleness as a condition of unredressed injury."[26] The concomitant contemporary ubiquity of rape as a metaphor for slavery thus serves a pornotropic function similar to Douglass's tale of the "piteous" Esther: it engenders Black femaleness as the embodiment of "general powerlessness"—the exceptionally abject within slavery's state of exception.[27]

The related discourses of Hemings as loving slave wife and Hemings as enslaved rape victim offer a case of what Spivak describes as legitimation by reversal.[28] Seemingly antithetical in their conclusions, both narratives rely on similar conceptions of love and desire, coercion and consent, sex and violence that construct interracial love in contradistinction to and exclusion of sexualized racial violence. As an ostensibly consensual relation, interracial love is presumed to transcend structural divisions—up to and including the racial demarcation of persons from property—and ameliorate even fatal relations of power. The remainder of this chapter challenges this presumption of the mutual exclusivity of love and violence, seeking instead other ways of understanding the story and figure of Sally Hemings that exceed and refuse these binary logics. Reading against the grain of Barbara Chase-Riboud's historical novel *Sally Hemings* and its sequel, *The President's Daughter*, I follow the double trace of erotic love and racial subjugation in order to reimagine the meanings of love and violence, death and freedom, in the context of African chattel slavery.

Reading *Sally Hemings*; or, The Miscegenetic Text

Released in 1979 to widespread popular attention and critical acclaim, the novel *Sally Hemings* by Barbara Chase-Riboud depicted a thirty-eight-year love affair between the famous master and enslaved concubine, briefly becoming a staging ground for the newest round of battle over the controversy that had ignited with the release of Brodie's bombshell psychobiography of Jefferson five years earlier. While the novel was a runaway best seller with more than one-and-a-half-million copies sold, the stakes of the debate over the truth of the tale far overreached the text itself, encompassing not only questions of *how* the history of Thomas Jefferson would be told but also questions about *who* had the right to produce the narratives that the nation tells about itself, and what form such a story should take. Like the historical figure herself, the fictional text of *Sally Hemings* functioned as an iconic representation of Black historical illegitimacy, disrupting existent white patrilineal biological and intellectual genealogies. Indeed, whether it be journalist and Jefferson scholar Virginius Dabney's dismissal of the text's "miscegenation of history and fiction" as constructing a "spurious" new genre he dubs "faction," or renowned Jeffersonian historian Merrill Peterson's characterization of it as "vulgar sensationalism masquerading as history," the past three decades of public and academic attention to the novel have been repeatedly circumscribed to the anxious contemplation not only of the interracial romance it was purported to depict but also of its miscegenative transgression of the seemingly stable boundaries between history and fiction.[29]

Within the field of literary studies, however, Chase-Riboud's novels of the Hemings family have received relatively little attention until recently.[30] More often read as historical romances than as neoslave narratives, *Sally Hemings* and *The President's Daughter* were as understudied by literature scholars as they were denounced by Jefferson researchers. The 1998 discovery of DNA linkages between Hemings's descendants and Jefferson's paternal line briefly spurred renewed attention to *Sally Hemings,* often couched in the rhetoric of historical vindication. However, it simultaneously seemed to signal the novel's apparent obsolescence: its (contested) worth as a historical record already impugned by its fictional nature, the novel-cum-history had now been superseded by the joint authority of scientific data and historical dates. In the end, the novel's perceived shortcoming was not that it attempted to "tell a suppressed historical truth" but that the historical truth it told was, after all, fictional.[31]

If the response to *Sally Hemings* in popular media and by early American historians has all too often emphasized the novel's failure to meet the standards of historical facticity, then its marginalization within African

American literary studies can be tied, at least in part, to its failure to adequately portray a kind of racial truth. As Barbara Christian's sympathetic, if critical, reading demonstrates, scholarly preoccupations with the historicity of *Sally Hemings* are inextricable from political anxieties about its racial authenticity. According to Christian, Chase-Riboud's desire to remedy the historical record impinges upon her attempt to exceed the limits of existent historical approaches, producing a narrative marked by elisions, exclusions, and half-told tales. The very character of the historical novel she seeks to write, Christian concludes, constrains Chase-Riboud; because her goal is to "rescue her heroine from myth, she cannot completely free herself from the conventional trappings of the historical novel."[32] Thus trapped in convention, Chase-Riboud's text fares poorly in Christian's comparison to other novels by African American women writers that stage a radical departure from the historical record to probe how maternal love and physical and sexual violence are traumatically intertwined in the complex internal life of "ordinary" slaves.[33] Ironically, then, it is the much-maligned faithfulness to the historical record that ostensibly impedes the capacity of *Sally Hemings* to represent the inner truth of gendered racial terror as experienced on the scale of the enslaved sexual/maternal body.

Yet Chase-Riboud was not the first African American novelist to tell the story of Jefferson's illicit affair through a strategic bricolage of fiction and documentary history; nor are the anxieties evoked by her novel unique. In the closing paragraph of her afterword to *Sally Hemings,* Chase-Ribaud comments on the resonances between her own text and the first-known novel by an African American, William Wells Brown's 1853 *Clotel; or, The President's Daughter.* "Although I read the original version only after I wrote this book," she notes, "I was touched to the quick by the recognition of cadences, themes, wellsprings of feeling."[34] Indeed, this sense of affinity with Brown's novel is evidenced in Chase-Riboud's later work: *Clotel* not only provides the title for the sequel to *Sally Hemings* but also haunts the pages of that sequel in a complex and dialogical intertextuality.

The set of critical preoccupations and discomforts spurred by Chase-Riboud's *Sally Hemings* since its publication are remarkably similar to those that shadowed Brown's *Clotel.* As Ann duCille has demonstrated in depth, despite its foundational status, *Clotel* remained, until recently, a largely understudied text, in large part due to questions about the novel's historical verisimilitude and unease with its ostensible racial politics.[35] Read alongside Brown's more famous nonfiction—his fugitive slave narrative, political treatises, and travel dispatches—the novel's invocation of the Jefferson/Hemings rumor was long dismissed as simple "sensationalism."[36] At the very least, the relationship to historicity in *Clotel* is an ambivalent one: while "its pages are liberally peppered with real-life incidents and historical events," it is equally rife with historical inaccuracies, large and small.[37]

Nor, duCille notes, has the novel's racial authenticity been uncontested. Rather, Brown's tale of two generations of (socially) forsaken (nearly) white femininity forced to travel a grueling path to love, marriage, and *freedom* was deemed by many Black activist-intellectuals too beholden to the literary conventions of the nineteenth-century sentimental novel to be "*true,* authentic, or certifiably 'black.'"[38] Positing a politics of Black liberation that finds its authority in sentimental appeal rather than historical fact or racial authenticity, *Clotel* lacked both the political immediacy and the authenticity of fugitive slaves' written memoirs, while its nearly white characters seemed designed to "appeal . . . to whites and to the black middle class, even as they stood in contradistinction to the black masses under siege."[39] An improper union of (white) sentimentality and Black testimony, historical sensationalism and literary romance, Brown's *President's Daughter,* like Jefferson's, was necessarily illegitimate.[40]

These commonalities between the critical treatment of *Clotel* and the public and scholarly responses to *Sally Hemings* demonstrate the abiding historical and racial anxieties that surround the disavowed figure of Sally Hemings. Just as significantly, they illuminate the integral, if not originary, character of miscegenetic transgression to the African American novel and, more generally, the Black aesthetic tradition.[41] If the radical traversal and reconfiguration of categories—Black and white, fact and fiction, intimacy and violence, aesthetics and politics—so notable in African American novelistic production finds its imaginative embodiment in the trope of the tragic mulatta, then its generic exemplar is, indeed, the neoslave narrative. Given this, how might a revisionary reading of Chase-Riboud's "illegitimate" union of national political history and sentimental popular fiction provide a provocative contribution to current understandings not only of the politics of interracial desire under slavery but also of the neoslave narrative as a revisionary literary form?

If we understand the function of the historical novel as not only to retell history but also to reconfigure the terms of history's telling, then how does *Sally Hemings* re-present the story of Thomas Jefferson, president, and Sally

Hemings, slave? On its surface, *Sally Hemings* tells the story of a "near white," beautiful and privileged mulatta protected from the more severe ravages of slavery by the love of her powerful master.[42] In its pages there are no depictions of explicit sexualized and gendered violence, or of the brutal consequences of contemporary attempts to grapple with the agonizing complexities of such genealogies, as there are in the texts discussed in previous chapters of this book. In the absence of these identifiable markers, *Sally Hemings* is easily read as a narrative of interracial "doomed romance" in which the novel's purported "endorse[ment] of the liaison" between Jefferson and his enslaved concubine works to efface the structures of sexualized and physical violence that intrinsically shaped relations of gender within African chattel slavery.[43] Simultaneously embedded in and disloyal to national historical narratives and/or racially authentic truths—a historical fiction that is at once too historical and too fictional—the novel's miscegenetic merging of the historical and the fictional, Black and white, has been deemed illegitimate by the standards of both historical facticity and fictional authenticity.

Love's Thrall

When Chase-Riboud's *Sally Hemings* is read with an eye to the complex relations of erotic desire, sexual domination, and raced and gendered commodification through which U.S. chattel slavery was built and reproduced, the structuring terms of the Jefferson/Hemings debate—love, freedom, violence, consent—become far from transparent. Chase-Riboud's depiction of Jefferson and Hemings's relationship unsettles the Manichean binary of love and coercion, opening the text to an interrogation of the meaning and limits of erotic love in the context of Black subjection. Therefore, rather than reading *Sally Hemings* as resolving the question of whether Hemings loved her master or consented to their sexual relationship, I approach it as a narrative of power and intimacy between enslaved concubine and American president that troubles the underlying premise that erotic love relies on or evidences the lover's capacity to consent and, thus, her relative individual freedom. Read against the grain in this way, Chase-Riboud's historical romance reveals the contours of a radically reconfigured conception of interracial love as it functions within the context of raced and gendered subjugation, in which the erotic love between master and slave neither mitigates white coercion nor reaffirms Black humanity. Indeed, the ties of love between Jefferson and Hemings in Chase-Riboud's novel are not only coeval with the bonds of ownership but also one and the same.

It is early in their sexual relationship that Sally Hemings realizes that Thomas Jefferson "like[s] owning her"; the "tender greed" that is Jefferson's love for his slave is as much the enactment of a desire to consume as it is the consummation of desire (*SH,* 124, 130). For Hemings is not merely Jefferson's property but his commodity, produced through the quotidian labor of "bringing [her] under his domination."

> He had formed and shaped her himself. . . . He possessed something he had created from beginning to end, without interference or objections or corrections. In a way, he had birthed her. . . . He had created her in his own image of womanly perfection, this speck of dust, this handful of clay from Monticello. "I love you," he said. (*SH,* 123)

If the recognition of the enslaved woman as a subject under the law depended on the understanding of her as a "commodity that could be bought and sold," then Hemings's existence as Jefferson's love object is equally reliant on her value as *his* commodity, produced through the unchecked exercise of his power over the ostensibly inert material that is his property.[44] In other words, Hemings can be Jefferson's "perfect *woman*" only because she seems to be the "perfect *slave,*" available to him for whatever productive and reproductive purposes he desires, including her own remaking (*SH,* 36, 43, emphasis added).

It is not Sally Hemings, however, but her brother James, Jefferson's chef and Sally's only relative in France, who first articulates the impossible coexistence of Jefferson's love and Hemings's freedom. Men like Jefferson, he notes, "don't free what they love" (*SH,* 130). For James, his sister's loss of her virginity to their master becomes inextricably tied to his own sexual-racial terror: dreams of immolation, genital violation, and beheading (*SH,* 109). With its implicit evocation of the rituals of lynching, James's recurring nightmare connects his sister's sexual blood to the bloody death of slaves, underscoring the omnipresent structures of racial violence from which interracial sex cannot be extricated. At the same time, James's visceral response to Sally's sexed and gendered thralldom illuminates his own heteromasculine investments. In an expression of what M. Jacqui Alexander has described as the "continuity between white imperial hetero-patriarchy . . . and black hetero-patriarchy," James's angry exhortations against his sister's "whoredom" reveal his own thwarted aspirations to remake her in his own insurrectionary image—a paternalistic desire at war with Jefferson's consuming desire to make her his concubine.[45]

If the master's love for a slave cannot be disentangled from his capacity to possess and consume the commodity that is *his,* nor can the slave's love for her master be extricated from the processes of domination and subjugation, objectification and recognition, that produced not only the master/slave relationship but also the subject categories of *master* and *slave* in and of themselves. "I have never heard you refer to him as anything else except 'the master,'" James observes incredulously. "Except that you make it sound like an endearment. . . . No wonder he loves you. If you can take the most ruthless word in the English language and turn it into an expression of love . . ." (*SH,* 197). Far from transcending (or even enduring) the omnipresent relations of coercion that characterize chattel slavery, Sally Hemings's love for Jefferson is expressed within and through the structuring discourses of chatteldom. On her tongue, the words of love between master and slave are revealed as sharing a lexicon not with the liberal vernacular of freedom—consent, will, choice—but with the idiom of subjugation.

From the description of their affair's inception, in which Jefferson "gives himself into [Hemings's] keeping," to Hemings's claim sixteen years later that she had "bound him to [her] as surely as [she] was bound to him," the text reiterates the "reciprocal sensuality," produced by the "exercise of total power," which renders Jefferson both Hemings's master and her thrall (*SH,* 80, 106, 266). How are we to read these moments of transubstantiation, when the violent love of the master is rearticulated as the masterly power of the slave?[46] Certainly, as Saidiya Hartman has deftly argued, the investing of the enslaved female with powers capable of producing an erotic mastery over her ostensible owner is exemplary of the rhetorics by which slaveholders' systematic deployment of sexualized violence as a means of individual and collective control of Black subjects was rendered not just legible but legitimate in the antebellum South.[47] Yet, when read in a different register, might Chase-Riboud's emphasis on the profound interdependence of master and slave also expose the structural and ideological underpinnings of the United States' slave economy as well as the nation's economy of racial meaning?

In contradistinction to antebellum slavery's paternalistic rhetoric, the material well-being of white slaveholders relied on the labor of their slaves, both skilled and unskilled but always uncompensated. Indeed, the emergence of the nineteenth-century industrial and mercantile economy of the

North was no less indebted to the legalized kidnapping and captivity of Black bodies and the hyperexploitation of Black labor than were the pastoral homes and agrarian industries of the antebellum southern plantocracy. In the broadest sense, African chattel slavery and the Atlantic and Pacific slave trades provided a significant portion of the foundational capital on which capitalist Europe and the Americas were built and with which they rose to global imperial status. Jefferson's individual psychic dependence on Hemings, then, can be read as index of a deeper and broader reliance on his slave *familia* to protect and preserve his "life and property," thus freeing him to father a nation whose own extensive and unpaid debt to captive and coerced slave labor has been long disavowed.[48]

Yet the subordination of master to slave and of whiteness to blackness can be read to have ontological as well as material resonances. That the necropolitical "creation of the Negro" coincided with the philosophical emergence of Enlightenment-era liberal humanism was not accidental. Rather, as I have argued throughout, the transmogrification of captive African to Black slave was crucial for liberalism's emergence: as a marker of the very limit of humanity, blackness became an essential social category against which white personhood and liberty could be measured.[49] In short, the precondition for the emergence of whiteness as "the characteristic, the attribute, the property of free human beings" was the codification of blackness as the embodiment of unlimited availability to commodification.[50] In this sense, Jefferson's consuming and dependent love for Hemings can be seen as the "positive condition of possibility" for the liberal humanist ideologies that he so ardently espoused, and for which he became a national icon.[51]

Making Love; or, Reproducing Death

Whether in its historical, fictional, or factional version, Sally Hemings and Thomas Jefferson's miscegenetic affair offers a différantial iteration of the republic's origin myth, a radical alterity that simultaneously structures and endangers the system of meaning in which it is embedded.[52] The love between Hemings and her master is not founded in bodily sovereignty or inalienable individual rights but is antithetical to them; it points not to the political power of equality under the law but to the erotic purchase of death-dealing hierarchies of power and difference; it does not mitigate Hemings's enslavement but reifies her status as a fetishized biocommodity, subject to social death.

If, as Patterson suggests, the "direct and insidious violence, the namelessness and invisibility, the endless personal violation, and the chronic inalienable dishonor" of social death make "authentic human relationship[s]," including those of "genuine" love, impossible, then what sense can be made of Chase-Riboud's fictional love between Sally Hemings and her master, embedded as it is in relations of mastery, objecthood, and submission?[53] Within the rubric of (hetero)normative romantic love, in which the coercive terror of slavery is rendered illegible by the rhetoric of tender romance, such a love is unimaginable.[54] It is only by disarticulating erotic love from its affiliation with liberal conceptions of individual free will that this unthinkable love can perhaps be comprehended. Jefferson's love for Hemings is not merely enacted through violence but is a form of violence itself; it exists only through the ultimate negation, or social death, of the love object. Hemings's love for Jefferson indexes the myriad forms of intimate labor—domestic, biological, sexual, and affective—through which enslaved Black females reproduced both the Black subjects and the Black social death that were the necessary preconditions for African chattel slavery's continuation. Rather than mitigating the conditions of her subjugation, then, Sally Hemings's erotic love relationship with Thomas Jefferson both codifies her position within a brutal lineage of three generations of enslaved concubines and evidences her oneness with the "ill-used . . . raped and scorned" Black women upon whose coerced productive and reproductive labor African chattel slavery both materially and discursively relied (*SH*, 304–5).

The depiction in *Sally Hemings* of interracial erotic love as inextricable from and complicit in the structures of chattel slavery makes available another revised understanding of social death that exceeds the limits of its juridical legacy as a form of suspended death sentence and its philosophical roots in Hegel's struggle to the death. As Chase-Riboud's narrative illustrates, when the dialectical struggle of master and slave enters the intimate arena of sexual and reproductive labor, it is not the subject unafraid of death but "the one who stop[s] loving, who stop[s] needing love," who emerges from the struggle victorious (*SH*, 352). That is, when the originary scene for the production of social death is relocated to the biopolitical terrain of miscegenetic heterosexuality, such a move demands a critical revision of traditional conceptions of social death as solely a phenomenon in which sovereign power both creates and reveals itself by making *die* or letting *live*. For if, in the context of African chattel slavery, the fundaments of love and death are not diametrically opposed but are instead alternative registers for the production of Black unfreedom, then sex, as well as blood—making *live* (love) and making *die*—can be understood as enactments of power through which the socially dead Black subject is produced. The collisions and collusions of blood and sex that characterized interracial sexual love and miscegenetic reproduction in the antebellum United States can then be understood to index what Foucault describes as modern racism's reinscription of "the thematic of sexuality in the system of law" through the "analytics of sexuality and the symbolics of blood."[55] At this material-discursive caesura of sex and death, "the real blood of chains and whips and hatchets" and "the blood of race, polluted, displaced, and disappearing in rape and miscegenation" converge to produce the necessary conditions for the production and reproduction of Black social death (*SH,* 306). Such a reading poses a challenge to popular bio- and necropolitical theorizations that understand the interpenetration of the politics of death with the politics of life through a model of war. Rather than tracing those "trajectories by which the state of exception and relation of enmity have become the normative basis of the right to kill" or articulating "the perception of the existence of the Other . . . as a mortal threat or absolute danger whose biophysical elimination would strengthen my potential to life and security," a Black reproductive reading of the material-discursive caesura of modern racism as it emerged in the context of antebellum slavery in the United States necessarily approaches it as operating on a logic of intimacy rather than enmity.[56]

Yet, as Foucault reminds us, the production of power also always engenders its opposition: the sociopolitical ramifications of Hemings and Jefferson's sexual encounter across the color line are double-edged.[57] For while the sexual love between master and slave instantiated the enslaved concubine's status as a socially dead slave, it concomitantly leveraged the laws of *partus sequiter ventrem* to reproduce in the commodified and subjugated bodies of their racially mixed offspring a delegitimation of the ostensibly distinct and finite boundaries between white and Black, free and unfree, human and inhuman, upon which racialized social death relied. Moreover, as I have argued throughout this book, the ideological maintenance of African chattel slavery, and most particularly the sexual commodification of the slave, required the construction of the slave as the "Black antiwill," that is, the antithetical alterity though which white free will was defined and substantiated.[58] To imagine the loving enslaved concubine demands contemplation of a form of will that engenders abjection rather than evidencing individual sovereignty. This *unfree* will both exceeds and unsettles naturalized distinctions between coercion and consent, (white) free will and Black will-lessness, proffering a profound challenge to the discursive systems of domination upon which Black enslavement relied.

In sum, a gendered revision of social death as both death-dealing and life-administering posits the enslaved Black concubine/mother as a necessary contradiction at the center of centuries-old legal and social narratives that have sought to fix the line between white freedom and Black unfreedom. This gendered revision of social death is a "vestibular cultural formation" at once outside and penetrative of both public and private spheres, and in which sexuality and maternity are simultaneously private intimacies and commodities available for public exchange.[59] The unstable subject/object of this formation, the concubine/slave/mother, emerges in the aporetic gaps of the history that disavows her: between the public sphere of political rights and the private worlds of sentiment and sexuality; between the discourse of (white) free will and that of (Black) social death.[60] As African chattel slavery's enabling danger, she is both a precondition for the reproduction of Black subjugation and a threat to the biopolitical control, evacuation of Black subjectivity, and ideals of racial purity that undergird white supremacy.

From Social Death to the Death of Blackness

If rather than constituting Black freedom, interracial erotic love enacts the positive conditions of possibility for the (re)production of Black social death as well as its ideological endangerment, then what might be the conditions for the production of Black liberation? For Sally Hemings, freedom is a mirage, a "vague glimmering" that cannot be banished but that neither manumission nor flight, recognition nor love, can achieve (*SH,* 94, 228). As Elizabeth Hemings—Sally's mother and enslaved concubine before her—comes to realize, not even legal emancipation can free one from the "dangers of blackness" or provide escape from white terrorism disguised as justice. In an ultimate rejection of the terms by which Black social death is produced and maintained, Elizabeth exercises the form of opposition available to her: to die on her own terms (*SH,* 285).[61]

For Nathan Langdon, the white census taker to whom an elderly Sally Hemings relates fragments of her past in the final years of her life, it is not physical death but the metaphysical transfiguration of Black into white that holds the potential for Hemings's freedom. In a grand gesture of infatuation and exemplary enactment of biopolitical governmentality, Langdon leverages his position as the county census taker to reclassify Hemings and her two youngest sons as white. Rather than earning her gratitude, however, his action provokes her rage.

> I'm tired, Nathan. I'm tired of white men playing God with my flesh and my spirit and my children and my life, which is running out. I thought you understood that. You've left me nothing of my own. Not even my color! (*SH,* 56)

Langdon's decision is, to Hemings, an act of rape—an assault so profound that it demands that descriptive that appears nowhere in her description of her relationship with Jefferson. Langdon's paternalistic act of ostensible liberation is in actuality a form of extirpation that robs her of "her mind, her thoughts, her feelings, her history" (*SH,* 57). By stripping Hemings of her blackness, Langdon seeks to produce a legalistic suture capable of eliding the incommensurabilities of meaning that Jefferson and Hemings's miscegenetic relationship exposes, and to obscure the exercise of Black unfree will that Hemings's love enacts.[62] Or, to put it differently, it is not the peril to Hemings as a free Black woman in a slave society that Langdon seeks to ameliorate; rather, it is the threat that her blackness poses to that society that he seeks to contain. Yet that same act of racial conversion, inscribed by Jefferson twenty-seven years earlier in the pages of his plantation roster when he listed Hemings as a white woman, is perceived by her not as a violation but as proof of "a past and a passion nothing could disavow," and as recompense for her servitude in the form of access to freedom for her children (*SH,* 273). The divergent and contradictory meanings in these two near-identical acts of racial alchemy encapsulate the complex and contradictory constructions of whiteness in Chase-Riboud's two historical novels of the Jefferson-Hemings family. For if the transmutation of Black into white provides an avenue of escape from the slave's inalienable status of social death, it concomitantly exacts an equally fatal cost: the death of blackness.

Where Sally Hemings and her mother, Elizabeth, perceive liberation's illusory character, her only daughter, Harriet, sees freedom as "a limitless labyrinth of possibilities," a "vague and indiscriminate" thing inextricable from the whiteness that she pursues and claims.[63] "There [is] no freedom without whiteness," Harriet knows, just as she understands that "to shed her slavehood was also to shed her color" (*SH,* 335). She imagines her passage to freedom and whiteness in the North as "peeling off slavehood like a dirty petticoat," a metaphor that encompasses the logics of sexual and racial objectification through which blackness is constructed, even in its shedding (*SH,* 333). As Harriet's younger brother Madison observes, the act of auto-miscegenation that is passing has both sexual and mortal resonances. Harriet's re-creation of herself as a white woman is simultaneously a form of sexual recommodification (the "selling" of herself in exchange for "whiteness") and of obliteration (the erasure of herself in exchange for freedom) (*SH,* 337; *PD,* 9). As a female fugitive slave passing for white, Harriet doubles her civic and psychic "annihilation"; no longer Jefferson's slave and never acknowledged as his daughter, she has ceased to exist within the legally recognized categories available to unmarried nineteenth-century women (*PD,* 15, 45). This reinscription of Harriet's illegitimacy and total evacuation of her identity is the precondition for her white existence.

Like all of Jefferson's children who passed into the white world, both the historical Harriet Hemings and the fictional protagonist of Chase-Riboud's *The President's Daughter* were required to sever—publicly at least—all connections with their enslaved past. The price of leaving the plantation *familia* was the total disassociation from one's still-enslaved family; to move beyond the control of the master required slipping between the fingers of history.[64] In other words, for the passing fugitive, the violent legal severing of past, present, and future kinship networks and isolation from any legitimated social order or "conscious community of memory" that Patterson dubs "natal alienation" is both transformed and reproduced. No longer a constituent element of slavery's social death, it is the initiating violence of the death of blackness.[65]

Harriet, however, is all too aware of the seeming inalienability of blackness under the laws of hypodescent. In her terrified mind, it is her fingerprints that come to signify the inextricability of her existence as a unique and individual subject from the ineradicable fact of her blackness, materialized in the sooty marks she leaves on her white lover's face when she touches him. As the bodily "autograph that cannot be counterfeited or disguised or hidden away," her fingerprints at once index the illegibility of race in the passing body and the inalienability of race from the Black subject (*PD,* 77–79). For Harriet, they signal both the always imminent betrayal of her doubled illegitimacy and the ineradicable history of kidnapping, captivity, and physical and sexual subjugation that form her origin story and from which she cannot free herself. "This [Middle] Passage," she realizes, "was my fingerprints" (*PD,* 155). Indeed, the burning off of her fingerprints in a scientific accident that scars her hands irreparably marks Harriet's final, full achievement of her goal of passing. In the absence of fingerprints, her fingertips are as "smooth and white as marble" (*PD,* 279). This final rite of passage enacts not so much a total erasure of her past life but its violent sublation: "In the center of my palm, where my life line lay, there remained scar tissue, crisscrossing its center as if laid on by a whip. I had seen such scars on runaways. But even these scars would soon fade, leaving only tracks of white" (*PD,* 279). With the burning off of her fingerprints and severing of her life line, the "injury of [Harriet's] birth" as a Black slave is negated (*PD,* 279), yet it remains, under erasure: the presence of its absence is marked first by the scars that connect her to her enslaved past and her continuing fugitive status and eventually by the dense track of white that both marks and conceals the trace of her blackness.[66]

This indissoluble relationship in alterity between physical death, social death, and the death of blackness is given form in *The President's Daughter* through Chase-Riboud's revisionary intertextual engagement with Brown's *Clotel.* Reading the fictionalized "biography" of her own life, in which Jefferson's daughter throws herself into the Potomac River to drown rather than be returned to slavery in the South, Harriet is struck by how Clotel's choice of death over re-enslavement mirrors her own predicament. "Hadn't I drowned?" she wonders. "Wasn't I dead? Hadn't I chosen oblivion rather than slavery?" (*PD,* 327).[67] Indeed, each daughter chooses a fatal path; while Clotel drowns herself in the "deep foamy waters of the Potomac," Harriet sinks "into [the] white world as into a watery grave" (*PD,* 61).[68] Yet there remains an instructive tension between the two texts: Brown's depiction of Clotel's suicide follows David Walker and others to suggest that, as the chapter's title posits, physical "death is freedom" to the enslaved and socially dead Black subject; Chase-Riboud's narrative, however, delineates a psychic and racial death of the Black subject from which not even physical death can save her (*PD,* 446).[69]

Both product and embodiment of a political-economic, juridical, and social relation that simultaneously "affirmed the self-identity and liberty of whites and, conversely, denied the self-identity and liberty of blacks," Harriet is "the killing field and the blood victim of these two strains" (*PD,* 23).[70] Her mulatta body is the overdetermined convergence point not only of Black and white but also of the twinned, contradictory fundaments of racialized slavery in the United States: the irremediable stain of blackness and the unassailable purity of whiteness. In the wake of their miscegenetic collision, Harriet is engendered as a signifier of racial meaning in excess of established discursive categories as well as the negation of that surplus and the ideological danger that it represents. Harriet's success at passing thus can no more be understood as a Black "exercise of liberty or self-identity" than interracial erotic love. Rather, it is a conscious act of contingent self-obliteration, chosen within the coercive conditions that predicate her nominal freedom from slavery's total objectification on the evacuation of her Black identity. Harriet's fugitive path traces the contours of an abiding unfreedom engendered in the social, sexual, economic, and imaginative interaction of white and Black, free and enslaved, human and inhuman, that is produced and maintained even—indeed, especially—through the very structures and actions that seek to ameliorate its consequences.

In the Afterlife of Sally Hemings

Like the historical-fictional women who populate its pages, this reading of *Sally Hemings* and *The President's Daughter* seeks to situate itself at those points of impossible convergence between diametrically opposed categories of meaning. By interrogating the seemingly stable dichotomies between history and fiction, erotic love and sexualized violence, Black social death and the nominal freedom of passing for white, my goal has been to reveal a set of heretofore elided incommensurabilities of meaning and to point to the political potential embedded in these effaced contradictions. For if the possibility of love between Sally Hemings and Thomas Jefferson demonstrates not the transcendent capacity of erotic love but the intransigence of material and discursive systems of sexualized violence and racialized commodification, then it also gestures to the potential for the exercise of unfree will to enable and destabilize the logics and processes of raced and gendered coercion and control within which such acts are embedded.

Yet if Chase-Riboud's novelistic renderings of Sally and Harriet Hemings provide an opportunity to reexamine the meaning of freedom and subjugation within African chattel slavery, so too do they enable a reconsideration of the possibility of Black liberation outside those structures. Harriet Hemings's imagined life does not only provide a lesson on the psychic travails of maroonage, passing, and loss of self. More important, it provides an opportunity to examine the enduring nature of Black unfreedom within the American racial state, in which the meaning of whiteness remains dependent on the status of blackness as and at the limit of the human. If, as Harriet and her mother discover, Black unfreedom cannot be stripped away, escaped, or transcended without the risk of self-annihilation, then the possibility of freedom perhaps lies elsewhere, in a more profound transgression—one that calls into question the very categories of Black and white, free and unfree, love and freedom, as they are understood, articulated, and leveraged.

The biding quality of Black unfreedom, as well as the high cost for even the most nominal forms of Black freedom in the wake of emancipation, has been of central concern to contemporary scholars of slavery's afterlife. The final chapter follows this enduring trace of Black unfreedom to consider how the discourses and structures of chattel slavery are reiterated and transformed in the twentieth century, through both the imagination and administration of Black reproductivity as well as the raced and gendered practices of social reproduction and welfare.

5

A Picture of Me and My Mother

Planned Parenthood, Precious, *and the Rationalization of Black Reproductivity*

In the winter months of 2010, more than sixty billboards displaying a striking grayscale close-up of a Black toddler's tearstained face appeared throughout Georgia's Dekalb and Fulton Counties. Flanking the arresting image, bold text in caution-tape yellow warned passersby that "BLACK CHILDREN ARE AN ENDANGERED SPECIES" (Figure 4). With their tagline of "toomanyaborted.com," the billboards marked the beginning of an extended antiabortion public crusade targeting African American communities. Originally conceived of and sponsored by Georgia Right to Life and the Atlanta-based Radiance Foundation—a self-described African American–led "educational life-affirming organization"—the tactics of toomanyaborted.com were quickly seized upon by African American pro-life groups from across the nation.[1] Within months, the highway shoulders and urban landscapes of the United States were dotted with sky-high renderings of vulnerable Black children, artful representations of Black male leaders from single-parent homes, and disembodied photographs of Black women's fecund wombs. In the following years, the localized roadside media project morphed into a national public awareness campaign that included additional billboards, bumper stickers, and T-shirts; DVDs, online videos, and televised public service announcements highlighting the vast disparity in abortion rates between African American and white women; and numerous free speaker series aimed at Christian-oriented, pro-life, and largely African American audiences nationwide. From the assertion by Life Always that "the most dangerous place for an African American is in the womb" to the Restoration Project's sensational "Abortion in the Hood" billboards declaiming abortion rights advocacy as the betrayal of Black communities by corrupt African American leaders, the widespread crusade used U.S. metropolitan areas as staging grounds for the revitalization of long-standing constructions of abortion as racial genocide, bringing renewed visibility to

Figure 4. The Radiance Foundation and Georgia Right to Life collaborated in creating this billboard and others like it to display in DeKalb County and, eventually, across the United States. Kendrick Brinson / *New York Times* / Redux.

pro-choice politics as emerging from and embedded in the politics of anti-Black racism.[2]

The intensive public attention garnered by this series of campaigns owed a great deal to the political moment in which they first emerged. In the eighteen months after the Radiance Foundation's first billboard appeared in the Atlanta metropolitan area, a pitched battle was fought on the floor of Congress over federal funding for reproductive planning and health-care services. The House of Representatives drafted a continuing budget resolution eliminating federal grants for reproductive planning services and reproductive health care and all federal funding for Planned Parenthood; passed H.R. 3, or the "No Taxpayer Funding for Abortion Act," which sought to expand the 1976 Hyde Amendment by disallowing the use of tax benefits to pay for abortions and narrowly delimiting the legal definition of rape and launched an extended investigation of Planned Parenthood's alleged misuse of state and federal funds for medical abortion provision programs.[3] While both H.R. 3 and the House budget resolution were eventually rejected by the Senate, they initiated a firestorm of public debate. Meanwhile, as the legislative battle over women's rights to reproductive autonomy—and particularly, legal, non-life-threatening access to abortions—once again occupied the national spotlight, more than forty states quietly passed some eighty local laws restricting access to reproductive planning services, including abortions.[4]

Following as it did on the heels of 2008 and 2009's extensive media coverage of African American church groups' involvement in local and national campaigns against the legalization of same-sex marriage, the widely publicized, Black-led antiabortion campaign focused on African American communities was frequently interpreted as another example of the ascendance of a new, albeit short-lived, political alliance between the Black and white Christian right that was founded on a common ground of religious traditionalism and sexual and gender conservativism and stymied by the white Christian right's key role in the 2016 presidential election of Donald Trump. Certainly, this popular reading cannot be taken lightly. However, to characterize the past decade's expressions of Black sexual conservatism as the transparent manifestation of "traditional" racial-cultural norms—or, conversely, as evidence of Black communities falling prey to the duplicitous machinations of white right-wing opinion makers—deeply misunderstands the historical and political conditions of its emergence. In the context of what Ferguson describes as the construction of the heteronormative home "over and against the very nonheteronormative irrationalities believed to define African American sexuality," historical and contemporary articulations of Black sexual and gender conservatism might be better read as exemplifying what Candice Jenkins has dubbed the Black middle class's "salvific wish" to limit the vulnerability of Black bodies, families, and homes to the racist incursions and violence this book has traced, by fostering Black spaces of "conventional domesticity, the heterosexual marriage coupling, and traditional nuclear family."[5] Like the sexual economy of chattel slavery before it, this oppositional economy of racial salvation is inherently gendered: it asks that Black women sacrifice bodily autonomy for "the 'ultimate' safety of the black community as a whole."[6] In so doing, Black-led antiabortion campaigns like the Radiance Foundation's strategically rearticulate what Rhonda Williams has argued are historical connections between Black nationalism and ideals of patriarchal domesticity. By deliberately invoking principles of racial solidarity that supplant any mention of Black women's rights or needs with images of charismatic masculine leadership or of children as vulnerable, innocent victims, these campaigns wage a "restrictive, disciplinary assault upon black bodies" couched in contemporary cultural nationalist rhetorics of the heteronormative family as "*the* sanctioned site for the reproduction of authentic racial ethnic culture."[7]

At the same time that Black antiabortion campaigns may be clear manifestations of sexual disciplining by the Black middle class, they cannot be dismissed solely as such. To do so would overlook the historical centrality of debate and dissension around technologies of reproductive control within political and cultural movements of Black people and other people of color for survival and self-determination—a conversation that has existed in tandem with feminist activism for access to birth control and family planning resources for more than a century. Within African American social and political formations, wariness of mainstream reproductive planning advocacy, policies, and programs reflects an understanding of the always fraught status of Black reproductivity within projects of U.S. nation building. A suspicion of contraceptive technologies' perceived utility for white supremacist efforts to control Black reproduction was articulated as early as 1934, when the Universal Negro Improvement Association, under the leadership of Marcus Garvey, unanimously passed a resolution that called upon people of African descent not to "accept or practice the theory of birth control such as being advocated by irresponsible speculators who are attempting to interfere with the course of nature."[8] Yet the most comprehensive critique of the racialized implementation of reproductive planning emerged decades later, when a number of Black nationalist platforms of the 1960s and 1970s denounced "family planning" projects as genocidal in intent and consequence. Their analysis was rooted in an understanding of how, in the century after emancipation, U.S. white supremacy had become dependent on the state-sanctioned and extralegal curtailment and containment of Black populations; the restriction of procreative increase was thus part of the same national project as segregation, lynching, and malign medical neglect and intervention.[9]

As Black activists and scholars have long contended, mainstream advocacy for and provision of family planning resources in the United States have consistently been imbricated with and implemented through a eugenic logic of social engineering intended to disproportionately delimit reproduction by poor people, white ethnic immigrants, and people of color.[10] Given that, as the previous chapters have argued, the expropriation and control of Black reproduction has been a vital technology in the production and maintenance of U.S. racial capitalism since its establishment, it is difficult to conceive of a Black liberatory political project that advocates state-supported family planning or reproductive autonomy without contending with what Dorothy Roberts has described as the dependence of white, middle-class women's reproductive liberty on wide-scale Black reproductive control.[11] To dismiss Black antiabortion activists' rhetoric of genocide wholesale, then, would require a disavowal of this extensive history and its contemporary ramifications.

At the same time—and often in the very same writings that highlight the centrality of anti-Black racism to reproductive planning—Black feminists have cogently argued that the ability of Black women and other people able to gestate to determine the timing and number of offspring that they bear is a necessary precondition for Black liberation; moreover, access to childcare, adequate financial resources to raise children, and freedom from interpersonal and state reproductive violence are integral elements of the economic, political, and social justice for which African American activists have fought.[12] Feminists have long contended that the unavailability of affordable family planning services disproportionately punishes poor women of color; given this, the effort by Black men and women to limit access to such services is founded in a political model that understands heteromasculine liberation to be achieved by maintaining the vulnerability of Black women and gender-nonconforming folk to the brutal vicissitudes of racial gendered capitalism.[13]

This conglomeration of competing narratives, strategies, and interests—the state deployment of technologies of reproduction to manage relations of race, gender, and capital; Black middle-class investments in individual propriety as a tool for collective safety; Black nationalist reclamations of heteropatriarchy as a defense against necropolitical violence; and Black feminist assertions of the need for reproductive autonomy as a necessary precondition for Black freedom—constitutes Black reproductivity at the turn of the twenty-first century. It remains as vexed and generative an arena for the production of political meaning as it has been since the codification of *partus sequitur ventrem* three hundred years earlier. In light of this longer and broader political context of Black reproduction that the previous four chapters have explored, how might we make alternative sense of these seemingly contradictory policies, practices, and discourses from which contemporary questions of Black reproductive rights, practices, and freedoms have reemerged?

To do so requires drawing upon the insights garnered so far regarding the workings of the Black reproductive to interrogate the ostensibly irresolvable conflict between (white) feminist demands for reproductive rights and Black (nationalist) critiques of racialized family planning policy. This binary conception of the dilemma of reproductive planning and policy exemplifies what Kimberlé Crenshaw has described as "political intersectionality," in which the ideological frameworks of feminist and antiracist political movements are each incommensurate with the complex political positions and desires articulated by women of color.[14] Within this limited (and limiting) paradigm, the unceasing crusade by religious and political entities to restrict reproductive autonomy as a tool for the control, punishment, and exploitation of women as well as the modern birth control movement's continued reliance on and complicity in systems of social control via the management of racialized reproduction remain the rock and the hard place between which Black women and other women of color are expected to navigate, using a finely tuned compass capable of measuring the relative dangers of these not-unrelated forms of raced and gendered violence. This fabricated impasse of race versus gender, or nation versus sisterhood, facilely elides the political reality that the admonishments of the Black conservative antiabortion movement, uncritical celebrations of choice and access by white (and nonwhite) middle-class family planning advocates, and Black pronatalist rhetorics of "aiding the REVOLUTION through [procreative] NATION BUILDING" all share a common logic in which the regulation, exploitation, and curtailment of Black women's reproduction remains the acceptable collateral damage for other people's freedom.[15]

Rather than reiterate this conundrum, what follows offers an alternative approach to the question of blackness and reproductive planning—one that evinces a profound suspicion of the binary logic that understands twentieth- and twenty-first-century reproductive politics as a long-standing conflict between state control and personal choice, social responsibility and individual autonomy. Building upon earlier discussions of Black reproductivity as a vexed and multilocated technology through which power and subjectivity are produced and enacted, I instead argue that both contemporary state policies of reproductive control and the mainstream political project of reproductive rights are forms of what Grace Kyungwon Hong has described as the contemporary neoliberal management of racial life's attendant exacerbation of racialized vulnerability to death.[16]

Whether it be the Radiance Foundation's exhortation of Black individuals and communities to "live a life of meaning" or Planned Parenthood's defense of its federal funding with its claim to "save women's lives," the purported protection and increased valuation of Black life emerges as an oft-repeated rationale for the surveillance, control, and production of knowledge around Black reprosexuality. These conjoined and contested rhetorics rely on what Hannah Arendt described as the ascendency, in the modern era, of life—and its protection and preservation—as a primary societal goal and unquestioned social good.[17] Concomitantly, and just as importantly, they collectively constitute a performative discourse through which the meaning(s) and value of life are delineated and hierarchized. As Black feminist activist and writer Beverly Smith observes,

> It occurred to me this morning that what the anti-abortion people mean by life and what I mean by life are two very different things. Life for them is mostly a biological phenomenon. They don't care about the quality of life for those babies and their mothers, who for many valid reasons don't want a child and or feel that they can't have a child, no matter how much they might want to have one. What I think we're fighting for are decent standards of life, including the potential for growth, for all people, including women.[18]

Smith's daybreak musings give insight into why reproductivity in general, and Black reproductivity in particular, remains a crucial terrain of late modern ideological struggle: the individual or collective reproductive body signifies a conspicuous convergence point on and through which modern reproductive technologies, policies, and discourses simultaneously rearticulate and reinstantiate the relational meaning and value of what Agamben names *zoe* ("mere" or "simple" biological life) and *bios* (human social life).[19] Amid the conflicting invocations of unborn lives, women's lives, and lives worth living, the relative value of different lives and of different *kinds of life* are parsed; the resulting calculus measures not only the value of white life versus that of Black life but also of fetal life versus maternal life, the protection of life versus the quality of life, future generations against contemporary survival. What is elided in antiabortion propagandists' and family planning advocates' opposing claims to valorize, preserve, or protect Black life, however, is the extent to which the vexed and uneven imbrication of biological life (*zoe*) and social life (*bios*) enacted by contemporary reproductive technologies and discourses exemplify and enable the biopolitical practice of *making live* through concomitant management of biological populations and disciplining of individual and collective social bodies, at the same time that they leverage the historical and contemporary sociocultural value that Black social, civil, and physical death has had, and continues to have, in the United States.

By juxtaposing the antiracist idiom central to the contemporary African American pro-life movement with pre–World War II discourses around reproductive control and reproductive planning in the United States, and with Lee Daniel's 2011 critically acclaimed film, *Precious: Based on the Novel "Push" by Sapphire,* this chapter traces the common logics around Black reproductivity that these seemingly divergent rhetorical projects share, and how shifts in political and economic contexts have required their rearticulation in new forms and lexicons. In what follows, I argue that an interested reading of the 1930s and 1940s birth control programming aimed at impoverished African Americans reveals the critical function that Black reproductivity has played in the rationalization of social, economic, and political life in the twentieth century. While acknowledging the centrality of nineteenth-century Anglo-American social and scientific theories of eugenics to the emergence of early and mid-twentieth-century raced reproductive control in the United States, what follows links the emergence of reproductive planning programs directed at African Americans to the state and civil society's interest in reharnessing Black reproductivity to the project of modern racial capitalism in the wake of Black emancipation. Such a reading understands the emergence of liberal Keynesian policy in the United States and the heightened focus of reproductive planning programs on the management of Black procreation to be not merely coincident but inextricably intertwined elements of U.S. projects of modernization, industrialization, and rationalization. At the same time, this rethinking of midcentury reproductive politics also enables a renewed and revised consideration of the contemporary politics of Black reproductivity at the current moment of late capitalism in crisis.

The Negro Project and the Negro Problem

In January 1939, the largest U.S. organization for birth control education and advocacy, the American Birth Control League (ABCL), and the preeminent institution for research on birth control methods and usage, the Birth Control Clinical Research Bureau (BCCRB), resolved a ten-year political rift by merging into a single national organization for the study and advocacy of family planning through reproductive technologies. The resulting institution, the Birth Control Federation of America (BCFA), went on to become the most well-known organization for family planning advocacy and provision in the United States: the Planned Parenthood Federation of America. In the same year as the merger, the reorganized federation initiated what became the Division of Negro Service (DNS) or, as it was more commonly known, the "Negro Project."[20] Funded by a $20,000 grant from the Albert Lasker family, the DNS was created to address what were seen as the problems of high rates of childbirth, maternal and child mortality, disease, and poverty among African Americans. Its keystone initiative was a multisite demonstration project on birth control education and provision for African Americans in the rural and urban South. Working out of two clinics in Nashville, Tennessee, and through one clinic each in South Carolina's Berkeley and Lee Counties, doctors, nurses, and social service workers attempted over a three-year period to determine if providing low-cost, low-technology birth control methods, and the attendant training in how to use them, could reduce the rate of unwanted pregnancy in Black communities. In addition to the regional demonstration project sites, the DNS also produced extensive public education and birth control advocacy materials—directed at African American community organizations, religious leaders, and medical professionals—that were widely distributed nationwide.

In the past forty years, the southern demonstration project of the DNS has become a critical area of inquiry and contestation in contemporary popular and academic discussions of race and racism in reproductive planning.[21] At a time when the national birth control movement still maintained close ties with the national and international eugenics movement, the focus of the DNS on reducing reproduction among low-income African American women was indicative of the vexed interconnection between feminist visions of reproductive autonomy and white supremacist efforts to maintain racial control over Black procreation.[22] From the project's origins in a 1938 proposal drafted by movement founder Margaret Sanger and BCFA secretary Mary W. Reinhardt, the DNS was built on the premise that "negroes present[ed] the great problem" underlying the South's disproportionate rates of poverty, low employment, and ill-health during and after the Great Depression.[23] Sanger and her colleagues relied heavily on popular racist stereotypes of the time to drum up financial and media support for the project, describing the "primitive state of civilization in which most negroes of the South live[d]," beset by low intelligence, sexual carelessness, and high rates of contagious disease.[24] Subsequent materials for the project cited the low rates of African American contraception usage and the high ratio of Black-to-white births in southern states, implicitly invoking white fears of race suicide to motivate local officials' involvement and support.[25]

Nor was the Negro Project egalitarian in its structure and implementation. Largely managed and controlled by white doctors, nurses, and professional family planning advocates, the demonstration project relegated African American participants to advisory and subordinate positions—sometimes due to a paternalistic lack of faith in their capacities and at other times for fear of alienating southern segregationist supporters.[26] While Black nurses, doctors, ministers, and social workers were actively recruited to help allay African American patients' "ignorance, superstitions, and doubts," Sanger's petition to hire a full-time African American medical staff member met with staunch opposition from the federation's central office and board members. With its narrow focus on reducing birth rates and its patronizing goal of "working out . . . the best methods of approach" for "the negro psychology," the southern demonstration project showed little interest in creating long-term social change in its target communities: when the Berkeley County site showed very minimal success in reducing pregnancy rates, the mediocre results were blamed on the poor compliance and superstitious nature of the Black participants and the demonstration site was moved to Lee County; a year later, the Nashville program's remarkable success led to a similarly swift discontinuation on the grounds that it had achieved its experimental goals. No further resources were provided to the women in either state who had relied on the project's services.[27]

As a number of scholars have noted, however, the ideological context from which the DNS emerged and within which it operated was more heterogeneous and contested than it might appear at first glance.[28] Alongside its sweeping generalizations regarding careless procreation by African Americans and dire warnings about the disproportionate growth of Black populations, Sanger and Reinhardt's proposal acknowledged the "special social and economic pressure" that African Americans faced in the form of "discrimination, hardship, and segregation" and described the DNS as a remedy for Black women's lack of contraceptive access due to Jim Crow policies at existing southern birth control clinics.[29] Moreover, some of the staunchest support of the DNS came from the strongholds of Black civil society, including the National Association for the Advancement of Colored People (NAACP), the National Council of Negro Women (NCNW), the National Urban League, and the National Medical Association (NMA). Not only was the National Advisory Council for the DNS composed of nearly thirty prominent and influential African American figures—a cohort that included NCNW founder and president Mary McLeod Bethune, NAACP executive director Walter White, Fisk University's Charles S. Johnson, and New York pastor and civil rights activist Rev. Adam Clayton Powell Jr.—but also project leader Florence Rose remained in regular communication with hundreds of African American doctors, nurses, social workers, educators, and news publishers across the nation for the duration of the project. Many of these individuals and institutions staunchly advocated for the DNS as a vital tool for addressing the consequences of structural racism by reducing child and maternal mortality, increasing employment and education levels, and improving the health and economic well-being of Black families.

Contemporary studies of twentieth-century reproductive politics have offered several frameworks for making sense of the seemingly conflicting ideologies behind the Negro Project. Many of the differences in interpretation are rooted in divergent understandings of the relationship among the project's centralized white administration, the African American medical providers and patients who used the project's onsite resources, and the middle-class luminaries of Black civil society who supported the DNS more broadly. For example, reproductive rights historian Linda Gordon has posited that despite Sanger's desire to create a "project for black uplift," the ingrained racism of the white leadership of BCFA, combined with their unwillingness to cede any substantive control or autonomy to local African American doctors and nurses (or to pay them for their services), robbed the program of its ability to address the structural issues of racism, poverty, and gender inequality.[30] Instead, she argues, the project "functioned to stabilize existing social relations," divorcing birth control education and provision "from any politics that might have given it a democratic meaning: women's rights, civil rights, or any social analysis of southern poverty."[31]

Analyses more attentive to the complex dynamics of race, class, and gender, however, suggest that the power relation between the white birth control establishment and African American patients and community leaders was neither as transparent nor as absolute as Gordon's brief summary suggests. Joanna Schoen has suggested that the DNS's demonstration project was one example of what she describes as the core contradiction of early and midcentury reproductive planning: a "liberal" desire to increase reproductive autonomy versus a "conservative" state project to reduce social service dependency through reproductive control. Far from being passive victims, she argues, Black women throughout the South strategically leveraged family planning programs' contradictory aims to garner the services and resources they needed to improve their lives.[32] The ideological conflicts within the DNS underscore the extent to which the antagonism between reproductive autonomy and reproductive control was inherently racialized. As Dorothy Roberts aptly sums up the distinction, "White eugenicists promoted birth control as a way of preserving an oppressive structure; Blacks promoted birth control as a way of toppling it."[33] For African American civil rights activists and advocates, the long-standing exclusion of Black women from reproductive health services was part of the larger system of racial segregation that produced extreme racial disparities in health, quality of life, and mortality, and advocacy for reproductive planning services was a form of advocacy for economic and political equality.

Particularly for early Black feminists such as Bethune and Dr. Dorothy Boulding Ferebee (founder of the Mississippi Health Project and president of African American sorority Alpha Kappa Alpha), the commitment to increasing contraceptive access for Black women was entirely congruent with existing opposition to forcible sterilization of Black women; both stances were part of a broader commitment to enable "each [Black] family to have ALL the children it can support and afford, *but no more*—in order to assure better health, greater security and happiness for all."[34] This oft-repeated phrase, first used by the NCNW in its 1941 resolution in support of family planning, hints at what Roberts characterizes as the "elitist" undercurrent to birth control advocacy among Black civil society—a subtext that, while not based in notions of inherent race-based difference, was informed by the eugenic thinking of the time.[35] From W. E. B. Du Bois to E. Franklin Frazier to George Schuyler, Black "race men" and women sought to determine which Black women should be reproducing, and at what rates, to improve the status of the race as a whole. In the end, Roberts argues, the eugenicist underpinnings of the prewar birth control movement could not be fully subverted or overcome. "In a society marked by racial hierarchy," she concludes, the principle of reproductive control and the linking of societal ills to rates of reproduction among the socially disadvantaged necessarily "produced policies designed to reduce Black women's fertility."[36]

How are we to make sense of the concurrent and contradictory impulses toward the maintenance of white supremacy and its overthrow, the practices of eugenic control and the ideals of antiracist, feminist autonomy that brought the Division of Negro Service into being? In what follows, I offer an alternative analysis of the ideological foundations and fissures of the DNS as juxtaposed with the BCFA's concurrent project, the Southern Conference on Tomorrow's Children. Read alongside the themes, rhetoric, and espoused goals of the Southern Conference, the DNS experiment in birth control education and provision for African Americans in the South appears as a fraught—and sometimes contradictory—project of liberal democratic rationalization articulated through a lexicon of industrial capitalism, social welfare, and reproductive management. Reading the two southern projects together illustrates how strategies, policies, and practices for the management of Black reproductivity facilitated the racial capitalist state's transition from the postemancipation creation of Black citizenship to the neoliberal management of racial life.[37]

Tomorrow's Children and the Race of Social Welfare

In November 1939, the newly consolidated BCFA sponsored the Southern Conference on Tomorrow's Children, an unprecedented region-wide conference on public health, maternal and child welfare, and birth control in the southern United States. The first of a series of annual regional conferences of the same name held in the South, the Midwest, and New England between 1939 and 1941, the three-day convention brought together "public health, welfare, medical, legal, religious, educational, and civic" groups to consider "certain problems which relate to the South's human resources tomorrow."[38] The conference planning committee—made up of southern businessmen, media publishers, state public health officials, medical professionals, academics, and longtime birth control advocates—cast its objectives in the broad and inclusive terms of "plan[ning] better opportunity in life for 'Tomorrow's Children'" and "defin[ing] our individual responsibility . . . relative to this problem."[39] At its core, however, the conference was a large-scale attempt by the BCFA to convince southern business leaders and public officials that birth control constituted a viable and valuable solution to the social and economic ills perceived to be besieging the South.

The Southern Conference took its name from a popular text among birth control advocates of the time: *Tomorrow's Children: The Goal of Eugenics.*

Authored by Ellsworth Huntington, Yale geographer and president of the American Eugenics Society, *Tomorrow's Children* had been published four years earlier as the society's new handbook. Its publication marked the ascendance of what came to be known as "the new American eugenics," ushering in a methodological and epistemological shift in the U.S. eugenics movement. As described at the society's 1936 annual meeting, this new, "distinctly American" model continued to promote the biological management of populations through "the careful selection of mates, carefully formulated marriage laws, the regulation of immigration, the universal use of birth control, and the segregation or sterilization of known carriers of hereditary defects." Yet according to the society's Board of Directors,

> The new American eugenics goes further than this. It holds that this rebuilding of the foundation of our inverted pyramid is not merely a biological but a social problem. The conscious recognition of this is perhaps the most vital point in the new American attitude toward eugenics. Existing social agencies provide the most direct and effective way to bring about the biological revolution which is the goal of eugenics. Eugenically, the central social institution is the home. Therefore, all other social agencies such as the church, the school, the state, the hospital, and the many institutions connected with business must be scrutinized to see how they influence the size of many diverse types of families.[40]

With its emphasis on conjoining "genetics, or the science of heredity" and "sociology, or the science of society," new American eugenics departed from the previous narrow application of Mendelian heredity and environmental determinism in favor of an increased interest in employing social analysis to address the problem of individual and cultural reproduction.[41] At the same time, the increased emphasis on the eugenic potential of social agencies and civic institutions expanded the arena of sexual and reproductive regulation beyond the traditional scales of body and home to entail all aspects of political and civil society.

To be sure, the new American eugenics was neither as novel nor as uniquely American as Huntington and the American Eugenics Society claimed. However, its ascendancy did mark a significant change in the U.S. eugenics movement—one that resonated with concurrent shifts in U.S. racial ideology and political economic policy. New American eugenics' attention to cultural as well as biological inheritance reflected the influence of changing sociological approaches to race—most notably the emergence of the Chicago School of urban sociology—which located the origins of racial difference in cultural deficiencies to be remedied by social incorporation rather than in innate genetic limitations. Its turn to state agencies and policies as valuable arenas for eugenic intervention was a response to the U.S. Keynesian turn under Franklin D. Roosevelt and the resultant expansion of state-funded public relief, infrastructure, and jobs programs as instruments to ameliorate the effects of the Great Depression. For eugenicists, the late 1930s network of social welfare, public health, and employment agencies provided an ideal mechanism for the increased integration of the quotidian administration of social life with the state regulation and curtailment of biological life. Rather than being what has popularly been considered the early peals of the U.S. eugenics movement's death knell, the social and cultural turn ushered in a period of eugenics' increasing assimilability into mainstream midcentury modes of biopolitical governmentality.

Huntington's new eugenicist catechism, with its forward-looking title, was "seized upon . . . with enthusiasm" by the organizers of the first southern regional conference for its "popular and scientific appeal" and capacity to convey the themes of the conference as a whole.[42] Indeed, one might suspect that part of the appeal of the text (and title) for conference organizers was the extent to which it mirrored their own political strategy for producing social change—albeit with a more conservative bent. For some speakers, including BCFA executive director Woodbridge Morris, the strategy forward was explicitly eugenic, requiring the creation of a "new social order" that combined active reproductive regulations with the contemporary "modern humanitarian movement" of New Deal public service agencies to ensure that "saving lives" and improving health did not allow "the unfit to inherit the earth."[43] But for most participants, the ideologies underpinning the Southern Conference were firmly grounded in a liberal democratic approach to merging the projects of social welfare and social engineering.

It is particularly telling that the first day's final keynote address was delivered by Alva Myrdal, noted Swedish feminist and birth control advocate. Myrdal's 1934 book, *Crisis in the Population Question,* which she coauthored with her husband, Gunnar Myrdal, has been widely described as the inspiration for much of the construction of the Swedish welfare state.[44] Faced with Sweden's declining birth rate and increasing numbers of working-class, non-Scandinavian immigrants, the Myrdals countered conservative politicians' demands for stringent birth control restrictions with a plan of their own: provide unfettered access to birth control but complement it with stringent population management, a broad range of social welfare policies to encourage reproduction among "healthy Swedes," and a proactive program of "social engineering to rationalize and modernize Swedish society."[45] The Myrdals' plan melded modern industrialism's demands for an increasingly rationalized society and social democratic ideals of a statewide social welfare system with eugenic strategies of social engineering. On the one hand, they advocated progressive social-economic initiatives, including full employment, income redistribution, parenting and housing subsidies, and free health care and daycare for children; on the other hand, they argued that meeting the needs of modern industrial society for a "higher quality of 'human material'" required a compulsory sterilization program to "root out all types of physical and mental inferiority within the population, both the mentally retarded and the mentally ill, the genetically defective and persons of bad character."[46] Like the new American eugenicists, the Myrdals had discovered what appeared to be the solution to the strains that racial capitalism and modern industrialization placed on nationalist projects of heteronormative reprosexuality: the perfect merger of social welfare and social engineering.

The platform outlined in the Myrdals' *Crisis in the Population Question* has much in common with the tenets of the postmerger BCFA as articulated through the conference theme of "tomorrow's children." At the core of the agenda was an investment in the racial capitalist state's project of rationalization as enacted through three principles: human welfare, industrialization, and reproduction.[47] Within this paradigm, the goals of the birth control movement were implemented through social welfare programs and agencies, and reproductive planning was posited, in and of itself, as a form of social welfare. In the context of "tomorrow's children," social welfare was defined as that which both ameliorates modern industrial capitalism's effects and enables the reproduction of the necessary conditions for its continuance and growth. As a technology of social welfare, the logic went, reproductive planning enables modernization through the production of a better labor force and the rational management of human life in the service of the public good, as defined through the interests of the modern nation-state and capital. Within this model, procreative sexuality—and particularly the reproduction and sexuality of poor and/or Black people—was a critical point of intervention. If, as Ferguson argues, the control of sexuality became a central preoccupation under the logic of modern rationalization because it was perceived to operate in opposition to rationality and labor, then procreative sexuality, as both the precondition for and antithesis to the efficient and productive labor on which modern industrial capital relied, became a key site for the resolution of that preoccupation through careful regulation and close management.[48]

Alva Myrdal's speech at the Southern Conference on Tomorrow's Children took place during Gunnar Myrdal's first year of research for the Carnegie Corporation project that culminated in *An American Dilemma,* in which Gunnar would argue for an intensive public education campaign to teach poor, rural Black Southerners the importance of birth control, observing that in the U.S. South, there were "a greater number of Negroes so destitute . . . that it would be better if they did not procreate."[49] Two years after her speech, Alva published *Nation and Family,* for which Daniel Patrick Moynihan would write the introduction to the 1968 U.S. edition, explaining its powerful influence on his own approach to social and family policy.[50] And—perhaps most telling for the purposes of this chapter—the conference at which she gave her keynote address took place just three months before the launching of the DNS's first demonstration clinic in Nashville, Tennessee. Given the multiple presentations on clinic planning and contraceptive education by doctors and nurses associated with the new demonstration clinics, the timing was unlikely to be coincidental; nor, one imagines, was the choice of Barry Bingham, president and publisher of the *Louisville Courier-Journal* and known social progressive, to present the opening keynote address, "The South's Tomorrow."[51]

Bingham's speech is notable for how it exemplified what Ferguson describes as "the ideological basis for the rationalization of American culture," including its valorization of industrial capitalism and Enlightenment ideals of humanist liberalism articulated as equality and freedom-as-rights.[52] Condemning the poll taxes that he noted were "disenfranchising 75 percent of its people" and "slowly breaking down respect for democracy," Bingham urged greater interracial cooperation between Black and white Southerners. Admonishing his compatriots for their focus on the "charming and cultured life that a few of our forefathers lived on the fabled plantations of antebellum days," he called for a "second reconstruction" to "force the South out of its agricultural rut" and into a "higher type of civilization" based in "industrial development."[53] He then closed his address with a rousing call for participants to address the broader social questions of Black poverty, disenfranchisement, ill health, and unemployment.

> I do not believe I need to reiterate to this audience the moral argument for fair treatment to Negroes. I want to make my point rather on the cold, hard, practical economic basis. As long as so great a proportion of our Negroes are ridden by poverty, ignorance, and disease, we can hope for no material advance in the civilization of the South. . . . Let me cite you this point: only by giving the Southern Negro better opportunities for education, health and a decent standard of living can we move over onto the Negro's shoulders his fair share of the burden of citizenship. The white South cannot carry that whole burden by itself. Let's make an investment in our Negro citizens and get a return in added social responsibility.[54]

Bingham's opening speech underscored the extent to which the liberal logic underlying the birth control movement's efforts to provide African Americans access to reproductive planning technologies both depended on and enacted the "burdened individuality" of free Black citizenship. As Hartman has argued, emancipation's granting the status of liberal individuals to Black subjects subjected them to the concomitant "individuating power of discipline, operating in conjunction with the sequestering and segregating control of Black bodies as a species body, permitted under the guise of social rights, and facilitated by the regulatory power of the state."[55] At the same time, Hartman notes, the construction of African Americans as free subjects simultaneously constituted them as subjects of capital, whose productive and reproductive capacities "could be quantified measured, exchanged, and alienated" in the service of the racial capitalist state.[56] Bingham's model for the "fair treatment [of] Negroes," with its emphasis on "cold, hard, economic" calculations and its rhetoric of investment and return, exemplifies the ideologies underlying the Southern Conference by linking the incorporation of African Americans into citizenship and social welfare systems with the ever-present demands of modernization and industrial capitalism.

In the context of the Southern Conference on Tomorrow's Children, then, the demonstration project of the Division of Negro Service can be read as an example of the role that the technologies of reproductive planning and control have played in the transformation from slavery's punitive systems of captivity, enslavement, and dispossession to the burdened individuality of nominal freedom, with its attendant regulation, containment, and subordination. Moreover, the Southern Conference's emphasis on Black reproduction demonstrates how emancipation and the ostensible incorporation of African Americans into liberal democracy was met with the rearticulation of Black sexuality and reproduction from a required form of coerced labor to an unregulated, and thus unproductive, threat to racial capitalism's demands for a productive labor force. As Bingham's keynote address illustrates, the result of "modern rationality's juxtaposition of labor against sexuality" was the particular "racialization of Black subjects" that emerged as the overarching discourse shaping the Negro Project.[57]

Nowhere is this more evident than in the exhibition materials for the national education campaign of the DNS. Created for the Afra-American Emancipation Exposition that was held in Chicago in the summer of 1940 to celebrate the progress of African Americans in the seventy-five years since emancipation, the large installation was designed to demonstrate to African American exposition attendees "the progress that could be made by the Negro race in health by birth control."[58] The exhibit was canceled in early July due to pressure from Catholic opponents to birth control; however, both the original installation and its smaller, three-foot-by-two-foot replicas were widely displayed in the following years of the Negro Project (Figure 5). Juxtaposing images of impoverished and bedraggled Black men, women, and children in desolate, rural environs with those of well-dressed Black families in modern schools, health centers, and homes, the exhibit's implication was clear: birth control was the overwhelming distinguisher between poverty, ill health, and rural desolation versus financial security, societal incorporation, and modernization. In large letters over the image of a clean-cut Black man hoisting a smiling and well-fed baby above his head, the exhibit's title and message were blazoned: "Tomorrow's Children: One-half of the nation's children are born into the poorest homes. Birth control gives the children of tomorrow a fair chance for happiness and a normal life."[59]

The Afra-American Emancipation Exposition exhibit was not the only aspect of the DNS publicity campaign to adopt the rhetoric of "tomorrow's children." The phrase appeared frequently in brochures and press releases for the years of the demonstration project, often accompanied by selected images from the original display. Interpreted in the context of Huntington's tract and the original Southern Conference on Tomorrow's Children, the prevalence of the term, and the visual images that supported it, offer insight into the politics of race and class subtending the Division of Negro Service. If the Negro Project's myriad images of happy, healthy, and responsibly

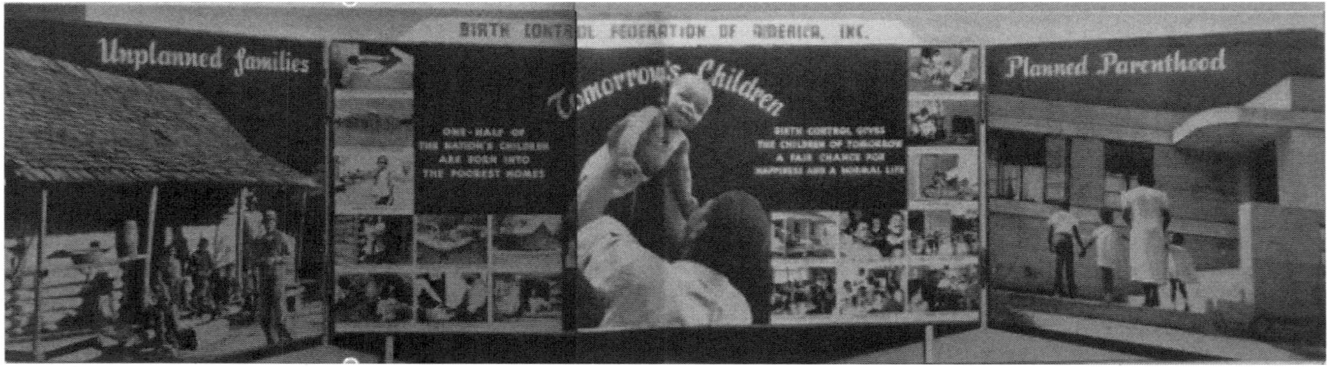

Figure 5. The Birth Control Federation of America's exhibit planned for the Afra-American Emancipation Exposition, Chicago, Ill., 1940. Planned Parenthood Federation of America Records (Part I), Sophia Smith Collection, Smith College, Northampton, Mass.

procreative Black families signal the well-managed life of the modern citizen that reproductive planning and control provides Black subjects who respond to the hail of industrial wage labor and the biopolitical management of life, then the counterposed images of the desolate, desperate, and hyperfertile rural Black poor demonstrate how the cost of "wild, unstable, and undomesticated" Black procreative sexuality is exiled "outside the bounds of the citizenship machine."[60] As exemplars of raced and classed difference, marked as deviance and punished by deprivation, they are foreclosed from incorporation into the middle class and, by extension, full status as subjects and citizens in the U.S. nation-state. Only by embracing modernization—code for their entailment into industrial capitalism's labor pool—can they hope to achieve full recognition and the benefits it promises.

It is this logic of incorporation that ties the political interests of the DNS and its cadre of African American middle-class supporters together. If, for the BCFA, birth control offered the ability to manage the populations that endanger heteronormative racial capitalism, for the leaders of African American civil society, Black self-regulation of reproduction marked the path to the political and economic enfranchisement necessary to sustain social and political life. More than half a century later, however, amid the rubble of late capitalist crisis, near-endless policies of reproductive surveillance, criminalization, and control have demonstrated the extent to which notions of full citizenship and political and economic incorporation are founded on the constitutive exclusion of Black subjects, even as the specter of unchecked Black deviance provides the context and pretext for the neoliberal management of racial life through the unceasing administration and regulation of Black reproductivity. It is this problematic with which the remainder of this chapter concerns itself.

Black Excess in the Post-Keynesian State

In the early pages of Sapphire's 1996 novel, *Push,* the protagonist, Claireece "Precious" Jones, remarks upon her illegibility within racial capitalism's frameworks of normativity, represented in this instance by the standardized educational achievement test.

> The tesses paint a picture of me and my muver—my whole family, we more than dumb, we invisible. One time I seen us on TV. It was a show of spooky shit, an' castles, you know shit be all haunted. And

> the peoples, well some of them was peoples an some of them was vampire peoples. But the real peoples did not know it till it was party time. You know crackers eating roast turkey and champagne and shit. So it's five of 'em sitting on a couch; and one of 'em get up and take a picture. Got it? When the picture develop (it's instamatic) only *one* person on the couch. The other peoples did not exist. They vampires. They eats, drinks, wear clothes, talks, fucks and stuff but when you get right down to it they don't exist.
>
> I big. I talk, I eats, I cooks, I laugh, watch TV, do what my muver say. But I can see when the picture come back I don't exist. Don't nobody want me. Don't nobody need me. I know who I am. I know who they say I am—vampire sucking the system's blood. Ugly black grease to be wipe away, punish, kilt, changed, finded a job for.[61]

In the critically acclaimed and award-winning 2009 film version of Sapphire's novel, *Precious,* Precious's musings on her damning test scores are stripped of all references to vampires, as is her piercing insight into the complex interplay of visibility and invisibility that Kara Keeling has noted is integral to the economy of blackness, and for which the unphotographable undead are a metaphor.[62] Effectively excising Precious's implicit indictment of a soon-to-be-post-Keynesian state that disavows both the existence of and its own reliance upon invisible, surplus, dispossessed racialized populations, screenwriter Geoffrey Fletcher and director Lee Daniels leave only Precious's comparison of herself and her mother to ugly Black grease—a comparison that is reinforced in the following scene's incessant images of Gabourey Sidibe's dark-skinned face smeared with grease from gorging on stolen fried chicken. If in Sapphire's novel, Precious and her mother are examples of what David Marriott describes as the spook that is produced through our racial paranoia as the embodiment of our fears or of what Christopher Peterson names the specter of our own being-toward-death, then in this cinematic version, Precious, Mary, and their family are waste products: the remaindered elements of an unequal society; the repugnant excess of an unhealthy body national.[63] The Precious of Sapphire's novel dreams of responding to her own erasure by screaming her continued existence across public venues from subway cars to television broadcasts, all the while knowing that her true value to the racial capitalist state lies in her social, civil, and physical death. Fletcher and Daniel's celluloid Precious makes no such claim to being but can only dream longingly of her own demise, fantasizing of dropped pianos or desks to end her seemingly pointless misery.

Reading this scene from *Precious* alongside and against Sapphire's original 1996 novel is not to idealize *Push* as a virtuous, politically progressive, Black feminist text that has been contaminated by or destroyed in Daniel's filmic rendering.[64] Rather, in juxtaposing the two, I follow Erica Edwards's argument that an understanding of the process and genre of adaptation is crucial to contemporary Black feminist critique of cultural production by, for, and about Black women.[65] Recognizing the points of conjuncture and departure between these two tales of Precious Jones demands that we consider the different political moments in which each cultural text came into being: *Push* was written and published amid the bipartisan state revanchism of Newt Gingrich's 1994 Contract with America and Bill Clinton's 1996 fulfillment of his campaign promise to "end welfare as we know it," whereas *Precious* was released amid a global economic crisis that ushered in the highest rates of African American unemployment in nearly three decades. Just as important, it draws attention to the distinction between text and film as media forms and particularly to the increasingly crucial role that visual technologies play in our interpellation as crucial participants in what Keeling has dubbed the socially necessary labor of affectivity—that is, the quotidian work through which images are consumed and social reality is created and reproduced in accordance with common sense and in the service of existing modes of exploitation and domination.[66] Like the DNS exhibit on "tomorrow's children," *Precious* can be read as an example of how visual technologies both produce sociocultural value and reproduce social relations via their investments in and visual rearticulation of the ideas and forms through which racial capitalism is reproduced.

Precious's test scores paint a picture not only of her but also of her mother and the rest of her family because her cinematic coming-of-age story, like most tales of individual obstacles, aspiration, and achievement, relies implicitly on commonsense notions of familial responsibility and hereditary lineage. Like pro-life rhetorics of personal responsibility, modern family planning celebrations of individual choice, and contemporary social welfare initiatives built on the promise of social reproductive control, her narrative of uplift elides the extent to which—poor, Black, and female—her ostensible ascendance to individual sovereignty occurs via the bio- and necropolitical management of her physical and social life. In this, *Precious* indexes a broader revision in U.S. policies, practices, and discourses of the

Black reproductive, in which the administration of the endangering excess of Black reproductivity simultaneously requires the rationing of Black biological life (*zoe*), the discipline of Black social life (*bios*), and the production of Black social, civil, and physical death as inextricable and dynamic technologies of power within the neoliberal racial state.

As the protagonist and narrator of the film that takes her name as its title, Precious demonstrates how the iconified Black female body is "systematically overdetermined" by the interwoven economies of violence, desire, and capital within which it is embedded.[67] As Precious takes her solitary walk through city streets imagining her own death, her body can be read as what Daphne Brooks would call an "ur-text of alienation": embodied evidence of the dispossessed status of Black subjects within the discourses and structures of white supremacy.[68] At the same time, her "black female corporeality" appears as a peripatetic and ubiquitous site of surplus in the dystopic urban landscape of early neoliberal austerity, an icon of the "superfluous and indispensable … surplus populations [that] fulfill and exceed the demands of capital."[69] If, as Nicole Fleetwood argues, Black female embodiment is characterized within dominant visual regimes as the body in excess, then Precious's fat, hyperreproductive body literalizes the concept of "excess *flesh*"—that is, not only in the sense of fat and muscle, bone and tissue but also as Spillers's "zero degree of social conceptualization."[70] Her body is the materialization of white supremacist racial fantasies of excessive Black corporeality, consumption, and reproduction. These racialized and gendered forms of surplus are constrained from their possible disruption of social norms, and thus rendered palatable for audiences, by her greatest form of excess: "the excessive burden of … suffering."[71] As an illiterate, lonely, HIV-positive survivor of incest at the hands of both her mother and her father, pregnant with her second child by her father at the age of sixteen, Precious evokes a legibility and emotional appeal to the audience that relies on their perception of her as embodying the conditions of "wounded" and "mortified flesh," demonstrating how the conditions through which blackness has become coherent and sympathetic remain affectively, if no longer legally, structured and contained by the logics of chatteldom.[72]

If her excessive misery makes Precious a legible and sympathetic character, her elimination of such excess constitutes the precondition for emergence as an appropriate cinematic heroine to multiracial and largely middle-class audiences. When Precious vomits her stolen fried chicken in the vestibule trash can of her new alternative school, she forcefully purges what Toni Morrison describes as the "funk"—that excessive blackness in behaviors, tastes, language, and phenotypical characteristics that indexes the excess that *is* blackness.[73] This moment of emesis marks the beginning of Precious's aspirations to a different kind of life—one in which her raced, classed, and gendered vulnerability to premature death are mediated by her accession to the biopolitical and disciplinary social regimes within which institutionalized domesticity and proper maternalism are deemed the appropriate vehicles for the protection and preservation of Black life.[74] Her purgative rite of passage is represented as yielding immediate rewards: entrance into the protected space of Ms. Rain's classroom. Following the path of a glowing white light and her light-and-bright instructor (played by Paula Patton), Precious responds to the maternalistic hail of the welfare state. In so doing, she "finds her voice," literally rendering herself legible as a regulated and burdened individual in the pages of her newly acquired journal.

It is, in large part, this spectacle of poor Black pathological misery and the healing power of nominal racial uplift that has caused both *Push* and *Precious* to be trenchantly critiqued as tired and problematic rehashings of Daniel Patrick Moynihan's 1965 report, *The Negro Family: The Case for National Action,* in which high rates of single-female-headed households in Black communities were purported to herald the emergence of a culture of emasculating Black matriarchs, absent fathers, and delinquent, if not criminal, Black male youth.[75] However, as a narrative of Black pathological reprosexuality set against the landscape of Ronald Reagan–era structural adjustment policies and seen through the lens of the early twenty-first century's conjuncture of national racial and socioeconomic polarization and advanced capitalist globalization and militarization, *Precious* reflects the extent to which contemporary contingent state strategies for the resolution of the post-1968 global hegemonic crisis and the post-Keynesian economic shift—austerity politics, carceral systematization, and limited class-based incorporation—require revised systems of rationalization and differentiation capable of justifying the regulation, containment, and abandonment of ever-expanding racialized surplus populations. *Precious* thus demonstrates a significant rearticulation of the familiar discourse: Moynihan's fantasies reach a new culmination point in the particular diseased subculture represented by Precious's mother, Mary. As the archetypal brutally violent, criminally lazy, sexually perverse, and conniving "welfare queen," Mary indexes a new Black matriarch, a chimera of shifting and unstable racial and sexual pathologies, who not only (re)produces sexually and gender-deviant lawless Black masculine thugs but also literally is one herself.

Mary is not only a malingering parasite on and unrepentant con of the welfare system or an unfit parent who vacillates between malign indifference, brutal physical violence, and vicious sexual competition and coercion; she is also an icon of racist fantasies of Black sexual deviance. From our first view of her in a white tank undershirt and front-tied head wrap that invokes in equal parts the popular imagination of the enslaved Black mammy and the unpalatable Black masculinity of hip-hop icon Tupac Shakur, Mary exemplifies how, as Jaime Schultz has argued, the mapping of racial-sexual anxieties about insurgent female masculinity onto the Black female body works alongside and in the service of racial-sexual fantasies around Black women's libidinal voraciousness and sexual availability.[76] Rather than opening the film up to the queer possibilities for a Black maternity performed otherwise, Mo'Nique's Oscar-winning portrayal of Mary cycles through trope after trope of racial-sexual deviance, from Black hypermasculine predation to hypersexual Black femininity, from brutal pathological maternity to abject wounded victimhood, until her character is evacuated of contextual meaning. As the abandoned and repugnant detritus of the post-Keynesian racial capitalist state, she is the product of "a national culture that disavows the configuration of her own racial, gender, class and sexual particularity and a mode of production that fosters her own formation," foreclosed from the processes of racial uplift and incorporation to which Precious, in her journey toward domesticated maternal subjecthood, is granted nominal access. She becomes a cinematic cipher imminently available for the viewer's reading of poor, Black, sexual monstrosity—the lurking vampire of racial capitalism.[77]

In the violent interactions between Precious and Mary, we gain insight into the film's heteropatriarchal rearticulation of the monstrous Black mother. If, as Hartman has argued, bodily availability for injury has long stood as the marker of Black unfree subjectivity and imminent criminal violence has rationalized the Black subject's constitutive availability for preemptive surveillance, punishment, and containment, then Precious and Mary's conjoined life-and-death struggle is a spectacle of the Black female body as a locus of gender-deviant brutal hypersexual masculinity, on the one hand, and excessive, wounded, maternal flesh, on the other. Mary's racialized sexuality marks her not only as "vestibular to culture" but also as the constitutive limit *of* culture—that which exists both *as* and *at* the limit of the human.[78] At the same time, by seeking to stymie the possible lines of flight located in the monstrous excesses that the film coaches us to abjure, *Precious* enacts a foreclosure of the "insurgent ground" that claiming the flesh might engender. The brutal violence to which Mary subjects her daughter demonstrates the dynamic networks of meaning through which Black bodies are both excluded from and necessary to the white heteropatriarchal calculus of normalcy and deviance, morality and perversion. As witnesses to their life-and-death struggle—and to a series of family snapshots of the two in better, more normative days—we measure what Keeling describes as "the value that [blackness] must carry in order to help rationalize a society in which white supremacy and bourgeois culture are inseparable."[79] The bruised and bleeding mother and daughter constitute not just the imminent failure of heteronormativity but also a necessary endangerment to the heteronormative categories of sex and gender that have been integral to the production and regulation of racial hierarchies.

If Precious's entrance into Ms. Rain's classroom marks the beginning of her transformation into an appropriate subject of domestic life, then her late-night departure from her mother's home marks its completion. At the beginning of the film, Precious's realization of her living death is rearticulated as her death wish; by the end, her role within the racial sexual capitalist state is transmogrified from that which should be wiped away, punished, or killed to being part of the domesticated surplus labor pool waiting patiently to be employed on a nonexistent date in her short-lived future. At the time of *Push*'s publication, the early death throes of the welfare state might still have been imperceptible to the novel's audience, leaving them open to the happy ending of disciplined domesticity and regulated labor that Precious is implicitly promised. By the 2008 cinematic release of *Precious,* the turn-of-the-twenty-first-century's historical conjuncture of state abandonment, carceral systematization, and advanced capital's military and economic globalization makes visible to all but the most Pollyanna of viewers Precious's inescapable entanglement in the state's ongoing shell game through which the regulation, containment, and abandonment of ever-expanding racialized surplus populations are justified through promises of incorporation and rationalization and practices of regulation and differentiation, even as the bare value of such surplus populations as policed, criminalized, and warehoused excess is exploited.

The resulting antagonism between Precious's status as living dead and the state's desire to protect and preserve the value of her bare life is sutured, if not actually resolved, through the implicit commentary of the faded billboard visible over Precious's head as she flees her mother's brutal violence with her newborn baby in her arms: in the top-right corner of the frame, an animal control service exhorts onlookers to "spay and neuter" (Figure 6). The cinematic juxtaposition of a homeless, Black teenage mother hunched beneath a larger-than-life reminder to prevent unchecked procreation among animals performs an elision of Black, female, and animal far beyond Douglass's rhetorical reach, revealing the brutal logic of Black reproductivity in the post-Keynesian era: even as the increased surveillance, criminalization, and control of Black reprosexuality are explained through the rhetorics of collective responsibility and social welfare, the preservation and proliferation of Black life continue to depend on the careful administration of Black living death on and through the Black female body. In this cinematic discursive shuttling between hypersexual excess and asexual void, sexual deviance and moral mimicry, the myriad and complex ways of living, loving, and even dying that Black women have forged in excess of this morality tale of vampires and welfare queens, teen moms and perverts, are

Figure 6. Precious leaves home on Christmas Eve; behind her, a painted wall exhorts the public to "spay and neuter." *Precious: Based on the Novel "Push" by Sapphire.* Directed by Lee Daniels. Lionsgate, 2009. Screenshot by author.

relegated outside the frame, unable to be imagined, let alone captured in images.

This space of excess, beyond and illegible to the governing logics of racial neoliberal systems of rationalization, is where Mary remains at the close of Daniels's film. In the end, it is Mary's abjection—her extended confession of alienation, progressive illness, and criminal culpability to Precious's racially illegible social worker, Mrs. Weiss—that distinguishes the conditions of bare life within which Precious survives as a victory for the audience to celebrate at the end of the film. Of course, as Edwards astutely argues, the containment of meaning in cultural production is rarely complete, even in this cinematic spectacle of Black feminine abjection.[80] In her accounting for herself to the agents of the state—agents of biopolitical management and necropolitical taxonomies, of welfare provisions and carceral surveillance—Mary poses a final question that remains surplus to the confession's function of categorization and containment, unable to be resolved, contained, or dismissed through the film's narratives of racial uplift by access to nominal domesticated survival. "Who was gonna love me?" she asks. In pausing to meditate on Mary's question, my intent is not to suggest the ameliorative or liberating qualities of love; rather, it is to underscore the conditions within which Mary's question becomes unanswerable, incomprehensible, the fugitive thought of the criminal subject. In asking it, Mary points to the structures of abandonment, the systems reliant on the expropriation of Black biological life and social death as the excess to be warehoused, criminalized, and sacrificed to maintain the crumbling material and ideological coherence of late neoliberal racial capitalism. She implicitly condemns the logics and grammars within which her sustenance, affective capacities, and sexual desires are incommensurate with and incidental to the workings of the state, in which her inevitable demise and her daughter's bare survival are as much the necessary conditions for and effect of the current mode of production and mode of life as the management of, education around, and medicalization of Black women's reproduction was a half century earlier.

Reproductive Control, Reproductive Freedom, Reproductive Justice

In 1979 the Committee for Abortion Rights and Against Sterilization Abuse (CARASA) published its first pamphlet, *Women under Attack*. In it, CARASA articulated a new approach to theorizing the politics of reproduction that sought to address the interlocking structures through which poor women and women of color's reproductive options were constrained, criminalized, and pathologized—a paradigm that it named "reproductive freedom." As the pamphlet defined it,

> Reproductive freedom means the freedom to have as well as to not have children. Policies that restrict women's right to have and raise children—through forced sterilization or the denial of adequate welfare benefits—are directly related to policies that compel women to have children, on the view that this is their primary human function. Both kinds of policies constitute reproduction control by the state and affect the rights of all women insofar as women are the producers of children.[81]

As an organization that centered an analysis of race, class, and gender as interconnected relations of power that shaped the conditions of reproduction, CARASA prioritized questions of procreative autonomy while also articulating its understanding of reproductive freedom as including a holistic set of concerns that shaped the conditions of reproduction, including welfare rights, subsidized childcare, public education, wage equality, workplace safety, and the elimination of sterilization abuse.[82] On the surface, the list of key issues outlined by CARASA bears a remarkable resemblance to that outlined by the Myrdals in *Crisis in the Population Question.* Yet, in contradistinction to the Myrdals' understanding of social welfare as an instrument for social engineering, CARASA conceived of state-supported social services as mechanisms not of modernization or incorporation but of ensuring social justice in the face of racial capitalism and heteropatriarchy. In so doing, the organizers constructed a vital political model for freedom that demanded individual autonomy and interrogated the collective social conditions upon which true freedom would rely. During the time the organizers collaborated, CARASA was faced with a disagreement over the role of sexuality in its political mission. While many of the organizers understood lesbian reproductive rights to be part of its larger agenda, others balked at the demand that sexual freedom more generally be central to its analysis of reproduction.[83] By 1983 the conflict had fractured the group, which dissolved soon after.

I offer this history of CARASA as one example of reproductive political organizing in the late twentieth century because it illustrates the possibilities—however short-lived—for thinking about Black reproductivity through the logic of freedom. I dwell on it to acknowledge the difficulties of articulating a political model of reproductivity capable of addressing the complex interaction of procreation, labor, and sexuality that make up Black reproductivity. While CARASA's platform of reproductive freedom has innumerable resonances with contemporary political frameworks of reproductive justice, its emphasis on freedom, as defined through collective responsibility, offers a provocative alternative to current human rights–based models for reproductive politics. In this model of reproductive freedom, framed by the shared project of a collective structuring of life's conditions, what space might be made available for those positioned as and at the limit of the human? Would a child like Precious or a woman like Mary find a form of collectivity that enabled their freedom? Or would the stigma of sexual deviance by which they are defined as poor, Black, and dying exceed the boundaries of the group's identification with a version of reproductivity in which the sexual remained peripheral?

In posing these questions, I return to the imperative with which this chapter began: to understand the connections across time periods and political movements that mark out the conditions for Black reproductive control and the possibilities for Black reproductive freedom. If the constraints on Black reproductive freedom emerge from not only the sexual conservatism of the New Right and the bureaucratic totalitarianism of modern liberal democracy under racial capitalism but also the normative investments of the radical left, then it is also the case that these points of friction—of contradiction and conflict—are where the leverage to achieve new models of freedom might best be applied. It is in those ephemeral, undecidable, and crisis-laden moments that we must turn to imagine an alternative model for Black reproductivity that is capable of producing a freedom for which we choose to fight.

Coda

Lest We Forget

Twenty-five years after *The Liberation of Aunt Jemima* was first displayed at Rainbow Sign, Betye Saar returned to the theme of Aunt Jemima—or at least, Aunt Jemima returned to haunt Saar's work. Between 1997 and 1998, Saar created a collection of more than twenty vintage washboards, to which she either adhered black-and-white photographs of Black women at work or attached brightly colored, gun-toting mammy figurines of various styles, eras, and sizes. The resulting series, *Workers + Warriors—The Return of Aunt Jemima,* brought together the meditations on "the endurance and dignity of memory" that had long preoccupied her "ancestral boxes" and the incitement to radical, liberatory change that had driven her more "political" series, such as *Exploding the Myth.*[1] In this sense, like many of the other contemporary narratives of Black unfreedom at the center of this book, *Workers + Warriors* was a dialectical aesthetic project that emerged at the conjuncture of the ethics of memory and the imperatives of the future to offer up to its audience both a revised theory of history and a radical theory of change.

When asked why she had returned to Aunt Jemima in her work, Saar instead explained why Aunt Jemima had returned to her: while liberated from slavery, Aunt Jemima remained a resistant captive to the renewed entailments of racial capitalism; her liberation was ongoing and unfinished. At the end of the twentieth century, Saar argued, the discourses and structures of racism not only had persisted but also were in the process of being rearticulated within a neoliberal mode of commodification that enabled the consumption of racial difference without accountability for the fatal hierarchies of power within which such difference remained embedded.[2] In this moment of renewed crisis, she explained,

> Aunt Jemima returns with newer, bigger weapons and a tougher attitude. She symbolizes the painful ancestral memories of the middle passage, of slavery, of Jim Crow, of segregation, and of

> continuing racism. Aunt Jemima is back with a vengeance and her message: America, clean up your act![3]

Within her explanation, Saar exposes the tensions between past and present, remembering and rebelling, which are at the heart of the series. In one register, Saar's washboards make visceral the painful history of Black women's productive and reproductive labor—the picking of cotton, the weaving of cloth, the washing of clothes—by evoking sensory memories or imaginations of aching backs, knuckles rubbed raw, and bruised knees. At the same time, she once again reconstitutes the domestic—fragmented, violent, vexed—as a generative place for the political work of Black liberation: a place where, rather than clean for white people, Black reproductive workers from days long past could be reanimated to demand that white America come clean. In the final pages of this book, then, I take up Saar's dialectic, turning to two of the assemblages within the *Workers + Warriors* series in order to lay out a few last thoughts on the reproduction of memory, freedom, and survival within the context of a Black feminist political and cultural project.

There is only one piece in the *Workers + Warriors* series that incorporates both photographic image and mammy memorabilia. *Lest We Forget: The Strength of Tears, the Fragility of Smiles, the Fierceness of Love* (1998) is a tripartite assemblage of three washboards (Figure 7). On the left, the sepia-stained image of a woman hunches over a washboard in a tub, surrounded by the implements of her trade. Her figure is barely discernable against the darkened zinc of the washboard's grooves; her face is pointed down, averted from the camera's lens; and her hands support her body, resting on the tub's edge. On the right, a rough wooden cutout of a smiling and round-faced mammy is the toiling launderer's mirror with a difference. Clad in a brightly colored and patterned kerchief and dress, she holds a semiautomatic machine gun in both hands. Pasted on her white apron is a red-and-white sticker reading, "Liberate Aunt Jemima." The two side panels are joined by a larger washboard. Ghosted on its corrugated surface is a faded but familiar print of a slave ship's enslaved cargo, confined head to foot in the ship's hold. The washboards' wooden supports serve as Saar's writing surface; framing each image are words stenciled in black print onto the upper and lower horizontals of the washboards' wooden frames. Read from top to bottom and left to right, the three panels read, "LEST WE FORGET . . . THE STRENGTH OF TEARS OF THOSE WHO TOILED . . . THE

FRAGILITY OF SMILES OF STRANGERS LOST AT SEA . . . THE FIERCENESS OF LOVE." Under the final frame, a ribbon of print runs, declaring that "EXTREME TIMES CALL FOR EXTREME MEASURES."

While assembled of nontraditional materials, *Lest We Forget* is composed in the form of a classic triptych: the three panels can be read separately as individual scenes but collectively constitute a larger and longer narrative. In place of the ecclesiastical depictions of Christ's life, death, and resurrection that populated triptychs of the fifteenth and sixteenth centuries, Saar offers what Arlene Raven has described as a "culturally subterranean . . . allegory long absent from the secular and sacred historical record"—a haunted genealogy of estrangement, of ephemeral joys lost, of lives at risk of being forgotten.[4] In this story of Black women's historical unfreedom and ongoing struggle for freedom, the ghostly memory of

Figure 7. Betye Saar, *Lest We Forget; The Strength of Tears, The Fragility of Smiles, The Fierceness of Love,* 1998. Mixed media on vintage washboard, 22¾ x 30¼ x 2 inches, signed. Collection of the Norton Museum of Art, West Palm Beach, Fla. Courtesy of the artist, Michael Rosenfeld Gallery LLC, New York, N.Y., and Roberts Projects, Los Angeles, Calif. Copyright Betye Saar.

chattel slavery and the Middle Passage functions as the central "site of synthesis," indexing the brutal expropriation of Black bodies, labor, and lives in the service of racial capitalism and the ongoing dehumanization and objectification from which Black women have fought and labored to liberate themselves.[5] Saar's resignification of the art form thus no longer imparts a tale of the miracle of messianic transcendence but instead is a memorial to and meditation on the double-edged practices and possibilities of transformation: the violent transfiguration of people into property and the as-yet incomplete process through which, in the afterlife of captivity, the formerly enslaved and their descendants have created their own freedom.

As in *The Liberation of Aunt Jemima,* Saar's memorial to those who work and fight for freedom locates the sphere of political transformation in the realm of the reproductive domestic. The left panel's portrayal of a working laundrywoman from the early twentieth century posits the quotidian hard labor of Black women domestic workers as inseparable from slavery's thoroughgoing permeation of the intimate spheres of body and home. Her unexpected pairing of "strength" and "tears" recasts a feminized affective signifier as a form of political strength, while her invocation of "those who toiled" recognizes that in the wake of emancipation, "women's success or frustrations in influencing the character of domestic labor would define how meaningful freedom would be."[6]

If the left panel engages the question of labor (work), the right panel raises the imminent specter of revolution (war). Despite her high-tech weaponry, the wooden mammy's bright-red smile evokes the Aunt Jemima of twenty-five years earlier, reminding viewers that the Black domestic is still a site of violence and opposition and that the women who have so often come to stand in as symbols of its imagined regime of raced and gendered order still joyfully enlist as domestic soldiers in its undoing. More than two decades later, in the face of new crises and opportunities, the descriptive phrase "the liberation of Aunt Jemima" has become an imperative: liberate Aunt Jemima. As viewers, we are no longer allowed simply to watch the domestic revolution underway; each of us who bears witness has been tasked with the project of liberation. At the same time, however, *Lest We Forget* pairs the exhortation that "extreme times call for extreme heroines" with a recollection of the fierceness of the love that Black women have exercised for their born and found kin—a love that refuses to be erased or recast by nostalgic white supremacist fables of nurturing Black surrogate mothers.

The genealogy of tears and toil, joy and loss, and love and liberation in *Lest We Forget* offers a visceral visual reminder of the "importance of miniscule movements, [shards] of hope, scraps of food, the interrupted dreams of freedom found in those spaces deemed devoid of full human life."[7] As such, it resonates with the central claim of this project: that neither the history of chattel slavery nor the ongoing political project of Black liberation can be extricated from the material-discursive assemblage that is the Black reproductive. Like Ursa Corregidora's blues, Saar's reproduction of the experiences of those who came before her is an iteration with a difference, a retelling of the story that enables a different, freer, ending. In this, like each of the neoslave narratives in this text, Saar's guard against forgetting becomes, concomitantly, an instrument by which to envision present and future possibilities of freedom.

• • •

Visually, Saar's *Gonna Lay Down My Burden* (1998) seems as compositionally simple as *Lest We Forget* is complex: A Black woman in a dark dress and headscarf and a white apron—a domestic worker—looks directly out from the washboard's uneven surface, unsmiling and unflinching (Figure 8). Her expression is hard to read. She appears to be caught midtask: Her right hand rests on the ironing board in front of her, thumb against the shirttail of the white man's shirt she is ironing. Her upper body leans forward toward the camera, other arm cocked back, while the pressing iron in her left hand remains suspended a few inches above the board. Over her head, the text on the washboard's top horizontal reads, "We was mostly 'bout survival." Just below it, another sticker commands us to liberate Aunt Jemima. The phrase from which the piece takes its name is stenciled along the bottom horizontal with neither punctuation nor capitalization: "gonna lay down my burden." While the majority of pieces in the *Workers + Warriors* series have been given a sepia wash, *Gonna Lay Down My Burden* is cast in shades of black and gray; the only splashes of color in the piece are the gold foil sticker with its red block letters and the orange-and-black butterfly wings affixed to a corner of the washboard's corrugated zinc surface.

The apparent simplicity of *Gonna Lay Down My Burden* is deceptive. The photographic image itself is enigmatic: its close cropping makes it nearly impossible to determine the setting or the woman's status—enslaved or emancipated, washerwoman, housekeeper, or maid—eluding any attempts to put things in their "proper" place. The woman's face is unreadable as she gazes back at viewers. Is she demanding an ethical accounting for the history of subordination and dispossession, the years of intimate violences, the freedom suspended beyond the reach of the frame? Her expression could be perceived as anger, resignation, or simply exhaustion. Is she looking out with a sense of weariness, or shared struggle? Like her facial expression, the iron in her tight grasp resists easy interpretation: held at the ready, it could be used as either domestic tool or potential weapon, and it reminds the viewer that in the context of chattel slavery and its ongoing afterlife, the domestic is at once a geographic locus of productive and reproductive labor as well as a terrain structured by the raced and gendered vulnerability to exploitation, dispossession, and violence. Frozen in the image, leaning toward the viewer in a pose of imminent action, the woman might have been be surprised into stillness, caught between one unknown action

Figure 8. Betye Saar, *Gonna Lay Down My Burden,* 1998. Mixed media on vintage washboard, 24 x 12½ x 2 inches, signed. Private Collection. Courtesy of the artist, Michael Rosenfeld Gallery LLC, New York, N.Y., and Roberts Projects, Los Angeles, Calif. Copyright Betye Saar.

and the next. To describe *Gonna Lay Down My Burden* as an artistic rendering of resistance acknowledges how this piece, like all of Saar's assemblages related to Aunt Jemima, repels the racist romanticizing of complaisant domestics or cheerful mammies. At least as significant, however, the deceptively simply piece resists easy interpretation or the ascription of meaning. There are no gun-toting mammies or declarations of war here. Instead, like many of the cultural texts discussed in this book, it demands modes of reading that are attentive to the contingent and the undecidable.

Take, for instance, the words stenciled on the bottom horizontal, below the woman's image: "Gonna lay down my burden." Commonly used in Black vernacular English, the phrase is also an alternate title and the opening lyric of a gospel song more commonly known as "Down by the Riverside." Originally a sung spiritual in enslaved Black communities, "Down by the Riverside" is frequently recorded and was a popular protest song for the civil rights and antiwar movements. While there are innumerable different versions, the most common includes three verses and a chorus.

> I'm gonna lay down my burden, down by the riverside
> Down by the riverside, down by the riverside
> Gonna lay down my burden, down by the riverside
> I'm gonna study war no more
>
> CHORUS:
> I ain't gonna study war no more, study war no more
> Ain't gonna study war no more
> I ain't gonna study war no more, study war no more
> Ain't gonna study war no more

Read literally, in the context of chattel slavery's reliance on dispossession and dehumanization to coercively maintain the hyperexploitation of labor, the song's allusions to the laying down of heavy burdens and crossing of rivers reference a series of material acts through which enslaved Black people emancipated themselves and escaped to the North.

Read together, however, the three verses of "Down by the Riverside" also anticipate a time of individual and collective spiritual rebirth. In subsequent verses, the singer vows to "put on my long white robes" and to "lay down my sword and shield," invoking the ritual of baptism and the advent of an age of peace, respectively. The gospel song's biblical source is found in Isaiah 2:4 (King James Version): "And he shall judge among the nations, and shall rebuke many people: and they shall beat their swords into plowshares, and their spears into pruninghooks: nation shall not lift up sword against nation, neither shall they learn war anymore." With its description of the conversion of the weapons of war into tools of husbandry and the end of strife between nations, Isaiah 2:4 can be read as a utopian promise. In the context of chattel slavery and continuing structures of Black unfreedom, however, the vow of the enslaved and subjugated to "lay down sword and shield" need not be read as a commitment to Christlike love or forgiveness in the face of brutal violence and terrorism. Instead, it is helpful to interpret the song's refrain to "study war no more" in the context of Sora Han's astute observation that "the United States is not at war. The United States *is* war."[8] The promise of the spiritual to "study war no more," then, is no meek acquiescence to the modes and agents of racial domination but a political and ethical rejection of the ongoing structures of brutality and terror, displacement and dispossession, that structure the U.S. racial and settler colonial state.

Furthermore, the book of Isaiah is composed of a series of prophecies foretelling the coming of the Messiah to the new Jerusalem. Within Christian traditions, Isaiah 2:4 is interpreted as prophesying an end time yet to come, in which the Messiah returns to distribute justice, redeem the subjugated, and usher them into the Kingdom of God. With its repeated refrain of laying down burdens and its invocation of messianic time, "Down by the Riverside" is a sonic performance of what I have referred to in the previous pages as the future anterior tense of Black liberation. As I have argued throughout, to engage in a politics of the future anterior requires the letting go—or laying down—of existing stable identities, presentist pragmatic stratagems, or current political certainties to surrender to the undecidable, the contradictory, or the contingent as the ethical precondition for a future possibility of freedom.

Where in *Gonna Lay Down My Burden* can the viewer locate the trace of the future anterior? We might turn to the slightly creased and tattered butterfly nearly hidden in the corner of the washboard. Its bright, outstretched wings, incongruous against the somber interior scene, index an imminent fugitivity: a line of flight from the "degraded present" to an ephemeral and evanescent freedom yet to fully manifest. We might also hear it in the imperative hail of the red-and-gold sticker to "liberate Aunt Jemima," a blunt reminder that our future freedom relies on the ongoing work to imagine new ways of being, even—or especially—from within regimes of raced and gendered subjugation. We might even glimpse it in the gaze of the woman poised over her ironing board, whose carefully composed face holds an air of waiting—whether patiently or expectantly—for something yet to arrive.

Throughout this book, I have argued that Black freedom emerges in the moment of crisis, the instance of aporia, the moment of jouissance, as the radical alterity of Black captivity, objectification, and dispossession. Such a claim is based on the understanding that freedom is neither external to nor a fugitive from systems of unfreedom; rather, it is Black unfreedom's effaced condition of possibility, the impossible experience and future-yet-to-be-imagined that surfaces to answer to the call of that which exceeds racial captivity's calculus of human and nonhuman, living and dead, free and unfree. In this sense, the practice of freedom comes into its own, however contingently, through material-discursive acts of reproduction gone awry—that is, from the fissures and gaps that open up in the track of Black unfreedom's ongoing différantial reiteration. It is this track that I have heretofore called "the trace of Black reproductivity." In concluding, however, I would like to entertain a different framing for that possibility of Black freedom that takes form in the suspended moment—a framing that borrows from Saar's own. "We was mostly 'bout survival," the dark text at the top of the washboard states baldly. In the context of a Black reproductive feminist politics, what is the relationship between survival and liberation? I suggest that when read through such a lens, survival in and of itself can be a liberatory practice.

• • •

In her 1978 poem "Litany for Survival," Audre Lorde describes Black feminism in the face of the death-dealing politics of racism and heteropatriarchy as a reproductive practice of the future anterior: "seeking a now that can breed / futures / like bread in our children's mouths." Yet Lorde knows that the parent's quest for a future freedom is without guarantees; rather, appearing in a flash in the moment of crisis—"this instant and this triumph"—the "future" names the fleeting possibility that emerges in the face of impossibility. "We were never meant to survive," she reminds us, twice.[9] This double-edged quality of survival—the spiritual and political sustenance of the future, on the one hand, and the radical impossibility of Black female life, on the other—is precisely the kind of radical undecidability that this book has sought to trace, in order to argue that even as the regimes and discourses that sustain Black reproductive subjugation are reiterated, revised, and reshaped, those ephemeral, aporetic instances of radical possibility—the possibility of freedom—also are continuously created anew.

In 1986, when asked to speak on "Sisterhood and Survival" for a conference on the Black woman writer in the African diaspora, Lorde takes a different approach. Survival, she suggests, is one name for the collective practice of freedom, a working toward "a future in which all people across the world [are] free."[10] A project of global freedom, of course, demands attention to the specifically entwined politics of race and gender, sexuality and class, that shape the conditions of possibility for Black women; indeed, as part of the Combahee River Collective, Lorde had argued that "if Black women were free, it would mean that everyone else would have to be free since our freedom would necessitate the destruction of all the systems of oppression."[11] Yet it also demands acting on the recognition "that we are not alone. . . . We are sisters, and our survival is mutual."[12] As a collective practice rooted in Black feminist politics of freedom, Lorde's concept of survival requires not only that we learn, as Erica Edwards suggests, "to imagine ever more ways of surviving, together, this sojourn" but also that we understand that the act of mutual survival is, concomitantly, a practice of "struggling," together, "for the future."[13]

The heart of this project lies in the abiding belief that in the never-ending crisis that is the afterlife of chattel slavery, it is only at those points of collision and convergence—the "split second between" brand name and Black bombshell, maternity and violence, making love and making die, unbroken skin and sexlessness—that the necessary and impossible means of imagining a different future, together, emerge. It is my hope that by seeking that instant of collision, that moment of convergence, where the politics and practice of survival meet the future possibility of Black freedom, we might be able to reproduce—to proliferate—a vision of the future that constructs, *right here and now,* ways to make life in the face of our constitutive vulnerabilities; tools for sharing our histories, our present precarious lives, and our future possibilities; and the means of refusing the quotidian wearing away at the fabric of our political imagination. In short, it is a belief that it is just such a politic that holds, at its core, the possibility of a freedom that encompasses us all.

Acknowledgments

It is a truism among those who know me that I am not an easy person to help, which makes it all the more wondrous that so many people have generously supported and guided me at every stage of what has been an unusually long process from idea to publication. From this project's beginning, Ruth Wilson Gilmore has served as mentor, reader, interlocutor, and friend. She continues to be a role model, demonstrating every day what it means to make through our labor the world we want to live in. José Davíd Saldivar shared with me his professional wisdom, his rigorous and original mind, and a belief that literature offers an irreplaceable window through which to make sense of what we experience and that for which we have no name. Shannon H. Jackson has always believed in my work and challenged my thinking.

During my time at the University of California, Berkeley, I received support from the Graduate Opportunity Program and the Ford Foundation Fellowship Program. The Marilyn Yarborough Dissertation Fellowship at Kenyon College provided me with much-needed time and space to think and to write. Since arriving at the University of California, San Diego, my research and writing toward this project have been supported by the Hellman Foundation, the University of California Humanities Institute, a Faculty Career Development Award, and two research grants from the UCSD Academic Senate. A Sophia Smith Collection Research Travel Grant enabled me to conduct additional research that greatly enriched the final manuscript.

For their help and guidance navigating archival material and permissions, I am grateful to Amy Hague and Kathleen Nutter at the Sophia Smith Collection and College Archives, Jack Eckert and the collections staff in the Center for the History of Medicine at Harvard University's Countway Medical Library, the staff of the Library of Congress Manuscript Division, and Jack Robertson and Anna Berkes at the Jefferson Library at Monticello. During my time at the Jefferson Library, Cinder Stanton and Leni Sorenson generously took time to share their knowledge of all things related to the enslaved African American community at Monticello; Cinder's willingness to open up her extensive personal papers to me was an unexpected and precious boon. Amy Hague at Smith College, Marjorie Van Cura and Dan Munn at the Michael Rosenfeld Gallery, and Jacob Vasa at Roberts Projects provided invaluable help acquiring images for publication. Closer to home, Peter Devine and the interlibrary loan desk at the UC San Diego Library hunted down and acquired reel after reel of microfilm on my behalf.

I have been happy to learn that conducting research need not be a solitary travail. A number of people have hosted and entertained me when I have been far from home. Asha and Shama Nadkarni and Jason Moralee have given me a home away from home in Northampton for as long as I've needed one, always with good cheer and often with very little notice. The Kaplan/Lowry family—Samantha, Matt, Sophia, Justin, and Scarlett—have provided a resting place and amazing family time in Boston. Lini Chakravorty and Leila and Narayan Neti fed and entertained me during lonely days in Charlottesville, and Felicia Lynch and Cheryl Robinson not only listened patiently to my research tales and conundrums but also provided directions, bus passes, and hot dinners during my time in Washington, D.C. My research assistants, Marilisa Navarro, Kai Small, and Maria Célleri, each helped make this book what it has become.

As a graduate student at Berkeley, I was lucky to have a student community that enriched my thinking and practice at every stage. Through discussion and study, protests and pro-seminars, Priya Kandaswamy, Kate Drabinski, Renu Cappelli, Jared Sexton, Frank Wilderson, Matt Richardson, and Omise'eke Natasha Tinsley each helped make me a stronger scholar, activist, and colleague. The programs in American Studies and Women's and Gender Studies at Kenyon College were my academic home for two years. I thank Peter Rutkoff and Laurie Finke for inviting me to join in their pedagogical project, and Ted Mason and Ric Sheffield for their unconditional commitment to my success. In the woods of Ohio, I found true treasures: Julian Sheppard coached me through my writing woes with patience, humor, and skill; Asha Nadkarni and Mrinalini Chakravorty were the best of friends and comrades, and intellectual interlocutors without compare. During my time at the University of Illinois, Mimi Nguyen, Fiona Ngo, Soo Ah Kwan, and Ruth Nicole Brown were not just a writing group but a respite from the storm. Karen Flynn, Rayvon Fouché, and Sharra Vostral opened their lives and homes to me on innumerable occasions; Sherie Randolph and Christopher Freeburg provided the perfect mix of hilarity, compassion, brilliance, and bracing reality checks; and Siobhan Somerville was, as she always is, a model for intellectual and political ethicality, offering astute counsel and a kind ear whenever needed.

I was lucky to find another intellectual and political home at the University of California, San Diego. Yen Le Espiritu, Curtis Marez, Shelley Streeby, Kalindi Vora, and Roshanak Kheshti generously read my work and shared their own. Natalia Molina and Adria Imada offered advice on matters large and small. Dayo Gore, my colleague in all things, has worn every hat I have asked of her with humor, patience, and a remarkable amount of understated wisdom.

Of course, any professor knows that we learn not only from our teachers and colleagues but also from our students. Many of the critical concepts and arguments in this book were first explored in my undergraduate seminars on the theory and politics of Black women's writing at Kenyon College and the University of Illinois, Urbana-Champaign, and in my graduate seminars on gender, sexuality, and race at UCSD. I also have had the honor of working alongside remarkable PhD students in Black gender and sexuality studies—Bayan Abusneineh, Maisam Alomar, LeKeisha Hughes, Lea Johnson, Tara-Lynne Pixley, Kai Small, Tezeru Teshome, and Xach Williams—whose own incisive analyses of my thinking and key texts have pushed me to think harder and anew, and made this book immeasurably better.

The rich intellectual terrain of Southern California provides a region-wide community of interlocutors. At the UC Humanities Research Institute's 2012 Research Seminar, Between Life & Death: Necropolitics in the Era of Late Capitalism, Grace Kyungwon Hong, Jodi Kim, Curtis Marez, Andrea Smith, Christine Hong, Alexander Hirsch, Lindsay Smith, and Thu-Huong Nguyen-Vo provided stirring conversation and critical feedback, enriching my thinking in relation to not only this project but also the politics of knowledge production more generally. The amazing women of the LOUD women of color writing collective—among them Macarena Gómez-Barris, Maylei Blackwell, Jayna Brown, Aisha Finch, Mishuana Goeman, Yogita Goyal, Arlene Keizer, Jodi Kim, Shana Redmond, Deb Vargas, and Tiffany Willoughby-Herard—read much of this manuscript at various stages and judiciously doled out staunch encouragement, nuanced critical feedback, and necessary reality checks in perfect measure. Grace Hong was not only first to suggest to me that this book might have a home at the University of Minnesota Press but also was a careful, engaged, and patient reader of my work. Sarah Haley has been a model of rigorous, ethical, and inspiring scholarship and a consistent advocate for the importance of this project. Erica R. Edwards and Dayo Gore read much of this book—sometimes more than once, often at short notice, and always with the perfect combination of generous spirits and rigorous eyes. The Black Studies Project at UCSD has been a source of infinite inspiration and motivation.

I have been blessed to have a family that has supported and nurtured my mind, body, and spirit along the way. My mother, Felicia Lynch, and father, Peter Kaplan, first taught me the meaning of justice and its unquantifiable value. My sister, Samantha Kaplan, was my first and always best friend; I am lucky we get to navigate the murky waters of academic politics together. Kay Hanson has been there since the beginning and has always offered her love and support. Diana Hayman was the first to suggest that I might be a scholar someday. Ari Wohlfeiler has been a political compass since we first met. Renu Cappelli's gentle spirit, humor, wisdom, and delicious food have sustained me for just as long. For more than fifteen years, Asha Nadkarni has been a serendipitous soulmate in all things intellectual and personal.

The process of completing this book has been far from quick and less than ideal; for quite a while, it became difficult to tell where the project ended and "real" life began. During those long, murky years, I was lucky to have people who stepped in with infinite compassion, hot meals, and the unshakable belief that things would get better—Arianne Miller, Dayo Gore, Roshy Kheshti, Sara Cassetti, Asha Nadkarni, Jenny Kelly, Marisol LeBron, Curtis Marez, Shelley Streeby, and Janet Jaffe. And in the end, Michelle Boyd not only coached me through the interminable process of letting go but also helped me rediscover the beauty and bravery of being both a writer and a badass. Without her, I cannot say for certain that this book would ever have reached print; my gratitude is only increased by the firm knowledge that she would vociferously disagree. My editor, Jason Weidemann, has remained steadfastly in my corner with remarkable patience, persistence, and generosity.

In the end, my deepest thanks are reserved for Kirstie A. Dorr. Not only has she read every word, listened to every argument, hashed through every conundrum, and pushed me to return to the page when I was ready to give it all up, but she has been an interlocutor, inspiration, and comrade for longer than this project has existed. Without her insights, her political and intellectual acuity, and her unshakable faith in the book that I was writing and the scholar that I am always working to become, this book, and my world, would be exponentially less.

Notes

Introduction

1. Krissah Thompson, "For Decades They Hid Jefferson's Relationship with Her. Now Monticello Is Making Room for Sally Hemings," *Washington Post,* February 19, 2017; Michael Cottman, "Historians Uncover Slave Quarters of Sally Hemings at Thomas Jefferson's Monticello," *NBC News,* July 3, 2017, https://www.nbcnews.com.

2. Gayatri Chakravorty Spivak tells us, "When one decides to speak of aporias, one is haunted by the ghost of the undecidable in every decision." The experience of aporia is both impossible and undecidable; not simply "a logical or philosophical problem like a contradiction, a dilemma, a paradox, [or] an antimony," it is that impossible experience that can neither be crossed nor remained in. Yet, as Spivak reminds us, this impossible experience is the condition of possibility of deciding and, therefore, the condition for the emergence of the ethical and the political. Gayatri Chakravorty Spivak, "A Moral Dilemma," *Theoria: A Journal of Social and Political Theory,* no. 96 (2000): 105–6.

3. Maria Mies, *Patriarchy and Accumulation on a World Scale: Women in the International Division of Labour* (London: Zed Books), x. While Mies is speaking specifically of the critical function of gender in the structuring of capitalism, Marxist feminists are not alone in observing the articulation of the economic with structures of race, gender, and sexuality in the formation of modern nation-states and the relations between them. Cedric Robinson's use of the term *racial capitalism* to describe how "racialism . . . permeate[d] the social structures emergent from capitalism" is exemplary of such an approach in the field of Black studies and has been formative to my own thinking. More recently, analytical approaches such as queer of color critique have elaborated an understanding of capital as "a formation constituted by discourses of race, gender, and sexuality" that both subtends and disorganizes heteronormativity. Cedric J. Robinson, *Black Marxism: The Making of the Black Radical Tradition* (Chapel Hill: University of North Carolina Press, 2000), 2; Roderick Ferguson, *Aberrations in Black: Toward a Queer of Color Critique* (Minneapolis: University of Minnesota Press, 2004), 11.

4. Ruth Wilson Gilmore, "Fatal Couplings of Power and Difference: Notes on Racism and Geography," *Professional Geographer* 54, no. 1 (2002): 16.

5. Here, I am thinking of blackness's multiplicity in resonance with Christina Sharpe's reading of "the wake" as the metaphor for blackness in the aftermath of slavery and the Middle Passage. Sharpe engages slavery's wake as "the track behind the ship, the disturbed flow (behind a body in motion/air or water)," a "state of wakefulness, consciousness," the "watch or vigil held beside the body of someone who has died," and "grief, celebration, memory, and those among the living who, through ritual, mourn their passing and celebrate their life." Thus, even as the wake of slavery continues to produce Black trauma and death, those of us who live "in, into, and through the wake" maintain an insistence on Black life. How we trace this potential for the engendering of new modes of thinking Black life amid the constraints of Black subjugation is one of the central political questions of this book. Christina Sharpe, *In the Wake: On Blackness and Being* (Durham, N.C.: Duke University Press, 2016), 3–11.

6. Lindon Barrett, *Blackness and Value: Seeing Double* (New York: Cambridge University Press, 2009), 17. Here I draw upon Barrett's argument that the discursive boundary between oppositional categories such as white and Black is both a site for and a result of the production of value. By positing blackness as the enabling term existing as and at the boundary of (white) humanity rather than whiteness's constructed Other, I seek to extend Barrett's useful critical interrogation of the binary logics of racialized differential value.

7. Saidiya V. Hartman, *Scenes of Subjection: Terror, Slavery, and Self-Making in Nineteenth-Century America,* Race and American Culture (New York: Oxford University Press, 1997), 57.

8. Mary Pat Brady, *Extinct Lands, Temporal Geographies: Chicana Literature and the Urgency of Space* (Durham, N.C.: Duke University Press, 2002), 52.

9. See, for example, Eric Williams, *Capitalism and Slavery* (Chapel Hill: University of North Carolina Press, 1994); Walter Johnson, *Soul By Soul: Life inside the Antebellum Slave Market* (Cambridge, Mass.: Harvard University Press, 1999); Stephanie Smallwood, *Saltwater Slavery: A Middle Passage from Africa to American Diaspora* (Cambridge, Mass.: Harvard University Press, 2007); and Edward Baptist, *The Half Has Never Been Told: Slavery and the Making of American Capitalism* (New York: Basic Books, 2014).

10. Cheryl I. Harris, "Whiteness as Property," in *Critical Race Theory: The Key Writings That Formed the Movement,* ed. Kimberlé Crenshaw et al. (New York: New Press, 1995), 279.

11. Karl Marx, *Capital,* vol. 1, *A Critique of Political Economy* (New York: Pelican Books, 1976), 8–10.

12. Frank Wilderson, *Red, White & Black: Cinema and the Structure of U.S. Antagonisms* (Durham, N.C.: Duke University Press, 2010), 18.

13. In this, I am following a path laid out by a body of theoretical work on blackness and modernity that includes Paul Gilroy, *The Black Atlantic: Modernity and*

Double-Consciousness (Cambridge, Mass.: Harvard University Press, 1993); and Hartman, *Scenes of Subjection.* Robinson reminds us that while racism's roots may lie in the "'internal' relations" of precapitalist Europe, its integral function increased dramatically under capitalism's production of power through the mobilization of difference. As "the development, organization, and expansion of capitalist society pursued essentially racial directions," he argues, "so too did social ideology." Robinson, *Black Marxism,* 2.

14. C. B. Macpherson, *The Political Theory of Possessive Individualism: Hobbes to Locke* (Oxford: Clarendon, 1962). See also Grace Kyungwon Hong, *The Ruptures of American Capital: Women of Color Feminism and the Culture of Immigrant Labor* (Minneapolis: University of Minnesota Press, 2006), 3–7.

15. Harris, "Whiteness as Property," 279.

16. Here I am following both Patricia Williams and Hong's reading of Williams to elucidate the workings of racialized dispossession. See Patricia J. Williams, *The Alchemy of Race and Rights* (Cambridge, Mass.: Harvard University Press, 1991), 219.

17. Gilmore, "Fatal Couplings," 16.

18. Hortense Spillers's conception of blackness's vestibularity is foundational to this project, as it is to much of the Black studies scholarship with which I am in conversation. While Spillers's most frequently cited reference to the vestibular is found in her renowned 1987 essay, "Mama's Baby, Papa's Maybe: An American Grammar Book," an earlier formulation found in 1982's "Interstices: A Small Drama of Words" offers the most explicit articulation of my argument here: "black is vestibular to culture. In other words, the black person mirrored for the society around her what a human being was *not.*" Both essays appear in Hortense J. Spillers, *Black, White, and in Color: Essays on American Literature and Culture* (Chicago: University of Chicago Press, 2003), 155, 207, 218.

19. Sharpe, *In the Wake,* 7–8, 14.

20. Hartman, *Scenes of Subjection,* 9; Barrett, *Blackness and Value,* 27; Manning Marable, *How Capitalism Underdeveloped Black America: Problems in Race, Political Economy, and Society* (Boston: South End, 2000), 105–30.

21. Hartman, *Scenes of Subjection,* 25; Ruth Wilson Gilmore, *Golden Gulag: Prisons, Surplus, Crisis, and Opposition in Globalizing California* (Berkeley: University of California Press, 2007), 28.

22. As a "configuration of meaning," *différance* names an iterative relationship of both difference and deferral, thus pointing to a "possibility of conceptuality" that simultaneously enables and destabilizes the relation between the signifier (in this case, blackness) and the signified (in this case, slavery). See Jacques Derrida, "Différance," in *Margins of Philosophy* (Chicago: University of Chicago Press, 1984), 1–28.

23. Saidiya V. Hartman, *Lose Your Mother: A Journey along the Atlantic Slave Route* (New York: Farrar, Straus and Giroux, 2007), 6.

24. For example, Gilroy has argued that the Black political culture that has emerged out of chattel slavery and settler colonialism constitutes a "variety of unhappy consciousness which demands that we rethink the meanings of rationality, autonomy, reflection, subjectivity, and power" with the understanding that "racial terror is not merely compatible with occidental rationality but cheerfully complicit with it." Gilroy, *Black Atlantic,* 56. We might read Gilroy's reference to G. W. F. Hegel's "unhappy consciousness" as also implicitly alluding to a Du Boisian conception of Black double-consciousness that both encompasses and exceeds the racial consciousness constituted through New World captivity and subsequent forms of unfreedom.

25. Robinson, *Black Marxism,* xxxi, 5.

26. Michel Foucault, *The History of Sexuality,* vol. 1, *An Introduction* (New York: Vintage Books, 1990), 103.

27. Alys Eve Weinbaum, *Wayward Reproductions* (Durham, N.C.: Duke University Press, 2004), 3–5. See also Dorothy E. Roberts, *Killing the Black Body: Race, Reproduction, and the Meaning of Liberty* (New York: Pantheon, 1997); and Nira Yuval-Davis, *Gender & Nation* (London: SAGE, 1997).

28. Michael Omi and Howard Winant, *Racial Formation in the United States: From the 1960s to the 1990s,* 2nd ed. (New York: Routledge, 1994), 56.

29. Omi and Winant, 56; Stuart Hall, "Race, Articulation, and Societies Structured in Dominance," in *Black British Cultural Studies: A Reader,* ed. Houston A. Baker and Manthia Diawara (Chicago: University of Chicago Press, 1996), 324–25.

30. This argument has been an integral part of Marxist feminist political and intellectual work over the past four decades. See, for example, Leopoldina Fortunati, *The Arcane of Reproduction: Housework, Prostitution, Labor and Capital* (New York: Autonomedia, 1995), 18; Mariarosa Dalla Costa and Selma James, *The Power of Women and the Subversion of the Community,* 3rd ed. (Bristol: Falling Wall, 1975); and Silvia Federici, *Caliban and the Witch: Women, the Body, and Reproduction* (New York: Autonomedia, 2004), 8.

31. Neferti X. M. Tadiar, *Things Fall Away: Philippine Historical Experience and the Makings of Globalization* (Durham, N.C.: Duke University Press, 2009), 34, 89.

32. Lee Edelman, *No Future: Queer Theory and the Death Drive* (Durham, N.C.: Duke University Press, 2004), 60; Jack Halberstam, *In a Queer Time and Place: Transgender Bodies, Subcultural Lives* (New York: New York University Press, 2005), 4.

33. Jack Halberstam, *The Queer Art of Failure* (Durham, N.C.: Duke University Press, 2011).

34. There have been a number of insightful engagements with Edelman's work in particular that have focused on the political possibilities enabled by disarticulating futurity from the imperatives of white (hetero)normativity, especially from within that body of scholarship broadly defined as queer of color critique. By queering the future—that is, positing "queer futurity" as the undecidable "not-yet" where

presently "impossible possibilit[ies]" might be imagined and manifested—thinkers such as Kara Keeling and José Esteban Muñoz have posited futurity as a terrain of political (im)possibility in ways that have been invaluable for my own work. Kara Keeling, "Looking for M—: Queer Temporality, Black Political Possibility, and Poetry for the Future," *GLQ* 15, no. 4 (2009): 565–82; José Esteban Muñoz, *Cruising Utopia: The Then and There of Queer Futurity* (New York: New York University Press, 2009), 11, 22, 83–96. Moreover, long before Edelman's *No Future* became a touchstone for thinking queerness and reproduction, queer-of-color scholars and activists had challenged the rhetorical opposition of the reproductive and the queer. See, especially, Cathy J. Cohen, "Punks, Bulldaggers, and Welfare Queens: The Radical Potential of Queer Politics," *GLQ* 3 (1997): 437–65; and Ferguson, *Aberrations in Black*, 32–39, 82–109.

35. Muñoz, *Cruising Utopia*, 92.

36. Edelman, *No Future*, 36.

37. Walter Benjamin, "The Work of Art in the Age of Mechanical Reproduction," in *Illuminations*, ed. Hannah Arendt, trans. Harry Zohn (New York: Schocken Books, 1968), 220.

38. Elin Diamond, *Unmaking Mimesis: Essays on Feminism and Theater* (New York: Routledge, 1997), v.

39. Fred Moten, *In the Break: The Aesthetics of the Black Radical Tradition* (Minneapolis: University of Minnesota Press, 2003), 4.

40. Hartman, *Scenes of Subjection*, 57–58.

41. See, for example, E. Williams, *Capitalism and Slavery*; Johnson, *Soul by Soul*; Baptist, *Half Has Never Been Told*.

42. Gilroy, *Black Atlantic*, 15.

43. Johnson, *Soul by Soul*, 78–116; Marie Jenkins Schwartz, *Birthing a Slave: Motherhood and Medicine in the Antebellum South* (Cambridge, Mass.: Harvard University Press, 2006), 9–32.

44. The concept of social death first appears in Orlando Patterson, *Slavery and Social Death: A Comparative Study* (Cambridge, Mass.: Harvard University Press, 1982). I discuss this conceptual framework in greater depth in chapters 1 and 2.

45. Johnson, *Soul by Soul*, 83–84, 86–88.

46. For more on the linkage between the management of slave reproduction and the emergence of the modern field of reproductive medicine, see Schwartz, *Birthing a Slave*; and Nicole Ivy, "Bodies of Work: A Meditation on Medical Imaginaries and Enslaved Women," *Souls* 18, no. 1 (2016): 11–31.

47. Patterson, *Slavery and Social Death*, 1–13.

48. Hartman, *Scenes of Subjection*, 94.

49. Gayatri Chakravorty Spivak, translator's preface, in *Of Grammatology*, by Jacques Derrida, trans. Gayatri Chakravorty Spivak (Baltimore: Johns Hopkins University Press, 1997), xvii. Derrida does not define the *trace*; indeed, to do so would

be to grant it a "proper name." He does, however, iterate numerous descriptions of it, including this extended one: "a common root, which is not a root but the concealment of the origin and which is not common because it does not amount to the same thing except with the unmonotonous insistence of difference, this unnameable movement of *difference-itself,* that I have strategically nicknamed trace " (93).

50. Jacques Derrida, "Signature Event Context," in *Margins of Philosophy*, 17.

51. Spillers, "Mama's Baby, Papa's Maybe," 206.

52. Spillers, 204–5.

53. Spillers, 207, 221–23.

54. Spillers, 228.

55. Arlene Keizer was the first to use the phrase *contemporary narratives of slavery* to discuss the body of literary production often referred to as neoslave narratives. As I detail in the following paragraphs, my own approach to such work—literary and otherwise—both relies on and differs from Keizer's. Arlene R. Keizer, *Black Subjects: Identity Formation in the Contemporary Narrative of Slavery* (Ithaca, N.Y.: Cornell University Press, 2004), 2–4.

56. Keizer, 2–4; Bernard W. Bell, *The Afro-American Novel and Its Tradition* (Amherst: University of Massachusetts Press, 1987), 289–90.

57. Ashraf H. A. Rushdy, *Neo-Slave Narratives: Studies in the Social Logic of a Literary Form* (New York: Oxford University Press, 1999), 3.

58. Joy James, "Introduction: Democracy and Captivity," in *The New Abolitionists: (Neo) Slave Narratives and Contemporary Prison Writings,* ed. Joy James (Albany: State University of New York Press, 2005), xxi–xxli; Dennis Childs, *Slaves of the State: Black Incarceration from the Chain Gang to the Penitentiary* (Minneapolis: University of Minnesota Press, 2015), 21.

59. Rushdy, *Neo-Slave Narratives,* 3–7, 231.

60. Keizer, *Black Subjects,* 11; Arlene R. Keizer, "Gone Astray in the Flesh: Kara Walker, Black Women Writers, and African American Postmemory," *PMLA* 123, no. 5 (2008): 1649–72.

61. Toni Morrison, *Beloved* (New York: Vintage International, 2004), 54.

62. I draw here on Avery Gordon's theory of haunting, in which she argues for the crucial function of the fictive—a category that far exceeds the fictional—for addressing the unspeakable and unthinkable traces, or "ghostly matters" of past and present social formations. I return to Gordon's theory of haunting and the fictive in chapter 2. Avery Gordon, *Ghostly Matters: Haunting and the Sociological Imagination* (Minneapolis: University of Minnesota Press, 1997).

63. Hartman, *Scenes of Subjection,* 100.

64. Patterson, *Slavery and Social Death,* 1–13.

65. Dorothy E. Roberts, *Killing the Black Body: Race, Reproduction, and the Meaning of Liberty* (New York: Vintage, 1997).

66. Patterson, *Slavery and Social Death,* 101.

67. Hartman, *Scenes of Subjection,* 6.

68. Chandan Reddy, *Freedom with Violence: Race, Sexuality, and the U.S. State* (Durham, N.C.: Duke University Press, 2011), 37–39; Wendy Brown, *States of Injury: Power and Freedom in Late Modernity* (Princeton, N.J.: Princeton University Press, 1995), 24.

69. Brown, *States of Injury,* 4; Audre Lorde, "Conference Keynote Address: Sisterhood and Survival," *Black Scholar* 13, no. 2 (March/April 1986): 6–7.

70. Hartman, *Scenes of Subjection,* 12–13.

71. Alexander G. Weheliye, *Habeas Viscus: Racializing Assemblages, Biopolitics, and Black Feminist Theories of the Human* (Durham, N.C.: Duke University Press, 2014), 132.

72. Gayatri Chakrovorty Spivak, "Ghostwriting," *Diacritics* 25, no. 2 (Summer 1995): 70–71.

73. Moten, *In the Break*, 8.

74. Brown, *States of Injury,* 9. In advocating a continued centering of the aesthetics of Black liberatory politics, my argument here resonates closely with and is informed by Moten, whose work exemplifies just such an approach. See Moten, *In the Break.*

75. Grace Kyungwon Hong, "The Future of Our Worlds: Black Feminism and the Politics of Knowledge in the University under Globalization," *Meridians: feminism, race, transnationalism* 8, no. 2 (2008): 107; Sharpe, *In the Wake,* 18, 22.

76. Hong, "The Future of Our Worlds," 108.

77. Griselda Pollock, "The Politics of Theory: Generations and Geographies in Feminist Theory and the Histories of Art Histories," in *Generations & Geographies in the Visual Arts: Feminist Readings,* ed. Griselda Pollock (New York: Routledge, 1996), xv.

78. Linda McDowell, *Gender, Identity, and Place: Understanding Feminist Geographies* (Minneapolis: University of Minnesota Press, 1999), 10.

79. For a thorough consideration of the gendered implications of the public/private and local/global divides, see Doreen Massey, *Space, Place, and Gender* (Minneapolis: University of Minnesota Press, 1994); Cathy N. Davidson and Jessamyn Hatcher, *No More Separate Spheres!* (Durham, N.C.: Duke University Press, 2002); and McDowell, *Gender, Identity, and Place.*

80. Evelynn Hammonds, "Black (W)holes and the Geometry of Black Female Sexuality," *differences: A Journal of Feminist Cultural Studies* 6, nos. 2–3 (1994): 139.

81. Spillers, *Black, White, and in Color,* 229.

82. Barbara Christian, "The Race for Theory," *Cultural Critique,* no. 6 (Spring 1987): 61.

1. Ain't Your Mama on the Pancake Box?

1. Dick Case, "Book Serves Up the Life of Syracuse's 'Aunt Jemima,'" *Syracuse Post-Standard,* November 3, 2002, http://syracusethenandnow.org.

2. There is little to suggest that this grand-scale theft of recipes occurred. However, given the other aspects of Hunter and Evans's well-documented grievance, and the commonness of such types of stories, the shameless appropriation that the recipe nabbing symbolizes has an apocryphal ring of truth, if not a factual one.

3. As I discuss later, the first woman to portray Aunt Jemima for publicity purposes was Nancy Green at the 1893 World's Columbian Exposition in Chicago; Aylene Lewis was still portraying Aunt Jemima on a daily basis at Aunt Jemima's Kitchen in Southern California's Disneyland as late as 1964.

4. Hortense J. Spillers, "Mama's Baby, Papa's Maybe: An American Grammar Book," in *Black, White, and in Color: Essays on American Literature and Culture* (Chicago: University of Chicago Press, 2003), 203–29; Christina Sharpe, *In the Wake: On Blackness and Being* (Durham, N.C.: Duke University Press, 2016), 25; Saidiya Hartman, "The Belly of the World: A Note on Black Women's Labors," *Souls: A Critical Journal of Black Politics, Culture, and Society* 18, no. 1 (January–March 2016): 168–69.

5. Cheryl I. Harris, "Whiteness as Property," in *Critical Race Theory: The Key Writings That Formed the Movement,* ed. Kimberlé Crenshaw et al. (New York: New Press, 1995), 279; Alexander G. Weheliye, *Habeas Viscus: Racializing Assemblages, Biopolitics, and Black Feminist Theories of the Human* (Durham, N.C.: Duke University Press, 2014), 4, 77–79.

6. As Cheryl Harris argues, the juridical and social codification of whiteness as a form of property emerges historically in contradistinction to the classification of Black people as property and Indigenous people as incapable of owning property. Weheliye pins the U.S. juridical precedent of "personhood-as-ownership" to the landmark 1857 Dred Scott case. C. Harris, "Whiteness as Property"; Weheliye, *Habeas Viscus,* 77–78. I expand on Harris's argument in chapter 4.

7. Given the enmeshment of heteropatriarchy and property, what is and is not juridically recognizable as grievable is profoundly gendered. See, for example, Saidiya V. Hartman, *Scenes of Subjection: Terror, Slavery, and Self-Making in Nineteenth-Century America,* Race and American Culture (New York: Oxford University Press, 1997), 81. I discuss this question of gender, law, and "negligible injury" at greater length in chapter 3.

8. Ian Haney Lopez makes this distinction between the law as juridical text and the law as practice or operation. See Ian Haney Lopez, *White by Law: The Legal Construction of Race,* 2nd ed. (New York: New York University Press, 2006), 80.

9. Weheliye, *Habeas Viscus,* 77. As Weheliye notes, while habeas corpus has been used successfully by racialized subjects and other persecuted and oppressed peoples to end their captivity, it also has been denied to racialized and persecuted groups greatly in need of its protections, most infamously in the cases of Japanese internment during World War II and the exemption of "unlawful enemy combatants" imprisoned at Guantánamo Bay. Weheliye describes these intentional failures of

the writ as examples of its use against minoritized subjects. I distinguish between these cases of malign neglect or juridical foreclosure and what I would argue is the constant common-sense deployment of the notion of "producing the body" as an antagonistic means of rejecting Black claims against institutions and the state.

10. Weheliye, 52.

11. Weheliye, 79. Spillers, "Mama's Baby, Papa's Maybe," 228.

12. Hortense Spillers et al., "'Whatcha Gonna Do?': Revisiting 'Mama's Baby, Papa's Maybe: An American Grammar Book': A Conversation with Hortense Spillers, Saidiya Hartman, Farah Jasmine Griffin, Shelly Eversley, & Jennifer L. Morgan," *Women's Studies Quarterly* 35, nos. 1–2 (Spring/Summer 2007): 300.

13. Riché Richardson, "Can We Please, Finally, Get Rid of 'Aunt Jemima'?," *New York Times,* June 24, 2015; Quaker Oats Company, "We Are Committed to Progress," accessed October 23, 2020, https://www.auntjemima.com.

14. Doris Witt, *Black Hunger: Food and the Politics of U.S. Identity* (New York: Oxford University Press, 1999), 25.

15. M. M. Manring, *Slave in a Box: The Strange Career of Aunt Jemima* (Charlottesville: University Press of Virginia, 1998); Witt, *Black Hunger*, 23.

16. Witt, *Black Hunger,* 22.

17. Quoted in Witt, 39.

18. For more on R. T. Davis's successful marketing strategy involving Aunt Jemima's ragdoll family, see Manring, *Slave in a Box,* 65.

19. Like the rest of Marquette's glowing history of Quaker Oats' rise to global supremacy, the chapter on Aunt Jemima lacks bibliographic information and citations, and few of his claims can be substantiated with any certainty. In the absence of other source material, however, it is hard to escape the Marquette narrative. While few scholarly works continue to turn to Marquette's text directly, the published work they do cite often lists Marquette as the original source for various historical details. For a more detailed critique of Marquette's brand history and its authoritative status, see Witt, *Black Hunger,* 25. For an example of how contemporary researchers negotiate the limits of Marquette's history, see Manring, *Slave in a Box,* 60–62.

20. Arthur Marquette, *Brands, Trademarks, and Good Will: The Story of the Quaker Oats Company* (New York: McGraw-Hill, 1967), 139–43. See also Manring, *Slave in a Box,* 60–65; and Witt, *Black Hunger,* 28–30.

21. Marquette, *Brands, Trademarks, and Good Will,* 143–49.

22. Manring, *Slave in a Box,* 75–78; Witt, *Black Hunger,* 25–26.

23. For an extended reading of Aunt Jemima's dual function as the unifier of North and South and the conjunction of modern mass production and antebellum pastoral nostalgia, see Jo-Ann Morgan, "Mammy the Huckster: Selling the Old South for the New Century," *American Art* 9, no. 1 (1995): 86–109; and Manring, *Slave in a Box,* 74, 119.

24. Witt, *Black Hunger,* 30; Jean Baudrillard, *Simulacra and Simulation,* trans. Sheila Faria Glaser (Ann Arbor: University of Michigan Press, 1994), 166.

25. Manring, *Slave in a Box,* 68–69; Witt, *Black Hunger,* 31.

26. Witt, *Black Hunger,* 31.

27. Rosalind Morris, "Introduction," in *Can the Subaltern Speak: Reflections on the History of an Idea* (New York: Columbia University Press, 2010), 3.

28. Weheliye, *Habeas Viscus,* 132.

29. Weheliye, 132.

30. The outcome of a collaboration between actor and author Breena Clarke and director Glenda Dickerson, *Re/membering Aunt Jemima: A Menstrual Show* was first published in 1993, and premiered at the National Black Arts Festival at Spelman College in 1994. I have not seen *Re/membering Aunt Jemima* onstage; it is very rarely produced. My description of the staging draws upon three different versions of the script, published in *Women and Performance: A Journal of Feminist Theory* 6, no. 1 (1993): 95–130; *Contemporary Plays by Women of Color: An Anthology,* ed. Kathy A. Perkins and Roberta Uno (New York: Routledge, 1996), 51–67; and *Colored Contradictions: An Anthology of Contemporary African-American Plays,* ed. Harry Elam and Robert Alexander (New York: Plume, 2006), 141–71. In each of these versions, the cast is described as being made up of "women"; contextually, each appears to presume a cast of cis women actors. This version of the opening song is from *Women and Performance,* 51. Hereafter, I refer to each version by the initials *WP, CP,* and *CC,* respectively.

31. Dickerson and Clarke, *Re/membering Aunt Jemima,* 141, 143 (*CC*).

32. Hartman, *Scenes of Subjection,* 57.

33. Lisa Anderson, *Black Feminism in Contemporary Drama* (Urbana: University of Illinois Press, 2008), 36.

34. Spillers, "Mama's Baby, Papa's Maybe," 204–5.

35. Combahee River Collective, "A Black Feminist Statement," in *Capitalist Patriarchy and the Case for Socialist Feminism,* ed. Zillah Eisenstein (New York: Monthly Review Press, 1978), 210.

36. Dickerson and Clarke, *Re/membering Aunt Jemima,* 51 (*WP*).

37. Elin Diamond, *Unmaking Mimesis: Essays on Feminism and Theater* (New York: Routledge, 1997), v.

38. Hartman, *Scenes of Subjection,* 57; Judith Butler, *Gender Trouble: Feminism and the Subversion of Identity* (New York: Routledge, 1999), 163–80.

39. Diamond, *Unmaking Mimesis,* v.

40. Dickerson and Clarke, *Re/membering Aunt Jemima,* 96 (*WP*), 34–35 (*CP*), 144–45 (*CC*).

41. Spillers, "Mama's Baby, Papa's Maybe," 203.

42. Priya Kandaswamy, "Gendering Racial Formation," in *Racial Formation in the Twenty-First Century,* ed. Daniel HoSang, Oneka LaBennett, and Laura Pulido (Berkeley: University of California Press, 2012), 36–38.

43. Dickerson and Clarke, *Re/membering Aunt Jemima,* 97 (*WP*); Orlando Patterson, *Slavery and Social Death: A Comparative Study* (Cambridge, Mass.: Harvard University Press, 1982), 1–13.

44. In the time that this project has been under way, the scholarship on social death has grown exponentially. In addition to Hartman, whom I engage in chapter 2, Christina Sharpe has also employed Patterson's theory of social death to read with and through Black women's writing. See, for example, Christina Sharpe, *Monstrous Intimacies: Making Post-Slavery Subjects* (Durham, N.C.: Duke University Press, 2010), 70, 93; and, for a profound revision of social death's afterlife, see Sharpe, *In the Wake.* For an application of social death to Black life in the aftertimes of chattel slavery, see Abdul R. JanMohamed, *The Death-Bound Subject: Richard Wright's Archaeology of Death* (Durham, N.C.: Duke University Press, 2005); Frank B. Wilderson, *Red, White & Black: Cinema and the Structure of U.S. Antagonisms* (Durham, N.C.: Duke University Press, 2010); and Jared Sexton, "The Social Life of Social Death: On Afro-Pessimism and Black Optimism," *InTensions,* no. 5 (Fall/Winter 2011): 1–47. For a rearticulation of social death as the contemporary condition of rightlessness, see Lisa Marie Cacho, *Social Death: Racialized Rightlessness and the Criminalization of the Unprotected* (New York: New York University Press, 2012). For an interrogation of the relationship between the political and the social in Patterson's work, see Fred Moten, "Blackness and Nothingness (Mysticism in the Flesh)," *South Atlantic Quarterly* 112, no. 4 (2013): 739–42.

45. Patterson, *Slavery and Social Death,* 1–13. In 1987, in Wappingers Falls, New York, teenager Tawana Brawley was found wrapped in a garbage bag, her clothes torn and burned, her body smeared with feces and marked with the words *KKK, nigger,* and *bitch.* She described herself as having been sexually assaulted by four white men, a claim that was later discounted by law enforcement and the courts in favor of an also unproven theory that the violence that Brawley experienced was self-inflicted. Regardless of at whose hands Brawley experienced these acts, their violent character and their embeddedness within the material-discursive structures of anti-Black misogyny is irrefutable.

46. Dickerson and Clarke, *Re/membering Aunt Jemima,* 98 (*WP*); Patterson, 5.

47. Dickerson and Clarke, *Re/membering Aunt Jemima,* 97 (*WP*); Julia Kristeva, *Powers of Horror: An Essay on Abjection* (New York: Columbia University Press, 1982), 2–3.

48. Dickerson and Clarke, *Re/membering Aunt Jemima,* 111 (*WP*).

49. Weheliye, *Habeas Viscus,* 38. Weheliye makes a similar argument regarding the utility and inadequacy of Patterson's model. On the whole, I find Patterson more useful to think alongside than Weheliye does, and thus he figures more centrally in this project. Moreover, while Weheliye attributes Patterson's shortcomings to his general disembodiment of the figure of the enslaved, I argue here, and more fully in the chapter that follows, that Patterson's form of disembodiment is in fact a

gendered construction of the slave and of slavery as transparently and normatively masculine.

50. Dickerson and Clarke, *Re/membering Aunt Jemima,* 161 (*CC*). The apocryphal tale of Sojourner Truth's thirteen children first appears in Frances Dana Barker Gage's 1863 version of Truth's "Ain't I a Woman?" speech at the Seneca Falls Convention. As Nell Irvin Painter demonstrates, this iconic portrayal of Truth's life and speech is more indebted to racist fantasies regarding Black women than to the historical record. It has, however, become part of the imagination of Truth as a popular historical symbol. See Nell Irvin Painter, *Sojourner Truth: A Life, a Symbol* (New York: W. W. Norton, 1997), 164–79.

51. Dickerson and Clarke, *Re/membering Aunt Jemima,* 149 (*CC*).

52. Dickerson and Clarke, *Re/membering Aunt Jemima,* 155 (*CC*).

53. "Federal Writers' Project: Slave Narrative Project," vol. 16, Texas, part 2, Easter-King, 1936, manuscript/mixed material, https://www.loc.gov.

54. Dickerson and Clarke, *Re/membering Aunt Jemima,* 51–52, 67 (*WP*).

55. For a longer discussion of the historical and cultural icons on whom Aunt Jemima's daughters are based, see Anderson, *Black Feminism,* 41–45, 48–52.

56. For more on the role of *nommo* in African diasporic cultural production, see Toni Cade Bambara, "Reading the Signs, Empowering the Eye: *Daughters of the Dust* and the Black Independent Cinema Movement," in *Black American Cinema,* ed. Manthia Diawara (New York: Routledge, 1993), 129–32.

57. Anderson, *Black Feminism,* 38; Dickerson and Clarke, *Re/membering Aunt Jemima,* 143 (*CC*).

58. Spillers, "Mama's Baby, Papa's Maybe," 204–5.

59. Dickerson and Clarke, *Re/membering Aunt Jemima,* 169 (*CC*).

60. Ruth Wilson Gilmore, *Golden Gulag: Prisons, Surplus, Crisis, and Opposition in Globalizing California* (Berkeley: University of California Press, 2007), 28.

61. Dickerson and Clarke, *Re/membering Aunt Jemima,* 168–69 (*CC*).

62. Sarah Haley, *No Mercy Here: Gender and the Making of Jim Crown Modernity* (Chapel Hill: University of North Carolina Press, 2016), 200; Fred Moten, *In the Break: The Aesthetics of the Black Radical Tradition* (Minneapolis: University of Minnesota Press, 2003), 1, 11, 256.

63. Dickerson and Clarke, *Re/membering Aunt Jemima,* 170 (*CC*).

64. Jane H. Carpenter, *Betye Saar,* The David C. Driskell Series of African American Art (San Francisco: Pomegranate, 2003), 26; Jane H. Carpenter, "Against the Flow: Betye Saar and Assemblage in the Age of Activism, 1965–74," *Bulletin: The University of Michigan Museums of Art and Archaeology* 13 (2000): 88–90.

65. A number of scholars discuss the particularities of the Black Arts Movement in the context of California in general and Los Angeles specifically. See Daniel Widener, *Black Arts West: Culture and Struggle in Postwar Los Angeles* (Durham, N.C.: Duke University Press, 2010); and Kellie Jones, "To/from Los Angeles with Betye Saar," in *Betye Saar: Extending the Frozen Moment* (Ann Arbor: University

of Michigan Museum of Art; Berkeley: University of California Press, 2005), 30. For examples of the specific use of the term *Black Art[s] West,* see Widener, *Black Arts West*; and Kellie Jones, "Black Art West: Thoughts on Art in Los Angeles," in *L.A. Object & David Hammons Body Prints,* ed. Connie Rogers Tilton and Lindsay Charlwood (New York: Tilton Gallery, 2011).

66. The Quaker Oats Company's 1968 redesign of the image of Aunt Jemima that appeared on all its packaging and in all its ads was a response to the political climate of the late 1960s. The new Aunt Jemima was significantly thinner and lighter skinned, and her head wrap was replaced with a wide cloth headband. Marilyn Kern-Foxworth, *Aunt Jemima, Uncle Ben, and Rastus: Blacks in Advertising, Yesterday, Today, and Tomorrow* (Westport, Conn.: Greenwood, 1994), 98–99.

67. Four of the pieces in the Exploding the Myth series incorporated the image of Aunt Jemima, including also *The Liberation of Aunt Jemima: Measure for Measure* (1973), *Liberation of Aunt Jemima: De Ole Folks at Home* (1973), and *Cocktail: Liberation of Aunt Jemima* (1973). For more on the series, see Sean M. Ulmer and Katharine Derosier Weiss, "Racial Imagery and Stereotypes," in *Betye Saar: Extending the Frozen Moment* (Ann Arbor: University of Michigan Museum of Art; Berkeley: University of California Press, 2005), 86–95; and Carpenter, "Against the Flow," 85–87.

68. Quoted in Jones, "To/from Los Angeles," 28.

69. Larry Neal, "The Black Arts Movement," *The Drama Review: TDR* 12, no. 4 (1968): 29; Hoyt Fuller, quoted in Alma Jean Billingslea-Brown, *Crossing Borders through Folklore: African American Women's Fiction and Art* (Columbia: University of Missouri Press, 1999), 24.

70. For the most thorough discussion of these various representations of Aunt Jemima in art of the 1960s and 1970s, see Michael D. Harris, *Colored Pictures: Race and Visual Representation* (Chapel Hill: University of North Carolina Press, 2003), 107–17.

71. Kimberly Wallace-Sanders, *Mammy: A Century of Race, Gender, and Southern Memory* (Ann Arbor: University of Michigan Press, 2008), 143.

72. Renee Montagne, "Life Is a Collage for Artist Betye Saar," NPR, December 28, 2006, http://www.npr.org.

73. "Betye Saar: National Visionary," National Visionary Leadership Project, accessed July 16, 2018, http://www.visionaryproject.org. See also M. Harris, *Colored Pictures,* 117; and Wallace-Sanders, *Mammy,* 143.

74. Ishmael Reed, "Betye Saar, Artist," quoted in Carpenter, *Betye Saar,* 44.

75. Quoted in Wallace-Sanders, *Mammy,* 143.

76. For a longer discussion about Black women's smiles simultaneously marking resistance to racial and gendered subjugation and being perceived and indicative of sexual availability and vulnerability, see Candice Marie Jenkins, *Private Lives, Proper Relations: Regulating Black Intimacy* (Minneapolis: University of Minnesota Press, 2007), 76–78.

77. Karla F. C. Holloway, *Codes of Conduct: Race, Ethics, and the Color of Our Character* (New Brunswick, N.J.: Rutgers University Press, 1995), 21. Like Holloway, who describes her grandmother's warnings about wearing red, I grew up in a household in which wearing red as a young Black woman was perceived to be risking even greater endangerment in the forms of increased surveillance, harassment, and possible predation—or so my grandmother taught my mother, and my mother taught me. Michael Harris also observes the red lips and clothing in *The Liberation of Aunt Jemima* in Harris, *Colored Pictures,* 117. While we draw different conclusions as to its effectiveness as an oppositional strategy, his own theorization of the symbolic implications of red clothing and open-mouthed smiles for Black women has helped me solidify my own thinking. See Michael Harris, "Memories and Memorabilia, Art and Identity: Is Aunt Jemima Really a Black Woman?," *Third Text* 12, no. 44 (2008): 25–26.

78. Jenkins, *Private Lives, Proper Relations,* 15–16.

79. Other L.A.-based African American artists working in assemblage at the time include Noah Purifoy, David Hammons, John Riddle, and John Outterbridge.

80. While today, the collection, replication, and display of so-called Black memorabilia have become a popular hobby and lucrative industry, it was far from the case when Saar first began scavenging and incorporating such items. For the history of this transition, see Kenneth W. Goings, *Mammy and Uncle Mose: Black Collectibles and American Stereotyping* (Bloomington: Indiana University Press, 1994).

81. M. Harris, *Colored Pictures,* 116. Harris is drawing here upon Henry Louis Gates Jr.'s theory of signifying, as elaborated in *The Signifying Monkey: A Theory of Afro-American Literary Criticism* (New York: Oxford University Press, 1988).

82. Jacques Derrida, quoted in Gayatri Chakravorty Spivak, *A Critique of Postcolonial Reason: Toward a History of the Vanishing Present* (Cambridge, Mass.: Harvard University Press, 1999), 426.

83. M. Harris, *Colored Pictures,* 118, emphasis added.

84. My theorization of the assemblage draws from Gilles Deleuze and Félix Guattari, *A Thousand Plateaus: Capitalism and Schizophrenia,* trans. Brian Massumi (Minneapolis: University of Minnesota Press, 1987); Jasbir Puar, *Terrorist Assemblages: Homonationalism in Queer Times* (Durham, N.C.: Duke University Press, 2007); and Weheliye, *Habeas Viscus.*

85. A number of scholars have written on the myth of the mammy. Some of the earliest examples include Herbert G. Gutman, *The Black Family in Slavery and Freedom* (New York: Pantheon Books, 1976), 443–44; Catherine Clinton, *The Plantation Mistress: Woman's World in the Old South* (New York: Pantheon, 1984), 202; and Deborah Gray White, *Ar'n't I a Woman? Female Slaves in the Plantation South* (New York: W. W. Norton, 1985), 55–61. On the myth of the mammy in the context of Aunt Jemima in particular, see Manring, *Slave in a Box,* 54–59.

86. White, *Ar'n't I a Woman?,* 61. See also Kimberly Wallace-Sanders, "The Body of a Myth: Embodying the Black Mammy Figure in Visual Culture," in *Black Womanhood: Images, Icons, and Ideologies of the African Body,* ed. Barbara Thompson (Hanover, N.H.: Hood Museum of Art, Dartmouth College, in association with University of Washington Press, 2008), 165; and Manring, *Slave in a Box,* 58.

87. Manring, *Slave in a Box,* 59.

88. Weheliye, *Habeas Viscus,* 6, 46–51; Deleuze and Guattari, *A Thousand Plateaus,* 10–15. For Deleuze and Guattari, the line of flight is the evanescent passage from the material to the immaterial as well as the instant of that passage. Accordingly, it has the ephemeral potential for transformation and escape. For a Black, queer, feminist take on the line of flight, see Kara Keeling, *The Witch's Flight: The Cinematic, the Black Femme, and the Image of Common Sense* (Durham, N.C.: Duke University Press, 2007).

89. Peter Clothier, *Betye Saar* (Los Angeles: Museum of Contemporary Art, 1984), 7–8.

90. A number of scholars have discussed Saar's work as simultaneously falling into and resisting such categorizations. In particular, see Clothier, 13, 25; Jones, "Black Art West," 29; and Carpenter, *Betye Saar.*

91. For discussions of several of these elements, see Carpenter, *Betye Saar,* 44–46; Jones, "Black Art West," 29; and James Christen Steward, "'Lest We Forget': The Liberating Art of Betye Saar," in *Betye Saar: Extending the Frozen Moment* (Ann Arbor: University of Michigan Museum of Art; Berkeley: University of California Press, 2005), 10.

92. Carpenter, *Betye Saar,* 44–46.

93. Clothier, *Betye Saar,* 13; Jones, "Black Art West," 29.

94. Quaker Oats Company, "We Are Committed to Progress"; Ramon Laguarta, "A Message from Our CEO," accessed October 23, 2020, https://www.pepsico.com.

95. Kirby Lauryen, "How to Make a Non Racist Breakfast," TikTok video, 37 seconds, June 15, 2020, https://www.tiktok.com; Tiffany Hsu, "Aunt Jemima Brand to Change Name and Image over 'Racial Stereotype,'" *New York Times,* June 17, 2020, updated September 27, 2020.

96. For a full discussion of multiculturalism as the management of difference within neoliberal racial capitalism, see Jodi Melamed, *Represent and Destroy: Rationalizing Violence in the New Racial Capitalism* (Minneapolis: University of Minnesota Press, 2011).

97. Quaker Oats Company, "We Are Committed to Progress."

98. Kate Rushin, "The Black Back-Ups," in *The Black Back-Ups* (Ithaca, N.Y.: Firebrand Books, 1993), 20.

99. See, for example, Michele Norris, "Quaker Oats Retires Aunt Jemima Character Named after Racist Stereotype," Weekend Edition, *NPR,* June 20, 2020, https://www.npr.org; Alexandra Olson and Matt Ott, "The End of Racist Pancakes?

Quaker Oats Retires Aunt Jemima," *Christian Science Monitor,* June 18, 2020, https://www.csmonitor.com; Nora McGreevy, "Quaker Oats to Retire Aunt Jemima after Acknowledging Brand's Origins as 'Racial Stereotype,'" *Smithsonian Magazine,* June 18, 2020, https://www.smithsonianmag.com.

2. Love and Violence / Maternity and Death

1. Wilma King, "'Mad' Enough to Kill: Enslaved Women, Murder, and Southern Courts," *Journal of African American History* 92, no. 1 (Winter 2007): 42–44, 55.

2. Harriet C. Frazier, *Slavery and Crime in Missouri, 1773–1865* (Jefferson, Mo.: McFarland, 2001), 120–21; King, "'Mad' Enough to Kill,'" 38–46.

3. "The Case of Margaret Garner," *Liberator (1831–1865)* 26, no. 18 (1856): 70; "The Criminal Charge against the Negroes," *National Era* 10, no. 480 (1856): 42; Henry C. Wright, "Letter from Henry C. Wright," *Liberator* 26, no. 15 (1856): 59; "Judge Leavitt," *Liberator* 26, no. 21 (1856): 1; "Ohio Fugitive Slave Case: Eloquent Speech from Lucy Stone," *National Era* 10, no. 478 (1856): 33; Mark Reinhardt, *Who Speaks for Margaret Garner?* (Minneapolis: University of Minnesota Press, 2010); Stephen Weisenburger, *Modern Medea: A Family Story of Slavery and Child-Murder from the Old South* (New York: Hill and Wang, 1998); Avery Gordon, *Ghostly Matters: Haunting and the Sociological Imagination* (Minneapolis: University of Minnesota Press, 1997).

4. Angela Y. Davis, "Reflections on the Black Woman's Role in the Community of Slaves," *Black Scholar* 13, nos. 1/2 (1971): 3–15. In addition to Davis, this rich body of work includes Jacqueline Jones, *Labor of Love, Labor of Sorrow: Black Women, Work, and the Family, from Slavery to the Present* (New York: Vintage, 1995); Hazel V. Carby, *Reconstructing Womanhood: The Afro-American Woman Novelist* (New York: Oxford University Press, 1987); Darlene Clark Hine, *Hine Sight: Black Women in the Re-Construction of American History* (Indianapolis: University of Indiana Press, 1997); Stephanie M. H. Camp, *Closer to Freedom: Enslaved Women and Everyday Resistance in the Plantation South* (Chapel Hill: University of North Carolina Press, 2004); and Jennifer Morgan, *Laboring Women: Reproduction and Gender in New World Slavery* (Philadelphia: University of Pennsylvania Press, 2007).

5. Some examples of the emerging scholarship on women's roles in violent revolts and insurgencies during the Middle Passage and in the Americas include Barbara Bush, "Defiance or Submission? The Role of the Slavewoman in Slave Resistance in the British Caribbean," *Immigrants & Minorities* 1, no. 1 (1985): 16–38; Rebecca Hall, "Not Killing Me Softly: African American Women, Slave Revolts, and Historical Constructions of Racialized Gender," *Freedom Center Journal* 2 (2010): 1–47; Aisha Finch, *Rethinking Slave Rebellion in Cuba: La Escalera and the Insurgencies of 1841–1844* (Chapel Hill: University of North Carolina Press,

2015); and Marjoleine Kars, "Dodging Rebellion: Politics and Gender in the Berbice Slave Uprising of 1763," *American Historical Review* 121, no. 1 (February 2016): 39–69. This body of work exemplifies the generative potential of feminist archival and historiographic work yet to be done in this arena.

6. Jeff Forret, *Slave against Slave: Plantation Violence in the Old South* (Baton Rouge: Louisiana State University Press, 2016), 336–38.

7. Eugene D. Genovese, *Roll, Jordan, Roll: The World the Slaves Made* (New York: Vintage Books, 1976), 496–98; Todd Savitt, *Medicine and Slavery: The Diseases and Healthcare of Black in Antebellum Virginia* (1978; repr., Urbana: University of Illinois Press, 2002), 120–29, 137–38; Michael Johnson, "Smothered Slave Infants: Were Slave Mothers at Fault?," *Journal of Southern History* 47, no. 4 (November 1981): 493–520.

8. Barbara Bush, "Hard Labor: Women, Childbirth, and Resistance in British Caribbean Slave Societies," in *More than Chattel: Black Women and Slavery in the Americas*, ed. David Barry Gaspar and Darlene Clark Hine (Bloomington: Indiana University Press, 1996), 193–217; Darlene Clark Hine, "Female Slave Resistance: The Economics of Sex," in *Hine Sight: Black Women and the Re-construction of American History* (Bloomington: Indiana University Press, 1994), 30–33; Frazier, *Slavery and Crime in Missouri*, 123–24.

9. Forret, *Slave against Slave*, 363; Frazier, *Slavery and Crime in Missouri*, 123; Emily West and Erin Shearer, "Fertility Control, Shared Nurturing, and Dual Exploitation: The Lives of Enslaved Mothers in the Antebellum United States," *Women's History Review* 27, no. 6 (2018): 1009.

10. Forret, *Slave against Slave*, 368.

11. Charles Pelot, South Carolina Mortality Schedules, Abbeville District, 1850, quoted in Johnson, "Smothered Slave Infants," 495.

12. Kenneth M. Stampp, *The Peculiar Institution: Slavery in the Antebellum South* (New York: Alfred A. Knopf, 1956), 306.

13. Some of the most influential texts in the field approach infanticide this way. See, for example, Eugene Genovese, *Roll, Jordan, Roll*, 496–98; Robert William Fogel and Stanley L. Engerman, *Time on the Cross: The Economics of American Negro History* (New York: W. W. Norton, 1974), 124–25; and Deborah Gray White, *Ar'n't I a Woman? Female Slaves in the Plantation South* (New York: W. W. Norton, 1985), 87–89.

14. Genovese, *Roll, Jordan, Roll*, 497.

15. West and Shearer, "Fertility Control," 1009.

16. As Hine notes, in his efforts to debunk the myth of the murderous Black slave mother, Genovese overlooks the reasons given by enslaved parents themselves for their admitted acts of infanticide. She muses, "Far from viewing such actions as murder, and therefore indicating these as lack of love, slave parents who took their children's lives may have done so out of a higher form of love and a

clearer understanding of the living death that awaited their children under slavery." Hine, *Hine Sight,* 33.

17. Kenneth F. Kiple and Virginia H. Kiple, "Slave Child Mortality: Some Nutritional Answers to a Perennial Puzzle," *Journal of Social History* 10, no. 3 (Spring 1977): 284–309; Savitt, *Medicine and Slavery,* 122–28, 137–38; Johnson, "Smothered Slave Infants," 493–520.

18. Hine, *Hine Sight,* 32.

19. Frazier, *Slavery and Crime in Missouri,* 121.

20. Morgan, *Laboring Women,* 178; *Cincinnati Daily Enquirer,* January 30, 1856, quoted in Reinhardt, *Who Speaks for Margaret Garner?,* 32; King, "'Mad' Enough to Kill," 43.

21. I borrow this notion of "the political art of individualizing disorder" from Allen Feldman, *Formations of Violence: The Narrative of the Body and Political Terror in Northern Ireland* (Chicago: University of Chicago Press, 1991), 109; and Ruth Wilson Gilmore, *Golden Gulag: Prisons, Surplus, Crisis, and Opposition in Globalizing California* (Berkeley: University of California Press, 2007), 25. While both use it to explore state and extralegal practices of arrest, it offers equally useful insights for thinking about so-called criminal madness.

22. Morgan, *Laboring Women,* 178.

23. Morgan, 178.

24. *Commonwealth v. Letty, a Negro Slave,* 182, Executive Papers, Governor James Pleasants, Pardon Papers, 1822, quoted in King, "'Mad' Enough to Kill," 43.

25. King, "'Mad' Enough to Kill," 43.

26. Frazier, *Slavery and Crime in Missouri,* 120–21; King, "'Mad' Enough to Kill,'" 38–46. Using the dates of Nelly's delivery, the overlapping gestation and postpartum dates of her slaveholder's wife, Nelly's reported confession, and court records, Frazier offers detailed and convincing evidence that Nelly was, indeed, impregnated by her late master.

27. Hilary Marland, "Getting Away with Murder? Puerperal Insanity, Infanticide, and the Defence Plea," in *Infanticide: Historical Perspectives on Child Murder and Concealment, 1550—2000,* ed. Mark Jackson (London: Routledge, 2002), 172.

28. Quoted in Forret, *Slave against Slave,* 163.

29. Forret, 363.

30. Forret, 163, 371–72; King, "'Mad' Enough to Kill," 43.

31. Marland, "Getting Away with Murder?," 172.

32. I. Loudon, "Puerperal Insanity in the 19th Century," *Journal of the Royal Society of Medicine* 88, no. 2 (February 1988): 78; James McDonald, "Puerperal Insanity," *American Journal of Insanity,* no. 4 (1847): 114, 116.

33. Hilary Marland, *Dangerous Motherhood: Insanity and Childbirth in Victorian Britain* (Basingstoke: Palgrave Macmillan, 2004), 6.

34. Marland, 198.

35. King, "'Mad' Enough to Kill," 43.

36. Hortense J. Spillers, "Mama's Baby, Papa's Maybe: An American Grammar Book," in *Black, White, and in Color: Essays on American Literature and Culture* (Chicago: University of Chicago Press, 2003), 228.

37. Weisenburger, *Modern Medea,* 172–73.

38. *Cincinnati Daily Enquirer,* January 30, 1856, quoted in Reinhardt, *Who Speaks for Margaret Garner?,* 31–32.

39. The case of Margaret Garner has been long recognized as a consummate example of the processes by which white abolitionist discourses functioned as means of muting and mediating the political articulations of slaves and former slaves. See, for example, Gordon, *Ghostly Matters*; and Reinhardt, *Who Speaks for Margaret Garner?*

40. Wright, "Letter from Henry C. Wright," 59.

41. Carol Pateman, *The Sexual Contract* (Cambridge, UK: Polity, 1988); Evelyn Nakano Glenn, *Unequal Freedom: How Race and Gender Shaped American Citizenship and Labor* (Cambridge, Mass.: Harvard University Press, 2002), 18–55.

42. Here I am paraphrasing Paul Gilroy, *The Black Atlantic: Modernity and Double-Consciousness* (Cambridge, Mass.: Harvard University Press, 1993), 56.

43. Quoted in Reinhardt, *Who Speaks for Margaret Garner?,* 112. See also Weisenburger, *Modern Medea,* 172–73. While we diverge in our conclusions, Weisenburger also addresses at great length the empathetic leveraging of conceptions of bourgeois white womanhood by white abolitionists such as Stone. See particularly Weisenburger, *Modern Medea,* 246–63.

44. For the origins of the phrase *cult of true womanhood,* see Barbara Welter, "The Cult of True Womanhood: 1820–1860," *American Quarterly* 18, no. 2, Part 1 (1966): 151–52. Reinhardt similarly explores the invocations of republican heroism by Garner's defenders; however, he gives little attention to how these discursive deployments of republicanism were concomitantly raced and gendered. Reinhardt, *Who Speaks for Margaret Garner?,* 36–37.

45. Spillers, "Mama's Baby, Papa's Maybe," 216. On the double-edged nature of white abolitionist empathy, see Saidiya V. Hartman, *Scenes of Subjection: Terror, Slavery, and Self-Making in Nineteenth-Century America,* Race and American Culture (New York: Oxford University Press, 1997), 19.

46. Michelle Oberman, "A Brief History of Infanticide and the Law," in *Infanticide: Psychosocial and Legal Perspectives*, ed. Margaret G. Spinelli (Washington, D.C.: American Psychiatric Publishing, 2003), 4.

47. Feldman, *Formations of Violence,* 5.

48. The promise of the *true story* has been widely used to market subsequent versions of the Garner story. See, for example, the tag line on the cover of Mark Reinhardt's *Who Speaks for Margaret Garner?* as well as the publicity for Weisenburger's *Modern Medea* and the 2005 Richard Danielpour opera based on the Garner case,

for which Morrison authored the libretto. Anthony Tommasini, "A Runaway Who Paid a High Price for Freedom," *New York Times,* September 13, 2007.

49. Feldman, *Formations of Violence,* 14.

50. Camp, *Closer to Freedom,* 3.

51. Jacques Derrida, *Of Grammatology,* trans. Gayatri Chakravorty Spivak (Baltimore: Johns Hopkins University Press, 1997).

52. Gordon, *Ghostly Matters,* 146, 50.

53. In reading *Beloved* as offering a political theory of slavery that enables imagination to take over where historical documentation ends, I am in the company of other feminist scholars working at methodological interstices. See Gordon, *Ghostly Matters,* 137–90; Tiya Miles, *The Ties That Bind: The Story of an Afro-Cherokee Family in Slavery and Freedom* (Berkeley: University of California Press, 2006), 59–63; and Arlene R. Keizer, *Black Subjects: Identity Formation in the Contemporary Narrative of Slavery* (Ithaca, N.Y.: Cornell University Press, 2004), 21–47.

54. Toni Morrison, *Beloved* (New York: Vintage International, 2004), 192. Further references are to this edition and are cited parenthetically in the text.

55. As I discuss later in this chapter, the masculine heroic slave is both an abolitionist and postemancipation trope. It is also the title of Frederick Douglass's only published work of fiction. Based on the 1841 uprising aboard the domestic slave ship the *Creole,* Douglass's novella exemplifies the gendered trope but is far from the only example. Frederick Douglass, *The Heroic Slave: A Cultural and Critical Edition,* ed. Robert S. Levine, John Stauffer, and John R. McKivigan (New Haven, Conn.: Yale University Press, 2015).

56. Claudia Tate, *Domestic Allegories of Political Desire: The Black Heroine's Text at the Turn of the Century* (New York: Oxford University Press, 1992), 81.

57. Frederick Douglass, *My Bondage and My Freedom* (1855), reprinted in *Autobiographies* (New York: Library of America, 1994), 286–87; Frederick Douglass, *Life and Times of Frederick Douglass* (1893), reprinted in *Autobiographies,* 591. In his most widely read autobiography, *The Narrative of the Life of Frederick Douglass* (1845), Douglass's description of his battle with Covey is quite brief. It is not until his later two memoirs, *My Bondage and My Freedom* and *Life and Times of Frederick Douglass,* that he relates the lengthier and more lyrical version excerpted here. As Gilroy observes, by the mid-1850s, Douglass had undertaken a revision of Enlightenment knowledge and practice to render it capable of recognizing and engaging Black humanity, which is reflected in his second two memoirs. See Gilroy, *Black Atlantic,* 59–61.

58. Gilroy, *Black Atlantic,* 60.

59. The lord/bondsman dialectic appears in G. W. F. Hegel, *The Phenomenology of Mind,* 2nd rev. ed. (Oxford: Clarendon, 1977), 114–18. The large body of work on the relationship between Hegel's dialectic and the ideologies and structures of chattel slavery is far too extensive to summarize here. I find these particular sources

useful: Gilroy, *Black Atlantic,* 58–70; Susan Buck-Morss, *Hegel, Haiti, and Universal History* (Pittsburgh: University of Pittsburgh Press, 2009); Shamoon Zamir, *Dark Voices: W. E. B. Du Bois and American Thought, 1888–1903* (Chicago: University of Chicago Press, 1995), 119–32; and Orlando Patterson, *Slavery and Social Death: A Comparative Study* (Cambridge, Mass.: Harvard University Press, 1982), 97–101. For an extensive exegesis of how this Hegelian dialectic structures Black subjectivity in slavery's aftermath, see Abdul JanMohamed, *The Death-Bound Subject: Richard Wright's Archaeology of Death* (Durham, N.C.: Duke University Press, 2005). On the suspension of execution in exchange for enslavement, see Peter Linebaugh and Marcus Rediker, *The Many-Headed Hydra: The Hidden History of the Revolutionary Atlantic* (Boston: Beacon, 2000), 58.

60. Gilroy, *Black Atlantic,* 60.

61. Tate, *Domestic Allegories of Political Desire,* 128, 81. For other discussions of masculinism in Douglass's narratives, see Gwen Bergner, "Myths of Masculinity: The Oedipus Complex and Douglass's 1845 Narrative," in *The Psychoanalysis of Race,* ed. Christopher Lane (New York: Columbia University Press, 1998), 241–60; Deborah McDowell, "In the First Place: Making Frederick Douglass and the Afro-American Narrative Tradition," in *African American Autobiography: A Collection of Critical Essays,* ed. William L. Andrews (Eaglewood Hills, N.J.: Prentice Hall, 1993), 192–214; and Maurice Wallace, "Constructing the Black Masculine: Frederick Douglass, Booker T. Washington, and the Sublimits of African American Autobiography," in *No More Separate Spheres!,* ed. Cathy N. Davidson and Jessamyn Hatcher (Durham, N.C.: Duke University Press, 2002), 82–107.

62. In the rearticulation of Garner's story into the narrative that is *Beloved,* her last name becomes the name of the slaveholding family who owned Sweet Home.

63. Sara Clarke Kaplan, "Love and Violence, Maternity and Death: Black Feminism and the Politics of Reading (Un)representability," *Black Women, Gender, and Families* 1, no. 1 (Spring 2007): 103.

64. Hazel Carby, *Reconstructing Womanhood: The Afro-American Woman Novelist* (New York: Oxford University Press, 1987), 22, 35.

65. Douglass, *My Bondage and My Freedom,* 175–77. While Douglass mentions in the previous chapter that Esther is his aunt, he never refers to her as such in the pivotal scene. In *Life and Times of Frederick Douglass* (1893), he repeats this revised 1855 version.

66. Douglass, *My Bondage and My Freedom,* 176–77; Spillers, "Mama's Baby, Papa's Maybe," 206. See also Weheliye's extension and rearticulation of pornotroping in Alexander G. Weheliye, "Pornotropes," *Journal of Visual Culture* 7, no. 1 (2008): 71–76.

67. Fred Moten, *In the Break: The Aesthetics of the Black Radical Tradition* (Minneapolis: University of Minnesota Press, 2003), 21.

68. Douglass, *My Bondage and My Freedom,* 176–77; Hartman, *Scenes of Subjection,* 88.

69. Moten, *In the Break,* 15; Weheliye, "Pornotropes," 72.

70. Bergner, "Myths of Masculinity," 242.

71. Gayatri Chakravorty Spivak, "Can the Subaltern Speak?," in *Marxism and the Interpretation of Culture,* ed. Cary Nelson and Lawrence Grossberg (Urbana: University of Illinois Press, 1988), 287.

72. Gayatri Spivak, "Subaltern Studies: Deconstructing Historiography," in *Selected Subaltern Studies,* ed. Ranajit Guha and Gayatri Chakravorty Spivak (New York: Oxford University Press, 1988), 31. I deploy Spivak's reading of the masculinism of South Asian subaltern studies well aware of the notable geographic and historical differences between the (post)colonial subaltern subject at the heart of subaltern studies and the slave subject under consideration here. This seemingly catachrestic application is founded in Ranajit Guha's avowal that the unique character of the South Asian colonial project was its formation as an autocracy of dominance without hegemony by, from, and in the interests of a bourgeois democratic state. While U.S. chattel slavery was formed *internal* to the U.S. liberal project and coexisted with an ongoing project of settler colonialism, it behooves us to remember that it, too, was a racial colonial structure of domination created by and for, and inextricable from, U.S. democracy. As such, the questions of power, history, and subjectivity that South Asian subaltern studies has long mulled over have continued insight to offer to scholars of U.S. slavery. See Ranajit Guha, *Dominance without Hegemony: History and Power in Colonial India* (Cambridge, Mass.: Harvard University Press, 1998).

73. The deconstructive concept of placing a word under erasure—what Derrida dubs *sous rature*—is not unrelated to Hegel's concept of sublation (or *Aufhebung*), in which one term negates the other while preserving it as an element within the resulting synthesis. The outcome of being placed "sous rature," however, is not synthesis but a relation of radical alterity, in which the trace of that which is "forever absent, . . . never to be found in its full being," structures the sign that remains present and visible. See Gayatri Chakravorty Spivak, translator's preface to Derrida, *Of Grammatology,* xi–xviii.

74. Hartman, *Scenes of Subjection,* 100, 98. In more recent work, Hartman has pointed to the constitutive role of enslaved reproduction. See Saidiya Hartman, "The Belly of the World: A Note on Black Women's Labors," *Souls: A Critical Journal of Black Politics, Culture, and Society* 18, no. 1 (January–March 2016): 166–73.

75. Spillers, "Mama's Baby, Papa's Maybe," 228.

76. Patterson, *Slavery and Social Death,* 5.

77. Spillers, "Mama's Baby, Papa's Maybe," 228.

78. Hartman, *Scenes of Subjection,* 98.

79. Spillers, "Mama's Baby, Papa's Maybe," 208.

80. Patterson, *Slavery and Social Death,* 2, 4.

81. Patterson, 17–34.

82. Spillers, "Mama's Baby, Papa's Maybe," 207.

83. Spillers, 206.

84. As Friedrich Engels reminds us, "The original meaning of the word *family* (*familia*) is not that compound of sentimentality and domestic strife which forms the ideal of the present-day philistines. . . . The term was invented by the Romans to denote a new social organism whose head ruled over wife and children and a number of slaves, and was invested under Roman paternal power with the rights of life and death over them all." Friedrich Engels, *The Origin of the Family, Private Property, and the State,* 2nd ed. (New York: International Publishers, 1972), 121.

85. Spillers, "Mama's Baby, Papa's Maybe," 218.

86. Feldman, *Formations of Violence,* 85, 89.

87. My thinking of the body and the home as the kinds of places for the dense and interconnected production and negotiation of raced and gendered meanings and relations relies on the work of materialist geographers, including Neil Smith's formative and widely used concept of "scale" as the socially constructed spatial distinctions through which sociopolitical contradictions are resolved, and the rigorous and extensive work of feminist geographers to enrich, complicate, and apply notions of scale to geographic analyses that center questions of race and gender. See Neil Smith, "Contours of a Spatialized Politics: Homeless Vehicles and the Production of Geographic Scale," *Social Text,* no. 33 (1992): 67–69; Doreen Massey, *Space, Place, and Gender* (Minneapolis: University of Minnesota Press, 2004); and Linda McDowell, *Gender, Identity, and Place: Understanding Feminist Geographies* (Minneapolis: University of Minnesota Press, 1999).

88. Feminist critiques of overly simplified notions of so-called separate spheres first emerged in the late 1990s and have been critical to the last two decades of feminist scholarship on domesticity. For vital work in this area, see Cathy N. Davidson and Jessamyn Hatcher, eds., *No More Separate Spheres!* (Durham, N.C.: Duke University Press, 2002); and Lora Romero, *Home Fronts: Domesticity and Its Critics in the Antebellum United States* (Durham, N.C.: Duke University Press, 1997).

89. Feldman, *Formations of Violence,* 39; Jean Franco, "Killing Priests, Nuns, Women, Children," in *On Signs,* ed. Marshall Blonsky (Baltimore: Johns Hopkins University Press, 1985), 415.

90. Spillers, "Mama's Baby, Papa's Maybe," 228.

91. Jacques Derrida, "Signature Event Context," in *Margins of Philosophy* (Chicago: University of Chicago Press, 1984), 314.

92. Derrida, 316; Antonio Gramsci, *Selections from the Prison Notebooks,* ed. Smith Quintin Hoare and Geoffrey Nowell (New York: International Publishers, 1971), 210. "A functional change in a sign system is a violent event. Even when it is perceived as 'gradual,' or 'failed,' or yet 'reversing itself,' the change can only be

operated by the force of a crisis. Yet if the space for a change (necessarily also an addition) had not been there in the prior function of the sign system, the crisis could not have made the change happen." Spivak, "Subaltern Studies," 4.

93. Judith Butler, *The Psychic Life of Power: Theories in Subjection* (Stanford: Stanford University Press, 1997), 130.

94. Spillers, "Mama's Baby, Papa's Maybe," 228–29.

95. Gilmore, *Golden Gulag*, 24–26; Kobena Mercer, *Welcome to the Jungle: New Positions in Black Cultural Studies* (New York: Routledge, 1994), 287–308; Ashraf H. A. Rushdy, *Neo-Slave Narratives: Studies in the Social Logic of a Literary Form* (New York: Oxford University Press, 1999), 23–52.

96. Toni Cade Bambara, *These Bones Are Not My Child*, ed. Toni Morrison (New York: Pantheon, 1999); Gilmore, *Golden Gulag*, 7, 17–24; Clarence Lusane, *Pipe Dream Blues: Racism and the War on Drugs* (Boston: South End, 1991).

97. Butler, *Psychic Life of Power*, 184–85.

98. John Vlach, quoted in Sharon Patricia Holland, *Raising the Dead: Readings of Death and (Black) Subjectivity* (Durham, N.C.: Duke University Press, 2000), 54.

3. Hysterical Bodies as Embodied History

1. To date, Prince's narrative remains the only known autobiography published by an enslaved woman from the British West Indies. Clare Midgley, *Women against Slavery: The British Campaigns, 1780–1870* (New York: Routledge, 1992), 87; Moira Ferguson, introduction to *The History of Mary Prince, a West Indian Slave, Related by Herself*, rev. ed., by Mary Prince, ed. Moira Ferguson (Ann Arbor: University of Michigan Press, 1997), 1.

2. Mary Prince, *The History of Mary Prince, a West Indian Slave, Related by Herself*, rev. ed., ed. Moira Ferguson (Ann Arbor: University of Michigan Press, 1997), 130–31. Further references are to this edition and are cited parenthetically in the text as *HMP.* See also Midgley, *Women against Slavery*, 90; and Jenny Sharpe, *Ghosts of Slavery: A Literary Archaeology of Black Women's Lives* (Minneapolis: University of Minnesota Press, 2003), 129.

3. Dwight A. McBride, *Impossible Witnesses: Truth, Abolitionism, and Slave Testimony* (New York: New York University Press, 2001), 95.

4. McBride, 95; Saidiya V. Hartman, *Scenes of Subjection: Terror, Slavery, and Self-Making in Nineteenth-Century America*, Race and American Culture (New York: Oxford University Press, 1997), 22.

5. McBride, *Impossible Witnesses*, 98, emphasis added.

6. For details on the legal and media battle surrounding Prince's *History*, see Prince, *History of Mary Prince*, 27–29; Sharpe, *Ghosts of Slavery*, 140–43; and Edlie L. Wong, *Neither Fugitive nor Free: Atlantic Slavery, Freedom Suits, and the Legal Culture of Travel* (New York: New York University Press, 2009), 58–59.

7. Kimberly Juanita Brown, *The Repeating Body: Slavery's Visual Resonance in the Contemporary* (Durham, N.C.: Duke University Press, 2015), 72; Adrienne Davis, "Don't Let Nobody Bother Yo' Principle: The Sexual Economy of American Slavery," in *Sister Circle: Black Women and Work,* ed. Sharon Harley (New Brunswick, N.J.: Rutgers University Press, 2002), 105.

8. Wong, *Neither Fugitive,* 59.

9. James Macqueen, "The Colonial Empire of Great Britain," *Blackwood's Edinburgh Magazine,* November 1831, 749.

10. For other discussions of the vital role that sexual propriety and feminine domesticity played in establishing the truth claims of enslaved women, see Ferguson, "Introduction," 4; Sharpe, *Ghosts of Slavery,* 120–21; and Wong, *Neither Fugitive,* 58–59.

11. Sharpe, *Ghosts of Slavery,* 139. See also Ferguson, "Introduction," 4.

12. Wong, *Neither Fugitive,* 56.

13. Hartman, *Scenes of Subjection,* 81, emphasis added.

14. Wong, *Neither Fugitive,* 59; Hartman, *Scenes of Subjection,* 86.

15. Hartman, *Scenes of Subjection,* 80.

16. I borrow this phrase from Kimberly Juanita Brown, "Black Rapture: Sally Hemings, Chica Da Silva, and the Slave Body of Sexual Supremacy," *Women's Studies Quarterly* 35, nos. 1–2 (Spring/Summer 2007): 45.

17. There is an extensive body of work on the strategic encoding of sexuality in Prince's *History.* In addition to sources already cited, see also A. M. Rauwerda, "Naming, Agency, and 'a Tissue of Falsehoods' in *The History of Mary Prince,*" *Victorian Literature and Culture* 29, no. 2 (2001): 397–411. The most notable example in the narrative itself is Prince's reported refusal of the demands of her former master, Mr. D—, that she attend him alone to bathe him when he was naked in his tub and her reference to him as an "indecent man" (*HMP,* 77–78).

18. Hartman, *Scenes of Subjection,* 18.

19. In a sense, this offers an extension of my argument in chapter 2: it is precisely this desire to obscure the sexual and reproductive in favor of a focus on forms of violence more easily understood as such to which Morrison calls attention when Sethe reveals to Paul D the details of the assault by schoolteacher's nephews. It bears saying that while I focus here on the strategic erasure of the sexual in women's narratives, the implications for all narratives—and indeed, all histories—of slavery are clear: if the disavowal of the sexualized aspects of chattel slavery was a rhetorical imperative for women narrators, it was no less urgent for male narrators to conceal their own experiences of sexualized violence—a category that, as I argue in this chapter and others have argued before, encompasses all forms of racialized violence in slavery.

20. This reading draws upon the arguments of Eileen Boris and Rhacel Salazar Parreñas in regard to what they dub "intimate labor" under late neoliberal capitalism.

Eileen Boris and Rhacel Salazar Parreñas, *Intimate Labors: Cultures, Technologies, and the Politics of Care* (Stanford: Stanford University Press, 2010), 1.

21. Gayl Jones, *Corregidora* (Boston: Beacon, 1975), 9. Further references are to this edition and are cited parenthetically in the text.

22. In this use of enjoyment, I am drawing upon Alexander Kojeve's reading of Hegel's lord/bondsman dialectic. See Alexander Kojeve, *Introduction to a Reading of Hegel* (New York: Basic Books, 1969).

23. Hortense J. Spillers, "Interstices: A Small Drama of Words," in *Black, White, and in Color: Essays on American Literature and Culture* (Chicago: University of Chicago Press, 2003), 155.

24. Kátia M. De Queirós Mattoso, *To Be a Slave in Brazil, 1550–1888* (New Brunswick, N.J.: Rutgers University Press, 1986), 13.

25. For an extensive discussion of the Atlantic slave trade's transformation of African captives to Atlantic commodities to New World slaves, see Stephanie Smallwood, *Saltwater Slavery: A Middle Passage from Africa to American Diaspora* (Cambridge, Mass.: Harvard University Press, 2007), 33–64, 153–81.

26. In Portuguese, "Dorita" can be translated to mean "little golden one." Christina Sharpe makes a similar observation about the significance of Dorita's name. Sharpe's reading of *Corregidora* shares profound commonalities with mine, in ways that elude and exceed citation. Ultimately, we diverge on our perception of the political value of hysteria in the Corregidora women's lives; however, Sharpe's incisive, thorough, and rigorous engagement of many of the same aspects of the text, and of my own work on it, has immeasurably enriched and generatively challenged my own. Christina Sharpe, *Monstrous Intimacies: Making Post-Slavery Subjects* (Durham, N.C.: Duke University Press, 2010), 40, 65.

27. It is difficult to make overarching generalizations about eighteenth- and nineteenth-century concubines in Brazil; the women involved—white, *mulata, cruila,* or *preta*—occupied diverse positions within a complex society structured through the articulation of Portuguese colonial ideologies of race, class, and gender. They exercised differing degrees of agency both when entering and negotiating such relationships. However, it is notable that as Portuguese property laws mandated that married women (or more precisely, their male relatives) had an equal claim to their husband's property, relations of concubinage often blocked poor women (or their families) from accessing the wealth of their extralegal long-term sexual partners. As well, while exact numbers are nearly impossible to obtain, and certainly varied from region to region, Kathleen Higgins argues that enslaved women in Brazil made up as many as one-third of those termed concubines by the state and the Catholic Church. See Muriel Nazzari, "Concubinage in Colonial Brazil: The Inequalities of Race, Class, and Gender," *Journal of Family History* 21, no. 2 (1996): 107–22; and Kathleen J. Higgins, *"Licentious Liberty" in a Brazilian Gold-Mining Region: Slavery, Gender, and Social Control in Eighteenth-Century Sabará, Minas*

Gerais (University Park: Pennsylvania State University Press, 1999), 112–13. In discussing the Portuguese and imperial Brazilian state's regulation of these sexual relations, I am following Louis Althusser in understanding the state to include both repressive and ideological apparatuses; in this particular case, the Catholic Church was, by far, the most active institution in reproducing and maintaining these codes. See Louis Althusser, "Ideology and Ideological State Apparatuses (Notes Towards an Investigation)," in *Lenin and Philosophy and Other Essays* (New York: New York University Press, 2001), 85–126.

28. Indeed, Monique Guillory makes a similar observation about the relationship in nineteenth-century New Orleans between free quadroons entering into relations of *plaçage* and enslaved "fancy girls" auctioned off for their sexual labors. Monique Guillory, "Under One Roof: The Sins and Sanctity of the New Orleans Quadroon Balls," in *Race Conciousness: African American Studies for the New Century,* ed. Judith Jackson Fossett and Jeffery A. Tucker (New York: New York University Press, 1997), 67–92.

29. *O Direito* (Rio De Janeiro) 35 (1884): 103–18, quoted in Robert Edgar Conrad, *Children of God's Fire: A Documentary History of Black Slavery in Brazil* (Princeton, N.J.: Princeton University Press, 1983), 281.

30. Conrad, 281.

31. Sharpe, *Ghosts of Slavery,* 143.

32. Indeed, the rare police or court attempts to invoke the Roman Code of Civil Law in order to clamp down on the "cancer of the prostituted slave" were ineffectual. When, for example, municipal judge Miguel José Tavares appointed "protectors" to remove enslaved prostitutes from their masters' control and find them shelter, his efforts proved to be short-lived and largely in vain. "The public depository, under pretext that it did not have a guarantee for what it might spend in feeding the deposited women, refused to accept them," Tavares reported to the Rio de Janeiro chief of police. "With great difficulty the private ones have accepted some. . . . This difficulty," he concludes, "caused me to exert great efforts, and creates major problems for me." "Relatorio do Chefe de Policia da Corte," in *Relatorio apresentado á Assembléa Geral Legislativa na Terceira Sessãode Decima Quarta Legislatura pelo Ministro e Secretario de Estado dos Negocios de Justiçia, Francisco Paula de Negrieros Sayão Lobato* (Rio de Janeiro, 1871), 21–22, quoted in Conrad, *Children of God's Fire,* 130–32.

33. Conrad, 280–81.

34. Conrad, 280–81.

35. Robert Brent Toplin, *The Abolition of Slavery in Brazil,* Studies in American Life, ed. Meier August (New York: Atheneum, 1972), xii, 266.

36. Carol E. Henderson, *Scarring the Black Body: Race and Representation in African American Literature* (Columbia: University of Missouri Press, 2002), 38.

37. Henderson, 38.

38. M. NourbeSe Philip, "A Genealogy of Resistance," in *A Genealogy of Resistance: And Other Essays* (Toronto: Mercury, 1997), 11.

39. Michel Foucault, *Language, Counter-Memory, Practice: Selected Essays and Interviews,* trans. Donald F. Bouchard and Sherry Simon (Ithaca, N.Y.: Cornell University Press, 1977), 139, 46.

40. Foucault, *Language, Counter-Memory,* 146.

41. Mary Karasch, "Damiana Da Cunha: Catechist and Sertanista," in *Struggle and Survival in Colonial America,* ed. David G. Sweet and Gary B. Nash (Berkeley: University of California Press, 1981), 109.

42. Sharpe astutely argues that sweat is a signifier of productive labor as well as of sexual labor and desire. If the residues of pain and violence are transferred to Ursa's face with Great Gram's slap, then as Sharpe notes, the sexual residue is transferred to her thighs when Great Gram rubs them. Sharpe, *Monstrous Intimacies,* 51–52.

43. Elizabeth Fox-Genovese, *Within the Plantation Household: Black and White Women of the Old South* (Chapel Hill: University of North Carolina Press, 1988), 468.

44. According to Naomi Zack, "It was the idea that mulattoes had mixed blood that stigmatized them in American history. This mixed blood was associated with physical debility, mental inferiority, and moral degeneracy." A central premise underlying such claims was "the presumed-inferior racial characteristics of blacks" that were passed on to mixed-race offspring via the rules of hypodescent—better known as the "one-drop rule." See Naomi Zack, *Race and Mixed Race* (Philadelphia: Temple University Press, 1993), 122. For a more detailed analysis of the discourses of seduction in slavery, see Hartman, *Scenes of Subjection,* 79–112.

45. A more detailed discussion of the ostensible seductiveness of the mulatta, as well as a far more extensive analysis of how the trope of the tragic mulatta is both deployed and destabilized in *Corregidora,* appears in Caroline A. Streeter, "Was Your Mama Mulatto? Notes toward a Theory of Racialized Sexuality in Gayl Jones's *Corregidora* and Julie Dash's *Daughters of the Dust,*" *Callaloo* 27, no. 3 (Summer 2004): 768–87. On ideas of the mulatto as sterile, like a mule, due to their so-called hybrid descent, see Zack, *Race and Mixed Race,* 122–23.

46. Elizabeth Yukins has made a similar argument about the symbolic function of the genitalia in this passage, stating that "the birthmark signifies a point where mind and body, past and future, self and family converge." Elizabeth Yukins, "Bastard Daughters and the Possession of History in *Corregidora* and *Paradise,*" *Signs: Journal of Women in Culture and Society* 28, no. 1 (2002): 228.

47. Michel Foucault, *The History of Sexuality,* vol. 1, *An Introduction* (New York: Vintage Books, 1990), 149.

48. Janet Beizer, *Ventriloquized Bodies: Narratives of Hysteria in Nineteenth-Century France* (Ithaca, N.Y.: Cornell University Press, 1994), 3.

49. For another, incisive reading of *Corregidora* through the lens of hysteria, see Sharpe, *Monstrous Intimacies,* 47–56.

50. Studies of *Corregidora* as a narrative of trauma include Yukins, "Bastard Daughters"; Naomi Morgenstern, "Mother's Milk and Sister's Blood: Trauma and the Neo-Slave Narrative," *differences: A Journal of Feminist Cultural Studies* 8, no. 2 (1996): 101–26; Bruce Simon, "Traumatic Repetition: Gayl Jones's *Corregidora,*" in *Race Consciousness: African American Studies for the New Century,* ed. Judith Jackson Fossett and Jeffrey A. Tucker (New York: New York University Press, 1997), 93–112; and Deborah Horvitz, "'Sadism Demands a Story': Oedipus, Feminism, and Sexuality in Gayl Jones's *Corregidora* and Dorothy Allison's *Bastard out of Carolina,*" *Contemporary Literature* 39, no. 2 (1998): 238–61.

51. Cathy Caruth, ed., *Trauma: Explorations in Memory* (Baltimore: Johns Hopkins University Press, 1995), 91; Cathy Caruth, *Unclaimed Experience: Trauma, Narrative, and History* (Baltimore: Johns Hopkins University Press, 1996), 5.

52. Caruth, *Trauma,* 11. The study of trauma has become, in the past thirty years, an extensive and theoretically rich field; it encompasses far more than I am capable of addressing here. My own approach to trauma is most deeply influenced by Caruth's work on trauma, history, and memory.

53. Paul Lerner and Mark S. Micale, "Trauma, Psychiatry, and History: A Conceptual and Historiographical Introduction," in *Traumatic Pasts: History, Psychiatry, and Trauma in the Modern Age, 1870–1930,* ed. Mark S. Micale and Paul Lerner (Cambridge: Cambridge University Press, 2001), 1–28.

54. There are innumerable sources that discuss the history of hysteria's classification as a uterine disease. I have found the following particularly useful: Ilza Veith, *Hysteria: The History of a Disease* (Chicago: University of Chicago Press, 1965); Beizer, *Ventriloquized Bodies;* Helen King, "Once upon a Text: Hysteria from Hippocrates," in *Hysteria beyond Freud,* ed. Sander Gilman et al. (Berkeley: University of California Press, 1993), 3–90.

55. Elaine Showalter, "Hysteria, Feminism, and Gender," in *Hysteria beyond Freud,* ed. Sander Gilman et al. (Berkeley: University of California Press, 1993), 290–91.

56. Charcot also used the terms *névroses traumatiques,* and *hystèro-traumatisme* to describe his male hysteric patients. See Jean-Martin Charcot, *Charcot the Clinician: The Tuesday Lessons (Leçons du mardi à la Salpêtrière, 1887–1888)* (New York: Raven, 1987), 43, 116–17; Lerner and Micale, "Trauma, Psychiatry, and History"; and Mark S. Micale, "Jean-Martin Charcot and Les Névroses Traumatiques: From Medicine to Culture in French Trauma Theory of the Late Nineteenth Century," in *Traumatic Pasts: History, Psychiatry, and Trauma in the Modern Age, 1870–1930,* ed. Mark S. Micale and Paul Lerner (Cambridge: Cambridge University Press, 2001), 115–39. For a consideration of the similar treatment of hysteria in the United States, see Lisa Cardyn, "The Construction of Female Sexual Trauma in

Turn-of-the-Century American Mental Medicine," in *Traumatic Pasts: History, Psychiatry, and Trauma in the Modern Age, 1870–1930,* ed. Mark S. Micale and Paul Lerner (Cambridge: Cambridge University Press, 2001), 172–202.

57. Sigmund Freud and Josef Breuer, "Studies on Hysteria (1893–1895)," in *The Standard Edition of the Complete Psychological Works of Sigmund Freud,* vol. 2, *1893–1895,* ed. and trans. James Strachey (London: Hogarth, 1955), 6–11.

58. Prior to the case of Dora, Freud's changing attitudes on the role of sexual trauma in the onset of hysteria can be traced through his lengthy correspondence with colleague and friend Wilhelm Fliess, collected in Sigmund Freud, *The Origins of Psychoanalysis: Letters to Wilhelm Fliess, Drafts and Notes (1887–1902),* vol. 1, ed. Marie Bonaparte, Anna Freud, and Ernst Kris (New York: Basic Books, 1954). Dora's sessions with Freud occurred in 1900, late into his reconsideration of the roots of hysteria. The ostensible facts, and later revisions, of Dora's case are well known: seventeen-year-old Dora—in reality a young Jewish woman named Ida Bauer—was brought to Freud by her father for treatment of her recurring "nervous" cough and loss of voice. From their sessions, a narrative emerged of Dora's sexual pursuit four years earlier by an older, married family friend, Herr K., and its toleration by her father, who was simultaneously conducting an affair with Herr K.'s wife. Freud found Dora's story suspect at its roots, and their sessions ended after only three months, when she refused to return for further treatment.

While Freud acceded that Dora's father might have been unwilling to examine Herr K.'s behavior too closely for fear of bringing attention to his own liaisons with Frau K., and that indeed Herr K.'s actions toward Dora bore all the marks of "lovemaking," he categorized Dora's suspicion that she had been "handed over to Herr K. as the price of his tolerating the relations between her father and his wife" as gross exaggeration, believed Dora to be in love with Herr K., and diagnosed Dora's choking to be a repetitive reliving of her response to Herr K.'s first sexual advances: a conversion of her repressed desire for the older man as a replacement for her own, forbidden father. It was when he finally confronted her with this "truth" and suggested that the best solution might have been for Dora to marry Herr K. and her father to marry Frau K. that Dora ended their sessions.

Perhaps most interesting to my argument here is Freud's inability to perceive the kisses and "embraces" that an adult family friend, Herr K., forced on a thirteen- to fourteen-year-old Dora as violent, nonconsensual, and possibly traumatic. "Her having felt so deeply *injured* by Herr K.'s proposal," he reflects, "seemed to me in general to need explanation, especially as I was beginning to realize that Herr K. himself had not regarded his proposal to Dora as a mere frivolous attempt at seduction." At the heart of it, it seems, lies his belief that Dora was exhibiting signs of hysteria *rather than* experiencing trauma. For the full description of the case, and Freud's interpretation of it, see "Fragment of an Analysis of a Case of Hysteria (1905 [1901])," in *The Standard Edition of the Complete Psychological Works of*

Sigmund Freud, vol. 7, *1901–1905*, ed. and trans. James Strachey (London: Hogarth, 1953), 1–122 (quote on 95). See also Hannah S. Decker, *Freud, Dora, and Vienna 1900* (New York: Free Press, 1991), xi, 118; and Charles Bernheimer and Claire Kahane, *In Dora's Case: Freud, Hysteria, Feminism* (New York: Columbia University Press, 1985).

59. One significant exception to this theoretical separation between hysteria theory and trauma theory is Judith Lewis Herman, *Trauma and Recovery* (New York: Basic Books, 1997).

60. Laura Briggs, "The Race of Hysteria: 'Overcivilization' and the 'Savage' in Late Nineteenth-Century Obstetrics and Gynecology," *American Quarterly* 52, no. 2 (2000): 246–73.

61. Some of the earliest examples of such crucial feminist revisions include the earlier work of the French feminist poststructuralists. See, for example, Hélène Cixous and Catherine Clément, *The Newly Born Woman*, trans. Betsy Wing (Minneapolis: University of Minnesota Press, 1986); and Luce Irigaray, *Speculum of the Other Woman* (Ithaca, N.Y.: Cornell University Press, 1985). More recent scholarship within the United States has both continued and expanded on the psychoanalytic approaches taken by Irigaray, Cixous, and Clément. See, for example, Claire Kahane, *Passions of the Voice: Hysteria, Narrative, and the Figure of the Speaking Woman, 1850–1915* (Baltimore: Johns Hopkins University Press, 1995); and Dianne Hunter, "Hysteria, Psychoanalysis, and Feminism: The Case of Anna O," in *Writing on the Body: Female Embodiment and Feminist Theory*, ed. Nadia Medina, Sarah Stanbury, and Katie Conboy (New York: Columbia University Press, 1997).

Cixous's work is illustrative of the precise limitation I am seeking to highlight here. In her reworking of hysteria, for example, she both argues that the hysteric is, in fact, "the typical woman in all her force" and, in an ill-thought move, borrows from Freud to describe the subjugation of women as a "dark continent trick," through which women have been taught "that hers is the dark region: because you are Africa, you are black." Interestingly, while Cixous expends a great deal of energy considering the consequences of such "terrifying myths" of female sexuality for "women," she shows remarkably little interest in the significance of such myths for the production of gendered *racial* difference, instead deploying blackness and whiteness as metaphors for subjugated white womanhood and dominant white patriarchy, respectively. There are, of course, feminist studies of hysteria that neither fall neatly into the schools of work described here nor replicate the missteps of such projects. Two excellent examples are Elin Diamond, *Unmaking Mimesis: Essays of Feminism and Theater* (New York: Routledge, 1997); and Showalter, "Hysteria, Feminism, and Gender."

62. Ruth Wilson Gilmore, "Tossed Overboard: Katrina, Mass Incarceration, and the Political of Abandonment" (paper presented at the Inaugural Lecture, Tufts Black Cultural Studies Seminar, Medford, Mass., September 28, 2005).

63. Foucault, *History of Sexuality,* 104–5.

64. Robyn Wiegman, *American Anatomies: Theorizing Race and Gender,* New Americanists (Durham, N.C.: Duke University Press, 1995), 53. Weigman is not alone in making this argument. See also E. Frances White, *Dark Continent of Our Bodies: Black Feminism and the Politics of Respectability* (Philadelphia: Temple University Press, 2001), 81–115; and Nancy Stepan, "Race and Gender: The Role of Analogy in Science," in *Anatomy of Racism,* ed. David Theo Goldberg (Minneapolis: University of Minnesota Press, 1990).

65. Diamond, *Unmaking Mimesis,* 6. The proliferation of the myth of the hypersexual Black female as a crucial element in the regulation of Black women's bodies has been extensively discussed in the body of Black feminist criticism cited throughout this book. Laura Briggs has discussed the racialization of hysteria more specifically; her approach varies from mine in emphasizing conceptions of the hysteric as "overcivilized," or white, in contradistinction with the bodies of nonwhite women, seen to epitomize savagery. See Briggs, "Race of Hysteria."

66. Freud and Breuer, "Studies on Hysteria," 240.

67. Showalter, "Hysteria, Feminism, and Gender," 292.

68. Spillers, "Interstices," 164.

69. Foucault, *History of Sexuality,* 149–50.

70. Spillers, "Interstices," 165.

71. Hirsch quoted in Yukins, "Bastard Daughters," 225.

72. "Dominick LaCapra defines a founding trauma as a historical event, such as the Holocaust, slavery, or apartheid, that comes to constitute a group's collective identity and becomes the basis for group members' individual identity." Yukins, 224.

73. On the collective nature of trauma and on trauma as historical transgression, see Caruth, *Unclaimed Experience,* 8, 66. See also Kai Erikson, "Notes on Trauma and Community," in *Trauma: Explorations in Memory,* ed. Cathy Caruth (Baltimore: Johns Hopkins University Press, 1995).

74. I discuss scale more fully in the notes to chapter 2.

75. Cixous and Clément, *Newly Born Woman,* 5.

76. Freud, *Origins of Psychoanalysis,* 215–16.

77. Cixous and Clément, *Newly Born Woman,* 147–48.

78. Dori Laub, "An Event without a Witness: Truth, Testimony, and Survival," in *Testimony: Crises of Witnessing in Literature, Psychoanalysis, and History,* ed. Shoshana Felman and Dori Laub (New York: Routledge, 1992), 78; Giorgio Agamben, *Remnants of Auschwitz: The Witness and the Archive* (New York: Zone Books), 85; Hortense J. Spillers, "Mama's Baby, Papa's Maybe: An American Grammar Book," in *Black, White, and in Color: Essays on American Literature and Culture* (Chicago: University of Chicago Press, 2003), 206; Laub, "An Event," 82.

79. On the impossibility of witnessing, see Laub, "An Event," 75–92; Dori Laub, "Truth and Testimony: The Process and the Struggle," in *Trauma: Explorations in*

Memory, ed. Cathy Caruth (Baltimore: Johns Hopkins University Press, 1995), 61–67; and Agamben, *Remnants of Auschwitz.*

80. Caruth, *Unclaimed Experience,* 83.

81. Diamond, *Unmaking Mimesis,* 5.

82. Luce Irigaray, *This Sex Which Is Not One* (Ithaca, N.Y.: Cornell University Press, 1985), 76.

83. Diamond, *Unmaking Mimesis,* 6.

84. Jacques Derrida, "Force of Law: The 'Mystical Foundation of Authority,'" in *Acts of Religion,* ed. Gil Anidjar (New York: Routledge, 2002), 244.

85. Laub, "Truth and Testimony," 69.

86. Caruth, *Trauma,* 4–5.

87. Veith, *Hysteria.*

88. Freud and Breuer, "Studies on Hysteria," 6.

89. Hartman, *Scenes of Subjection,* 19.

90. Ralph Ellison, *Shadow and Act* (New York: Random House, 1964), 78–79. See also Gayl Jones, *Liberating Voices: Oral Tradition in African American Literature* (Cambridge, Mass.: Harvard University Press, 1991), 191.

91. As translators of French psychoanalytic texts have frequently remarked, there is no adequate English translation of *jouissance*; in fact, part of its usefulness as a concept is its complexity of meaning. It includes "enjoyment," as in the enjoyment of property and rights; in French vernacular, it also refers to the moment of orgasm. As Betty Wing has observed, "It is therefore, a word with *simultaneously* sexual, political, and economic overtones." Furthermore, unlike pleasure—defined by Freud as the absence of tension or discomfort—jouissance is satisfaction delayed or denied; tension is increased rather than dispelled. In this sense, then, jouissance is desire enacted through compulsive unpleasure, the death drive; "in that respect, it is *beyond* the pleasure principle." Betsy Wing, glossary to *The Newly Born Woman,* by Hélène Cixous and Catherine Clément, trans. Betsy Wing (Minneapolis: University of Minnesota Press, 1986), 165; Alan Sheridan, "Translator's Note," in *The Four Fundamental Concepts of Psychoanalysis: The Seminar of Jacques Lacan, Book 11,* by Jacques Lacan, ed. Jacques-Alain Miller (New York: W. W. Norton), 281. On the particular ethical, psychic, and political work of feminine jouissance, see Jacques Lacan, *The Four Fundamental Concepts of Psychoanalysis: The Seminar of Jacques Lacan, Book 11,* ed. Jacques-Alain Miller (New York: W. W. Norton, 1998). In relation to hysteria, see Cixous and Clément, *Newly Born Woman,* 165.

92. Houston A. Baker, *Blues, Ideology, and Afro-American Literature: A Vernacular Theory* (Chicago: University of Chicago Press, 1984), 8.

93. For example, Spillers has suggested that, in general, the domain of music is a rare opportunity for the exposition of "the poetry of black female sexual experience." More specifically, Hazel Carby has argued that female blues singers "reclaimed female sexuality from being an objectification of male desire to a representation of

female desire," while Angela Davis has described the blues as a venue in which women could be in control of their sexuality in a way that sought to exploit neither herself nor her partner. See Spillers, "Interstices," 165; Hazel Carby, "It Just Be's Dat Way Sometime: The Sexual Politics of Women's Blues," *Radical America* 20, no. 4 (1986): 20; and Angela Y. Davis, *Blues Legacies and Black Feminism: Gertrude "Ma" Rainey, Bessie Smith, and Billie Holiday* (New York: Pantheon Books, 1998), 14.

94. I use *whore* with the intent of evoking both the degrading connotations of the word and the precise ways in which it operates as an identity rather than as an activity or form of labor. In this sense, it is not dissimilar to my understanding of the codification of blackness in the social category of the "slave."

95. Spillers, "Interstices," 167.

96. Angela Davis, *Blues Legacies,* 12.

97. Monique David-Ménard, *Hysteria from Freud to Lacan: Body and Language in Psychoanalysis* (Ithaca, N.Y.: Cornell University Press, 1989), 40–44.

4. Our Founding (M)Other

1. James T. Callender, "President Again," *Richmond Recorder,* September 1, 1802, 2.

2. Eugene A. Foster et al., "Jefferson Fathered Slave's Last Child," *Nature* 396, no. 6706 (1998): 27–28.

3. Frasier D. Neiman, "Coincidence or Causal Connection? The Relationship between Thomas Jefferson's Visits to Monticello and Sally Hemings's Conceptions," *William and Mary Quarterly,* 3rd ser., 57, no. 1 (2000): 198–210.

4. In addition to numerous individual essays and commentaries, several of the most sustained analyses exemplifying this approach appear in Jan Ellen Lewis and Peter S. Onuf, eds., *Sally Hemings and Thomas Jefferson: History, Memory, and Civic Culture* (Charlottesville: University of Virginia Press, 2000); and the special forum "Thomas Jefferson and Sally Hemings, Redux," *William and Mary Quarterly,* 3rd ser., 57, no. 1 (2000): 121–210.

5. Nathan Irvin Huggins, quoted in Annette Gordon-Reed, "Engaging Jefferson: Blacks and the Founding Father," *William and Mary Quarterly,* 3rd ser., 57, no. 1 (2000): 174. See also Orlando Patterson, "Jefferson the Contradiction," *New York Times,* November 2, 1998, A27. Patterson's hypothesis that the "longevity of the relationship not only humanizes Jefferson" for African Americans but also causes Black people to "feel less alienated from him" speaks precisely to the limitations of a notion of social death rooted solely in enmity that I critique in this chapter.

6. Throughout this chapter, I use terms such as *affair, relationship,* or *erotic love* advisedly, given that blackness as a category marks the limit of social relationality. Yet while Spillers wisely cautions us to consider "the very real possibility that sexuality, as a term of implied relatedness, is dubiously appropriate, manageable, or

accurate to *any* of the familial relationships under a system of enslavement," it is this chapter's argument that, like kinship, neither sexuality nor erotic desire—nor even love—are unmade by the forces of domination, commodification, and captivity; rather, those intimate relations are reconstituted in and through chatteldom's violent processes of objectification, even as the structures of slavery themselves are concomitantly reproduced through these modes of intimate violence. Hortense J. Spillers, "Mama's Baby, Papa's Maybe: An American Grammar Book," in *Black, White, and in Color: Essays on American Literature and Culture* (Chicago: University of Chicago Press, 2003), 221.

7. In part, this popular connection was due to the Jefferson/Hemings report's release the weekend before the 1998 national midterm election. Attendant historical rehashings of previously dismissed nineteenth-century rumors, printed accusations by venomous political rivals, and mock impeachments resonated all too closely with the titillating accounts of Oval Office peccadillos, special prosecutorial investigations, and presidential denials that had occupied the national stage for the past year. While Clinton supporters such as historian Joseph Ellis suggested that the revelation of Jefferson's "frailties and imperfections" might serve to make his namesake's transgressions seem "less aberrant and more palatable" by demonstrating that "presidential indiscretions are a longstanding, historically based thing," conservative political commentators found the timing of the report suspiciously convenient and decried attendant analysis as "political spin" attuned to the "White House party line: . . . we are all sinners, so forget this impeachment stuff." E. S. Lander and J. J. Ellis, "Founding Father," *Nature* 396, no. 6706 (1998): 13–14; Joseph J. Ellis, "When a Saint Becomes a Sinner," *U.S. News & World Report,* November 1998, 67–69; William Safire, "Sallygate," *New York Times,* November 2, 1998.

8. Joseph J. Ellis, "Jefferson: Post-DNA," *William and Mary Quarterly,* 3rd ser., 57, no. 1 (2000): 125–38; Jan Ellen Lewis, "The White Jeffersons," in *Sally Hemings & Thomas Jefferson: History, Memory, and Civic Culture,* ed. Jan Ellen Lewis and Peter S. Onuf (Charlottesville: University of Virginia Press, 1999), 127–60; Peter S. Onuf, "'Every Generation Is an 'Independent Nation': Colonization, Miscegenation, and the Fate of Jefferson's Children," *William and Mary Quarterly,* 3rd ser., 57, no. 1 (2000): 153–70.

9. Jefferson-Hemings Scholars' Commission, "Individual Views of Prof. Mayer," in *Report on the Jefferson-Hemings Matter* (Charlottesville: Thomas Jefferson Heritage Foundation, 2001), 288–90, Jefferson Library Research Reports, courtesy of the Thomas Jefferson Foundation.

10. The elevated stakes of the scholarly debate were made clear when the then-named Thomas Jefferson Memorial Foundation issued the long-awaited report of its Scholar's Research Committee, announcing that it had revisited and revised the foundation's previous dismissal of the purported relationship between Hemings and Jefferson. Furthermore, the committee reported that upon review and in light of

the DNA results, it found there to be a strong likelihood that Jefferson had fathered all of Hemings's children. Professional and amateur Jefferson scholars from across the nation decried the report, accusing the foundation of suppressing dissenting opinion and being poor custodians of Jefferson's legacy. Subsequently, a number of the dissenters formed a new institution, the Thomas Jefferson Heritage Foundation, which soon after issued its own extensive scholarly report decrying the possibility of Jefferson having fathered any—let alone all—of Hemings's children. To follow this chronology, see Thomas Jefferson Memorial Foundation, *Report of the Research Committee on Thomas Jefferson and Sally Hemings* (Charlottesville, Va.: TJMF, 2000), Jefferson Library Research Reports, courtesy of the Thomas Jefferson Foundation; as well as Herbert Barger, "Monticello Not True to Jefferson," *Daily Progress*; Maria Samminiatelli, "New Panel to Reconsider Jefferson-Hemings Evidence"; Jefferson-Hemings Scholars' Commission; *Report on the Jefferson-Hemings Matter*; and James P. Lucier, "Fable of Tom and Sally," all in Jefferson Library files on Sally Hemings, courtesy of the Thomas Jefferson Foundation.

11. "From the Port Folio," *Richmond Recorder*, September 1, 1802, 2; Scot A. French and Edward L. Ayers, "The Strange Career of Thomas Jefferson: Race and Slavery in American Memory, 1943–1993," in *Jeffersonian Legacies*, ed. Peter S. Onuf (Charlottesville: University of Virginia Press, 1993), 424.

12. Boyd quoted in French and Ayers, "Strange Career of Thomas Jefferson," 433.

13. Boyd quoted in French and Ayers, 433.

14. French and Ayers, 431.

15. Dianne Swann-Wright, ed., "Sally Hemings," special issue, *Footsteps: African American History*, November 1999; Shannon Lanier and Jane Feldman, *Jefferson's Children: The Story of One American Family* (New York: Random House, 2000); Joe Smydo, "Fisher Family Meets the President," *Pittsburgh Post-Gazette*, May 6, 2001, 154.

16. D. Dominick Lombardi, "Black Artists Confront History," *New York Times*, May 9, 1999. Roderick A. Ferguson, *Aberrations in Black: Toward a Queer of Color Critique* (Minneapolis: University of Minnesota Press, 2004), 6, 12.

17. I discuss the term *possessive individualism* in greater depth in the introduction. See also C. B. Macpherson, *The Political Theory of Possessive Individualism: Hobbes to Locke* (Oxford: Clarendon, 2010); and Grace Kyungwon Hong, *The Ruptures of American Capital: Women of Color Feminism and the Culture of Immigrant Labor* (Minneapolis: University of Minnesota Press, 2006), 3–7.

18. Ferguson, *Aberrations in Black*, 12–14.

19. Cheryl I. Harris, "Whiteness as Property," in *Critical Race Theory: The Key Writings That Formed the Movement*, ed. Kimberlé Crenshaw et al. (New York: New Press, 1995), 279.

20. Harris, 283.

21. Anonymous, *Jefferson Journal* 1, no. 1 (March 2002), personal papers of Lucia "Cinder" Stanton, Charlottesville, Virginia (hereafter CSP), emphasis added.

22. On the right to exclusion as a key characteristic of property, see Harris, "Whiteness as Property," 283. On the Monticello Association's multiyear conflict with the descendants of Sally Hemings and its votes to exclude all Hemings descendants from membership in the association, see, for example, Anita Hamilton, "A Family Divided," *Time,* July 5, 2004. My understanding of this also comes from personal communication with Lucia (Cinder) Stanton, June 2012.

23. Ellis, "Jefferson," 127.

24. Philip D. Morgan, "Interracial Sex in the Chesapeake and the British Atlantic World," in *Sally Hemings and Thomas Jefferson: History, Memory, and Civic Culture,* ed. Jan Ellen Lewis and Peter S. Onuf (Charlottesville: University of Virginia Press, 2000), 75; Gordon-Reed, "Engaging Jefferson," 179–80.

25. Ellen Goodman, "Not Even DNA Tests Can Reveal How Sally Felt," *Houston Chronicle,* November 8, 1998.

26. Saidiya V. Hartman, *Scenes of Subjection: Terror, Slavery, and Self-Making in Nineteenth-Century America,* Race and American Culture (New York: Oxford University Press, 1997), 101.

27. Frederick Douglass, *My Bondage and My Freedom* (1855), reprinted in *Autobiographies* (New York: Library of America, 1994), 177; Spillers, "Mama's Baby, Papa's Maybe," 206. I discuss Douglass's tale of Esther at length in chapter 2.

28. Gayatri Chakravorty Spivak, *A Critique of Postcolonial Reason: Toward a History of the Vanishing Present* (Cambridge, Mass.: Harvard University Press, 1999), 167–69.

29. Ashraf H. A. Rushdy, "'I Write in Tongues': The Supplement of Voice in Barbara Chase-Riboud's 'Sally Hemings,'" *Contemporary Literature* 35, no. 1 (1994): 105–6; French and Ayers, "Strange Career of Thomas Jefferson," 437. For the critical response of historians and Jeffersonian scholars to *Sally Hemings,* see French and Ayers, "Strange Career of Thomas Jefferson," 436–44; and Annette Gordon-Reed, *Thomas Jefferson and Sally Hemings: An American Controversy* (Charlottesville: University of Virginia Press, 1998), 181–83.

30. Earlier exceptions to this general trend include Barbara Christian, "'Somebody Forgot to Tell Somebody Something': African-American Women's Historical Novels," in *Wild Women in the Whirlwind: Afra-American Culture and the Contemporary Literary Renaissance,* ed. Joanne M. Braxton and Andrée Nicola McLaughlin (New Brunswick, N.J.: Rutgers University Press, 1990), 326–41; and Rushdy, "'I Write in Tongues.'" More recently, a generative body of literary criticism on *Sally Hemings* has emerged. See, for example, Cherise A. Pollard, "Self-Evident Truths: Love, Complicity, and Critique in Barbara Chase-Riboud's *Sally Hemings* and *The President's Daughter,*" in *Monuments of the Black Atlantic: Slavery and Memory,* ed.

Joanne M. Braxton and Maria I. Diedrich (Münster: LIT Verlag, 2004), 117–30; Suzette Spencer, "Historical Memory, Romantic Narrative, and Sally Hemings," *African American Review* 40, no. 3 (Fall 2006): 507–31; Salamishah Tillet, "Freedom in a Bondsmaid's Arms: Sally Hemings, Thomas Jefferson, and the Persistence of African American Memory," in *Sites of Slavery: Citizenship and Racial Democracy in the Post-Civil Rights Imagination* (Durham, N.C.: Duke University Press, 2012), 19–50; and Kimberly Juanita Brown, "Black Rapture: Corporeal Afterimage and Transnational Desire," in *The Repeating Body: Slavery's Visual Resonance in the Contemporary* (Durham, N.C.: Duke University Press, 2015), 18–56.

31. Ann duCille, "Where in the World Is William Wells Brown? Thomas Jefferson, Sally Hemings, and the DNA of African-American Literary History," in "History in the Making," special issue, *American Literary History* 12, no. 3 (2000): 453.

32. Christian, "'Somebody Forgot to Tell,'" 335–36.

33. Christian, 330, 36.

34. Barbara Chase-Riboud, *Sally Hemings: A Novel* (New York: Viking, 1979), 370. Further references are to this edition and are cited parenthetically in the text as *SH*. Chase-Riboud was not alone in this late discovery of Brown's original text; as Henry Louis Gates Jr. and Ann duCille each note, the 1853 version of William Wells Brown's novel—which Brown revised and republished three more times—was not released in the United States until 1969. Gates suggests that this is in no small part owed to this original version's scandalous rehashing of nineteenth-century rumors that Thomas Jefferson had had several children by Sally Hemings, including a daughter sold on the auction block. Henry Louis Gates Jr., introduction to *Three Classic African-American Novels,* ed. Henry Louis Gates Jr. (New York: Vintage Classics, 1990), x; duCille, "Where in the World," 445.

35. Both duCille and Giulia Fabi have made this argument in convincing detail. See duCille, "Where in the World"; and M. Giulia Fabi, introduction to *Clotel; or, The President's Daughter,* by William Wells Brown, ed. M. Giulia Fabi (New York: Penguin, 2004), vii–xxviii.

36. Fabi, introduction to *Clotel,* xxi.

37. DuCille, "Where in the World," 445. The most notable of these inaccuracies is the premise of the novel itself: the (false) rumor that Jefferson sold his enslaved "quadroon" daughter on the auction block. In fact, Harriet Hemings—the only female child of Jefferson and Hemings to survive to adulthood—was provided with money and stagecoach passage to escape slavery when she reached twenty-one. As best we know, upon reaching the North, she lived the remainder of her life as a white woman. Brown, *Clotel;* Gordon-Reed, *Thomas Jefferson and Sally Hemings,* 245–58.

38. DuCille, "Where in the World," 253.

39. DuCille, 253.

40. Certainly, as Christian points out, a similar argument could be made regarding other texts from the same time period, most particularly Harriet Jacobs's *Incidents in the Life of a Slave Girl.* Christian, "Somebody Forgot to Tell," 341.

41. For a related argument regarding the miscegenetic within the aesthetics of the Black radical tradition, see Fred Moten, *In the Break: The Aesthetics of the Black Radical Tradition* (Minneapolis: University of Minnesota Press, 2003), 70–71.

42. Hemings is described by Isaac Granger Jefferson, former enslaved blacksmith at Monticello, as "mighty near white." Isaac Jefferson, *Memoirs of a Monticello Slave—Dictated to Charles Campbell in the 1840s by Isaac, One of Thomas Jefferson's Slaves* (Charlottesville: University of Virginia Press, 1951), 10. Throughout the novel, Chase-Riboud frequently reiterates how fair-skinned and physically attractive Hemings is.

43. Gordon-Reed, "Engaging Jefferson," 178; Ellis, "Jefferson," 128.

44. Jenny Sharpe, *Ghosts of Slavery: A Literary Archaeology of Black Women's Lives* (Minneapolis: University of Minnesota Press, 2003), 143.

45. M. Jacqui Alexander, *Pedagogies of Crossing: Meditations on Feminism, Sexual Politics, Memory, and the Sacred* (Durham, N.C.: Duke University Press, 2005), 25.

46. Spencer, "Historical Memory," 521.

47. For incisive examples of such a reading, see Hartman, *Scenes of Subjection,* 86–94; and Spencer, "Historical Memory," 521.

48. Friedrich Engels, *The Origin of the Family, Private Property, and the State,* 2nd ed. (New York: International Publishers, 1972), 121. For Jefferson's reliance on his slaves, see Lucia Stanton, "'Those Who Labor for My Happiness': Thomas Jefferson and His Slaves," in *Jeffersonian Legacies,* ed. Peter S. Onuf (Charlottesville: University of Virginia Press, 1993), 147–80.

49. I offer a more extended consideration of "the creation of the Negro" as an objectified signifier of "limited humanity" in the introduction. See also Cedric J. Robinson, *Black Marxism: The Making of the Black Radical Tradition* (Chapel Hill: University of North Carolina Press, 2000), 4; Frantz Fanon, *Black Skin, White Masks,* trans. Richard Philcox (New York: Grove Press, 1968), 109, 112; and Hartman, *Scenes of Subjection,* 6.

50. Harris, "Whiteness as Property," 279.

51. Jacques Derrida, "Signature Event Context," in *Margins of Philosophy* (Chicago: University of Chicago Press, 1984), 314.

52. For a working definition of *différance,* see note 22 in this book's introduction. See also Jacques Derrida, "Différance," in *Margins of Philosophy,* 1–28.

53. Orlando Patterson, *Slavery and Social Death: A Comparative Study* (Cambridge, Mass.: Harvard University Press, 1982), 12.

54. Spencer, "Historical Memory," 517.

55. Michel Foucault, *The History of Sexuality,* vol. 1, *An Introduction* (New York: Vintage Books, 1990), 149–50.

56. Achille Mbembe, "Necropolitics," trans. Libby Meintjes, *Public Culture* 15, no. 1 (2003): 16; Michel Foucault, *"Society Must Be Defended": Lectures at the Collège de France, 1975–1976* (New York: Picador, 2003), 213.

57. Foucault, *History of Sexuality,* 95–96.

58. Patricia J. Williams, *The Alchemy of Race and Rights* (Cambridge, Mass.: Harvard University Press, 1991), 213.

59. Spillers, "Mama's Baby, Papa's Maybe," 218.

60. I extend this discussion of the reliance of liberal political theory on the raced and gendered geography of separate spheres in the introduction. See also Carol Pateman, *The Sexual Contract* (Cambridge, UK: Polity, 1988).

61. As I have argued elsewhere, the embrace of physical death by the enslaved can be read as a categorical rejection of the total domination that constituted the ideological precondition for their continued existence as physically living, socially dead slaves. In short, they used their bodies to precipitate structural and discursive crises by calling into question the very foundations on which chattel slavery—and liberal humanism—relied. Sara Clarke Kaplan, "Love and Violence/Maternity and Death: Black Feminism and the Politics of Reading (Un)representability," *Black Women, Gender, and Families* 1, no. 1 (Spring 2007): 99–101.

62. In this use of *suture,* I am following in the path of Ernesto Laclau and Chantal Mouffe in their extension of Jacques-Alain Miller's use of the term. Ernesto Laclau and Chantal Mouffe, *Hegemony and Socialist Strategy: Towards a Radical Democratic Politics,* 2nd ed. (New York: Verso, 2001).

63. Barbara Chase-Riboud, *The President's Daughter* (New York: Crown, 1994), 4–5. Further references are to this edition and are cited parenthetically in the text as *PD.*

64. Lewis, "White Jeffersons," 157; Onuf, "Every Generation," 166–67; Gordon-Reed, "Engaging Jefferson," 181–82.

65. Patterson, *Slavery and Social Death,* 5.

66. My use of *sublation* here is deeply influenced by Derrida's concept of sous rature. For more on the relationship between sublation and sous rature, see chapter 2, note 73. See also Gayatri Chakravorty Spivak, translator's preface to *Of Grammatology,* by Jacques Derrida, trans. Gayatri Chakravorty Spivak (Baltimore: Johns Hopkins University Press, 1997), xi–xviii. Pollard offers a related reading of the significance of Harriet Hemings's fingerprints and their erasure. Pollard, "Self-Evident Truths," 125.

67. Pollard also points to this scene as critical to understanding the cost that Harriet pays for passing. However, her approach differs from mine in its focus on the stakes of the construction of "history, psychology, truth, and representation." Pollard, "Self-Evident Truths," 124–25.

68. Brown, *Clotel,* 196.
69. Brown, 194.
70. Harris, "Whiteness as Property," 285.

5. A Picture of Me and My Mother

1. The Radiance Foundation, "Our Vision and Mission," accessed March 11, 2011, http://www.theradiancefoundation.org; The Radiance Foundation, "Vision & Mission," accessed November 7, 2011, http://www.toomanyaborted.com; Shaila Dewan, "Anti-Abortion Ads Split Atlanta," *New York Times,* February 5, 2010; Associated Press, "Atlanta Billboards Link Race, Abortion," Fox News, February 14, 2010, http://www.foxnews.com.

2. Life Always, "About Life Always," accessed February 2, 2012, http://thatsabortion.com; "'The Most Dangerous Place for an African-American Is in the Womb': Black Politician Criticises Anti-abortion Billboard," *Daily Mail Online,* February 24, 2011, https://www.dailymail.co.uk; Naeesa Aziz, "New Anti-Abortion Billboard Points Fingers at Black Leaders," *BET,* August 16, 2011, https://www.bet.com.

3. Sandhya Somashekhar and Philip Rucker, "GOP's Latest Proposal for Planned Parenthood Funding," *Washington Post,* April 8, 2011; Aimee Miles, "A Guide to GOP Proposals on Family Planning Funds," *Kaiser Health News,* March 9, 2011, https://khn.org; Ryan Grim, "Government Shutdown Threatened by Republicans over Planned Parenthood," *Huffington Post,* April 7, 2011 (updated June 7, 2011), https://www.huffpost.com; Sandhya Somashekhar, "Legislative Proposal Puts Abortion Rights Supporters on Alert," *Washington Post,* February 1, 2011; Noam Levey and Rosie Mestel, "Komen, Planned Parenthood and Congress: What's the Status?," *Los Angeles Times,* February 1, 2012; Susan B. Anthony List, "Rep. Stearns Launches Investigation of Planned Parenthood," September 28, 2011, https://www.sba-list.org.

4. Guttmacher Institute, "State Laws and Policies," accessed February 2, 2012, http://www.guttmacher.org.

5. Roderick A. Ferguson, *Aberrations in Black: Toward a Queer of Color Critique* (Minneapolis: University of Minnesota Press, 2004), 104; Candice Marie Jenkins, *Private Lives, Proper Relations: Regulating Black Intimacy* (Minneapolis: University of Minnesota Press, 2007), 19–20.

6. Jenkins, *Private Lives, Proper Relations,* 13–14.

7. Jenkins, 25; Rhonda M. Williams, "Living at the Crossroads: Explorations in Race, Nationality, Sexuality, and Gender," in *The House That Race Built,* ed. Wahneema Lubiano (New York: Vintage, 1998), 140, 44. Erica Edwards brilliantly explicates how visual depictions of charismatic, Black masculine leadership rendered it the synecdochal representation of Black political modernity. Erica R. Edwards,

Charisma and the Fictions of Black Leadership (Minneapolis: University of Minnesota Press, 2012), 37, 42–48, 72.

8. Robert G. Weisbord, *Genocide? Birth Control and the Black American* (Westport, Conn.: Greenwood, 1975), 43.

9. Jennifer Nelson, *Women of Color and the Reproductive Rights Movement* (New York: New York University Press, 2003), 85–111. It should be noted that this was not a universal critique among Black nationalists. Weisbord argues that Malcolm X was in favor of birth control access for African Americans, although he (rightly) noted the racism of contemporary population control campaigns and observed that more interest would probably be generated by an emphasis on "planning" rather than "control." Weisbord, *Genocide?*, 99.

10. Angela Y. Davis, *Women, Race & Class* (New York: Vintage Books, 1983), 202–21; Dorothy E. Roberts, *Killing the Black Body: Race, Reproduction, and the Meaning of Liberty* (New York: Vintage, 1997), 56–103; Loretta Ross, "Raising Our Voices," in *From Abortion to Reproductive Freedom: Transforming a Movement*, ed. Marlene Gerber Fried (Boston: South End, 1990), 141.

11. Roberts, *Killing the Black Body*, 3–6, 299–302.

12. Byllye Avery, "A Question of Survival/A Conspiracy of Silence: Abortion and Black Women's Health," in *From Abortion to Reproductive Freedom: Transforming a Movement*, ed. Marlene Gerber Fried (Boston: South End, 1990), 76; Toni Cade Bambara, "The Pill: Genocide or Liberation?," in *The Black Woman: An Anthology*, new ed., ed. Toni Cade Bambara (New York: Washington Square Press, 2005), 203–12; Davis, *Women, Race & Class*, 202; Ross, "Raising Our Voices," 140; National Black Women's Health Project, "Reproductive Rights Position Paper: National Black Women's Health Project," in *From Abortion to Reproductive Freedom: Transforming a Movement*, ed. Marlene Gerber Fried (Boston: South End, 1990), 291.

13. Some of the most compelling versions of this argument emerge from Black feminist activist-thinkers writing in direct response to the call by men in Black nationalist movements for Black women to "dump the pill." See, in particular, Bambara's influential essay "The Pill: Genocide or Liberation?," which first appeared in August 1969 in the Black nationalist magazine *Onyx*, as well as the 1968 collective response by Black women in Mount Vernon, New York, to the Black Unity Party of Peekskill, New York. Bambara, "The Pill," 203–12; "A Response by Black Sisters," September 11, 1968, repr. in *Poor Black Women*, ed. Patricia Robinson (Boston: New England Free Press, n.d.), n.p., Women's Liberation Movement Print Collection, Digital Collections, Duke University, https://repository.duke.edu/dc/wlmpc/wlmms01008.

14. Kimberlé W. Crenshaw, "Mapping the Margins: Intersectionality, Identity Politics, and Violence against Women of Color," in *Critical Race Theory: The Key Writings That Formed the Movement*, ed. Kimberlé Crenshaw et al. (New York: New Press, 1996), 282.

15. Black Unity Party (Peekskill, N.Y.), "Birth Control Pills and Black Children," in Robinson, *Poor Black Women,* n.p.

16. Grace Kyungwon Hong, *Death beyond Disavowal: The Impossible Politics of Difference* (Minneapolis: University of Minnesota Press, 2015), 7–8.

17. Hannah Arendt, *The Human Condition* (Chicago: University of Chicago Press, 1958), 313–14. Jodi Kim first pointed out this connection to Arendt's discussion of life as the highest good. Jodi Kim, email to author, February 20, 2012.

18. Beverly Smith, "Choosing Ourselves: Black Women and Abortion," in *From Abortion to Reproductive Freedom: Transforming a Movement,* ed. Marlene Gerber Fried (Boston: South End, 1990), 84.

19. Giorgio Agamben, *Homo Sacer: Sovereign Power and Bare Life* (Stanford: Stanford University Press, 1998), 1–12. See also Alexander G. Weheliye, "Pornotropes," *Journal of Visual Culture* 7, no. 1 (2008): 68.

20. Histories of the ABCL, the BCCRB, and their subsequent merger as the BCFA are many. Some of the notable ones consulted for this project include Linda Gordon, *The Moral Property of Women: A History of Birth Control Politics in America,* 3rd ed. (Urbana: University of Illinois Press, 2007); Carole R. McCann, *Birth Control Politics in the United States, 1916–1945* (Ithaca, N.Y.: Cornell University Press, 1994); Margaret Sanger, *Margaret Sanger: An Autobiography* (New York: W. W. Norton, 2004); and Rickie Solinger, *Pregnancy and Power: A Short History of Reproductive Politics in America* (New York: New York University Press, 2005).

21. A number of feminist scholars of reproductive politics have written on the Division of Negro Service and particularly its southern demonstration project. See especially Gordon, *Moral Property of Women,* 233–36; McCann, *Birth Control Politics in the United States,* 160–73; Roberts, *Killing the Black Body,* 76–79; Davis, *Women, Race & Class,* 214–15; and Johanna Schoen, *Choice & Coercion: Birth Control, Sterilization, and Abortion in Public Health and Welfare,* Gender and American Culture (Chapel Hill: University of North Carolina Press, 2005), 44–52. For representations of the Negro Project among Black antiabortion activists, see, for example, *Maafa 21: Black Genocide in 21st Century America,* written/directed/produced by Mark Crutcher (Life Dynamics, 2009), DVD; Life Education and Resource Network, "Planned Parenthood," accessed September 8, 2012, http://www.blackgenocide.org; and The Radiance Foundation, "The Mother of Planned Parenthood" and "The Negro Project," both accessed on February 2, 2012, http://www.toomanyaborted.com.

22. While the extent and sincerity of Margaret Sanger's personal commitment to eugenics has been an issue of considerable debate in recent years, the intimate history of the two movements is undeniable. Prominent eugenicists such as American Eugenics Society president Henry Pratt Fairchild and Clarence J. Gamble were long-standing members of the Board of Directors for the ABCL and the Research Bureau; employees and officers of all three organizations had been active

participants in each other's panels, roundtables, and conferences for a number of years; and in 1933 the ABCL and the American Eugenics Society had even briefly considered an institutional merger. In the context of this chapter, the question of Sanger's individual beliefs regarding eugenics is of considerably less interest than the institutional stance of BCFA and the structural politics of the birth control movement more generally. However, for a more detailed discussion of Sanger's complex and much-debated relationship to eugenics, see Alexander Sanger, "Eugenics, Race, and Margaret Sanger Revisited: Reproductive Freedom for All?," *Hypatia* 22, no. 2 (2007): 210–17; McCann, *Birth Control Politics in the United States,* 99–134; Roberts, *Killing the Black Body,* 72–81; and Gordon, *Moral Property of Women,* 196–201.

23. Margaret Sanger and Mary W. Reinhardt, "Birth Control and the Negro," draft, July 1939, box 24, folder 13, Florence Rose Papers, Sophia Smith Collection, Smith College, Northampton, Mass. (hereafter FRP-SSC).

24. Sanger and Reinhardt, "Birth Control and the Negro."

25. "Family Planning—Tomorrow's Children: Challenging Facts," box 82, folder 2, and Fred Hogue, "Social Eugenics," *Los Angeles Times,* October 22, 1939, box 47, folder 6, both in Planned Parenthood Federation of America Records (Part I), Sophia Smith Collection, Smith College, Northampton, Mass. (hereafter PPFA-SSC).

26. Schoen, *Choice & Coercion,* 51. For an example of the former, see "Clarence Gamble to Mary Rinehart" [*sic*], November 1, 1939, box 29, folder 16, FRP-SSC; for the latter, see Woodbridge E. Morris to Prentiss Wilson, April 11, 1941, box 96, folder 9, PPFA-SSC.

27. Clarence J. Gamble to Margaret Sanger, November 27, 1939, Clarence Gamble papers, 1920–1970s (inclusive), 1920–1966 (bulk), H MS c23, Harvard Medical Library, Francis A. Countway Library of Medicine, Boston, Mass. (hereafter CGP-CLM), located in Margaret Sanger Papers Microfilm Edition: Collected Documents Series, reel C07, frame 1078; Robert Seibels, "Pregnancy Spacing for the Rural Public Health," South Carolina State Board of Health, 1942. See also Schoen, *Choice & Coercion,* 49–50.

28. Gordon, *Moral Property of Women,* 236; Roberts, *Killing the Black Body,* 77–78, 82–83; Schoen, *Choice & Coercion,* 47–51.

29. Sanger and Reinhardt, "Birth Control and the Negro."

30. Gordon, *Moral Property of Women,* 235–36.

31. Gordon, 236.

32. Schoen, *Choice & Coercion,* 7, 12, 37, 45.

33. Roberts, *Killing the Black Body,* 86.

34. Florence Rose, "Activities Report, November 30–December 13, 1941," December 13, 1941, Margaret Sanger Papers, Manuscript Division, Library of Congress, Washington, D.C. (hereafter MSP-LCC), located in Margaret Sanger Papers Microfilm Edition: Library of Congress Series, reel 117, frame 654.

35. Roberts, *Killing the Black Body,* 85.

36. Roberts, 81.

37. The connection I am making here between the founding of the DNS, the advent of the Negro Project, and the organization of the southern regional conference is not only based on coincident timing. Conference presentations emphasized consideration of the so-called Negro problem in the South, members of the National Advisory Council for the DNS were tapped to sit on the conference's Steering Committee, and much of the preliminary research from the various demonstration sites for the Negro Project were first presented at the Southern Conferences of 1940–42. Moreover, as I detail below, from its very first session, the conference aligned itself with a vehement call to increase birth control service provisions to African Americans in the southern United States.

38. "Suggestions for Southern Regional Conference," June 22, 1939, box 83, folder 16, PPFA-SSC; "Conference on Tomorrow's Children," publicity brochure, n.d. (early 1939), box 7, folder 138, CGP-CLM. Archived materials on the series of regional conferences sponsored by the BCFA under the title "Tomorrow's Children" are sparse and relatively scattered, making it difficult to ascertain exactly how many were held. I have found documentation of at least six conferences: Atlanta, Georgia (1939); Cambridge, Massachusetts (1939, 1941); Chapel Hill-Durham, North Carolina (1940); Chicago, Illinois (1941); and Nashville, Tennessee (1941). See "Invitation to the Third Southern Conference on Tomorrow's Children," n.d. (April–Sep. 1941), box 40, folder 665, CGP-CLM.

39. "Conference on Tomorrow's Children," publicity brochure, n.d.

40. American Eugenics Society, "American Eugenics," May 7, 1936, reel 41, frame 570, MSP-LCC .

41. Ellsworth Huntington et al., *Tomorrow's Children: The Goal of Eugenics* (New York: John Wiley & Sons, 1935), 9–10.

42. Marguerite Benson to Ellsworth Huntington, May 19, 1939, box 83, folder 16, PPFA-SSC; Ellsworth Huntington to Marguerite Benson, May 25, 1939, box 83, folder 16, PPFA-SSC.

43. Woodbridge Morris, "Who Shall Inherit the Earth?," November 10, 1939, box 83, folder 16, PPFA-SSC.

44. Walter A. Jackson, *Gunnar Myrdal and America's Conscience: Social Engineering and Racial Liberalism, 1938–1987* (Chapel Hill: University of North Carolina Press, 1994), 75; Hedvig Ekerwald, "The Modernist Manifesto of Alva and Gunnar Myrdal: Modernization in Sweden in the Thirties and the Question of Sterilization," *International Journal of Politics, Culture, and Society* 14, no. 3 (Spring 2001): 545.

45. Jackson, *Gunnar Myrdal,* 75–77; Ekerwald, "Modernist Manifesto," 545–54.

46. Quoted in Jackson, *Gunnar Myrdal,* 78. *Crisis in the Population Question* has never been published in English. It is worth noting that compulsory sterilization

continued in Sweden under the auspices of the welfare state until it was exposed in 1997. See Ekerwald, "Modernist Manifesto," 545.

47. Citing Herbert Marcuse, Ferguson defines rationalization via Max Weber's conception of it as "how 'the specifically Western idea of reason is reified in a system of material and intellectual culture (economics, technology, 'way of life,' science, art), which is fully developed in industrial capitalism.'" Ferguson, *Aberrations in Black,* 83. My own reading of (reprosexual) rationalization under industrial capitalism in the next pages is deeply indebted to Ferguson's.

48. Ferguson, 84.

49. Quoted in James B. McKee, *Sociology and the Race Problem: The Failure of a Perspective* (Champaign: University of Illinois Press, 1993), 239–40.

50. Alva Myrdal, *Nation and Family: The Swedish Experiment in Democratic Family and Population* (Cambridge, Mass.: MIT Press, 1968).

51. "Southern Conference on Tomorrow's Children," program, November 9–11, 1939, box 7, folder 138, CGP-CLM.

52. Ferguson, *Aberrations in Black,* 90.

53. William E. Cole, "Side Glances at the Conference on Tomorrow's Children," winter 1940, box 83, folder 16, PPFA-SSC; "Bingham Says South's Ills Holding All of U.S. Back," *Atlanta Constitution,* November 10, 1939, p. 6, box 7, file 148, CGP-CLM.

54. Barry Bingham, "The South's Tomorrow," November 9, 1939, box 83, folder 16, PPFA-SSC.

55. Saidiya V. Hartman, *Scenes of Subjection: Terror, Slavery, and Self-Making in Nineteenth-Century America,* Race and American Culture (New York: Oxford University Press, 1997), 117.

56. Hartman, 117.

57. Ferguson, *Aberrations in Black,* 84.

58. "Fifteen Thousand Attend Exposition of Negro Advance," *Chicago Tribune,* July 19, 1940, reel 113, MSP-LCC.

59. "Planned Parenthood," n.d., ca. 1940, box 139, file 2406, CGP-CLM.

60. Ferguson, *Aberrations in Black,* 87.

61. Sapphire, *Push: A Novel* (New York: Vintage, 1997), 31.

62. Kara Keeling, "Joining the Lesbians: Cinematic Regimes of Black Lesbian Visibility," in *Black Queer Studies: A Critical Anthology,* ed. E. Patrick Johnson and Mae Henderson (Durham, N.C.: Duke University Press, 2005), 217–20.

63. David Marriott, *Haunted Life: Visual Culture and Black Modernity* (New Brunswick, N.J.: Rutgers University Press, 2007), 1, 17; Christopher Peterson, *Kindred Specters: Death, Mourning, and American Affinity* (Minneapolis: University of Minnesota Press, 2007), 51.

64. Indeed, it is worth noting that the controversy around *Push* as both a literary and political project has been around for as long as the novel has been in print.

65. Erica R. Edwards, "Tuning into *Precious*: The Black Women's Empowerment Adaptation and the Interruptions of the Absurd," *Black Camera* 4, no. 1 (2012): 83–84.

66. Kara Keeling, *The Witch's Flight: The Cinematic, the Black Femme, and the Image of Common Sense*, Perverse Modernities (Durham, N.C.: Duke University Press, 2007).

67. Daphne Brooks, *Bodies in Dissent: Spectacular Performances of Race and Freedom, 1850–1910* (Durham, N.C.: Duke University Press, 2006), 7.

68. Brooks, 7.

69. Ferguson, *Aberrations in Black*, 15.

70. Nicole R. Fleetwood, *Troubling Vision: Performance, Visuality, and Blackness* (Chicago: University of Chicago Press, 2010); Hortense J. Spillers, "Mama's Baby, Papa's Maybe: An American Grammar Book," in *Black, White, and in Color: Essays on American Literature and Culture* (Chicago: University of Chicago Press, 2003), 206.

71. Achille Mbembe, *On the Postcolony* (Berkeley: University of California Press, 2001), 199. For a thorough analysis of how the overlapping projects of European colonialism, African chattel slavery, and racial science linked fatness and blackness as signifiers of dangerous excess, greed, savagery, and disease, see Sabrina Strings, *Fearing the Black Body: The Racial Origins of Fat Phobia* (New York: New York University Press, 2019).

72. Hartman, *Scenes of Subjection*, 94.

73. Toni Morrison, *The Bluest Eye* (New York: Vintage, 2007), 83. See also Grace Kyungwon Hong, *The Ruptures of American Capital: Women of Color Feminism and the Culture of Immigrant Labor* (Minneapolis: University of Minnesota Press, 2006), 59.

74. Ruth Wilson Gilmore, *Golden Gulag: Prisons, Surplus, Crisis, and Opposition in Globalizing California* (Berkeley: University of California Press, 2007), 19; Hong, *Ruptures of American Capital*, 57–59.

75. Daniel Patrick Moynihan, *The Negro Family: The Case for National Action* (Washington, D.C.: Office of Policy Planning and Research, U.S. Department of Labor, 1965).

76. Jaime Schultz, "Reading the Catsuit: Serena Williams and the Production of Blackness at the 2002 U.S. Open," *Journal of Sport & Social Issues* 29, no. 3 (2005): 348–49.

77. Ferguson, *Aberrations in Black*, 11.

78. Hortense J. Spillers, "Interstices: A Small Drama of Words," in *Black, White, and in Color: Essays on American Literature and Culture* (Chicago: University of Chicago Press, 2003), 155. On surveillance, punishment, and containment, see Hartman, *Scenes of Subjection*, 94.

79. Keeling, *The Witch's Flight*, 95.

80. Edwards, "Tuning into *Precious*," 85.

81. CARASA, *Women under Attack: Victories, Backlash, and the Fight for Reproductive Freedom*, rev. ed., ed. Sue Davis (Boston: South End, 1988), 3.

82. Nelson, *Women of Color*, 137, 148.

83. My analysis of CARASA's platform draws upon Nelson, *Women of Color*; CARASA, *Women under Attack*; and Rebecca M. Kluchin, *Fit to Be Tied: Sterilization and Reproductive Rights in America, 1950–1980* (New Brunswick, N.J.: Rutgers University Press, 2009), 184–213.

Coda

1. Peter Clothier, *Betye Saar* (Los Angeles: Museum of Contemporary Art, 1984), 7–8, 13, 25.

2. I take this summary of Saar's concerns from Betye Saar, "Unfinished Business: The Return of Aunt Jemima," in *Betye Saar: Workers + Warriors—The Return of Aunt Jemima* (New York: Michael Rosenfeld Gallery, 1998), 3; "Betye Saar: National Visionary," National Visionary Leadership Project, accessed July 16, 2018, http://www.visionaryproject.org; and Jane H. Carpenter, *Betye Saar*, The David C. Driskell Series of African American Art (San Francisco: Pomegranate, 2003), 58–62. It bears noting that Saar's frustrated claim that Black art was becoming a commodified spectacle of objectified Black subjugation designed for white consumption was very entangled with her vehement critiques of the work of Kara Walker, and its broad critical success. The relationship between Walker's and Saar's notions of racial memory and commemoration, archetype and iconoclasm, has been written about elsewhere and requires a much more thorough consideration than is possible here.

3. Saar, "Unfinished Business," 3.

4. Arlene Raven, "Mostly 'Bout Survival," in *Betye Saar: Workers + Warriors—The Return of Aunt Jemima* (New York: Michael Rosenfeld Gallery, 1998), 8.

5. Raven, 8.

6. Tera W. Hunter, *To 'Joy My Freedom: Southern Black Women's Lives and Labors after the Civil War* (Cambridge, Mass.: Harvard University Press, 1997), 26.

7. Alexander G. Weheliye, *Habeas Viscus: Racializing Assemblages, Biopolitics, and Black Feminist Theories of the Human* (Durham, N.C.: Duke University Press, 2014), 12, 13.

8. Quoted in Andrea Smith, "Heteropatriarchy and the Three Pillars of White Supremacy: Rethinking Women of Color Organizing," in *The Color of Violence: The INCITE! Anthology*, ed. INCITE! Women of Color Against Violence (Boston: South End, 2006), 69.

9. Audre Lorde, "A Litany for Survival," in *The Black Unicorn: Poems* (1978; repr., New York: W. W. Norton, 1995), 31–32.

10. Audre Lorde, "Conference Keynote Address: Sisterhood and Survival," *Black Scholar* 13, no. 2 (March/April 1986): 5.

11. Combahee River Collective, "A Black Feminist Statement," in *Capitalist Patriarchy and the Case for Socialist Feminism,* ed. Zillah Eisenstein (New York: Monthly Review Press, 1978), 215.

12. Lorde, "Conference Keynote Address," 5, 7.

13. Erica R. Edwards, *Charisma and the Fictions of Black Leadership* (Minneapolis: University of Minnesota Press, 2012), 194; Lorde, "Conference Keynote Address," 6.

Index

Page numbers in italic refer to figures.

SARA CLARKE KAPLAN is associate professor of ethnic studies and critical gender studies at the University of California, San Diego, and cofounder of UCSD's Black Studies Project. Her work has been published in several journals, including *American Quarterly, American Literary History, Callaloo,* and the *Journal of Black Women, Gender, and Families.*